SUMER AND THE SUMERIANS

Mesopotamia produced one of the best-known ancient civilisations, with a literate, urban culture and highly developed political institutions. Writing primarily for a non-specialist audience but drawing on the most up-to-date historical and archaeological sources, Harriet Crawford reviews the extraordinary social and technological developments in the region over a period of two millennia, from 3800 to 2000 BC. She describes the physical environment and discusses architecture, trade and industry, the development of writing, and changes in social and political structures. The final chapter examines the shift in power during this period from the 'temple' to the 'palace'.

SUMER
AND THE
SUMERIANS

HARRIET CRAWFORD

Institute of Archaeology, University of London

CAMBRIDGE
UNIVERSITY PRESS

Published by the Press Syndicate of the University of Cambridge
The Pitt Building, Trumpington Street, Cambridge CB2 1RP
40 West 20th Street, New York, NY 10011–4211, USA
10 Stamford Road, Oakleigh, Victoria 3166, Australia

First published 1991
Reprinted 1991, 1992

Printed in Great Britain by The Bath Press, Avon

British Library cataloguing in publication data
Crawford, Harriet
Sumer and the Sumerians
1. Sumerian civilisation
I. TITLE
935'.01

Library of Congress cataloguing in publication data
Crawford, Harriet E.W.
Sumer and the Sumerians/Harriet Crawford.
p.   cm.
includes bibliographical references.
ISBN 0 521 38175 4. – ISBN 0 521 38850 3 (pbk.)
1. Sumerians.   2. Iraq – Antiquities.   I. Title.
DS72,C73   1990
935–dc20 89-77395 CIP

ISBN 0 521 381754 hardback
ISBN 0 521 388503 paperback

SE

CONTENTS

ILLUSTRATIONS

PREFACE

This book is intended for students, and especially for students beginning to study the archaeology and history of the ancient Near East. The changes which took place on the Mesopotamian plain between the Tigris and Euphrates rivers in the fourth and third millennia BC are of crucial importance in understanding subsequent developments in Western Asia and beyond. A range of major innovations in both technology and social development is attributed to this period and it is these innovations which will be described in the following chapters. Where evidence is available from adjacent geographic areas, which complements or extends that from Mesopotamia, it too will be included.

There are several ways of approaching such a study. One is the straightforward chronological account traditionally favoured by historians and archaeologists, which tries to describe a society in its entirety from genesis to extinction. More recently, authors have begun to isolate specific aspects of a society, taking one stimulus such as trade, or one theme such as the ecological background. The role of that specific factor in the development of the society is then explored.

This book attempts to combine these approaches and looks at a number of major themes, beginning with the physical environment and the historical background. There follows a description of how the environment was used, with sections on agriculture, irrigation and settlement pattern. Next is a chapter on the built environment and the use of space within the settlements; this includes a section on public buildings and on domestic housing. The best evidence for the reconstruction of everyday life comes, ironically, from the funerary remains. The industries which underpinned the Mesopotamian economy and provided the goods for the essential export trade are examined, and the penultimate chapter traces the development of writing, which was intimately linked to the economic development. Finally, there is a summary of the changes in the fine arts.

Each of these topics is followed throughout the two thousand years covered by the book. An attempt is then made in the concluding chapter to bring all these different themes together, and to isolate a number of major trends which can be seen in most, if not all, of the areas described. The most important thread, which links many of the topics discussed, seems to be the change which took place on the southern plain of Mesopotamia from a temple-dominated, politically fragmented pattern of city-states, to one of tight centralised control in which power was in the hands of a single divine ruler backed by a massive bureaucracy. The effects of this political transformation can be traced in almost every aspect of the material culture, as well as in the social system.

The emphasis in this book is on description rather than on explanations, because more accurate description of the archaeological phenomena is the essential basis for any attempt at understanding or explanation. Our evidence is still fragmentary, but the quantity is increasing at a rapid rate, largely as a result of rescue work ahead of major development schemes such as the Saddam dam in northern Iraq. The first task must be to try and incorporate this mass of often rather inchoate new information into our existing framework. The framework itself may have to be modified to accommodate the new facts, but, once this has been done, attempts at explanation can begin.

It is hoped that the thematic approach adopted in this book may throw new light on the period from about 3800 to 2000 BC by providing a different perspective. By assembling the evidence in this slightly different way, it may, perhaps, delineate more sharply some characteristics of the civilisation which is often loosely described as Sumerian. It is also hoped that this approach will provide easily accessible comparative data for people interested in particular aspects of the cultures of other archaeological areas.

Many people have helped me to write this book, colleagues and students have helped me with advice, and I am extraordinarily grateful to all of them for their generous help. It has been particularly stimulating to work with scholars in the adjacent disciplines of ancient history and ancient language and it is perhaps to Mark Geller and Amelie Kuhrt that I owe the greatest debt. I am also most grateful to Dr Uwe Finkbeiner, the Chicago University Press, to Dr Julian Reade, and the Trustees of the British Museum for permission to use illustrations of which they hold the copyright. Kate Morton, Neville Parker and Tessa Rickards drew the illustrations for me with endless patience and great skill and Georgina Herrmann allowed me to use two of her excellent photographs. Finally, the idea of presenting the material in a thematic way came from Peter Richards at the Cambridge University Press and made the writing of the book stimulating and exciting for me. I hope it may do the same for the reader.

Chapter 1

THE REDISCOVERY OF THE ANCIENT NEAR EAST: THE PHYSICAL ENVIRONMENT

Ever since the advent of Christianity, the Levant and especially the lands of the Bible have exerted a special fascination.

After the last crusade, English contacts with the Near and Middle East became somewhat tenuous, although a few ships continued to ply between Europe and the Holy Land; information about the lands of the Bible became even sparser and the stories about them increasingly apocryphal. The numerous editions of the travels of Sir John Mandeville, possibly written by an enterprising entrepreneur who never left his own fireside, remained a standard work for many years, there being nothing to replace it (Moseley 1983). It was only in the nineteenth century, when Britain established direct political relations with the Ottoman provinces, that it again became possible for curious individuals to travel moderately freely in Syria, Palestine and Iraq. J.S. Buckingham, writing in 1827, claims to be the first person for a century to publish his travels in these countries, and he found it sensible to travel dressed as an Arab and to act as a Muslim. The dangers involved were many and real, coming from both men and beasts, as Austen Henry Layard found even fifty years later when he too adopted Muslim dress and customs for his journeys.

In spite of the problems, the spate of travellers gathered momentum during the nineteenth century, spurred on by a great interest in the lands of the Old Testament and by a more practical need to find the least demanding route to the commercial El Dorado of India. Diplomats and military men, often distinguished scholars, contributed to the growing fever of interest in the lands of Assyria and Sumer, the home which Abraham had left at the beginning of his wanderings.

Much of the activity generated by this interest centred on the British Residency in Baghdad after the appointment of Claudius Rich as first British Resident in 1808. The Turkish authorities, though capricious, were usually prepared, as part of the complicated give and take of diplomatic exchange, to allow enterprising Europeans to explore the great mounds of Mesopotamia, and the first spectacular results of their initiative began to appear in London and Paris in the mid-nineteenth century. These men undoubtedly did much damage – they were licensed plunderers – but they equally certainly saved some magnificent pieces from destruction (Lloyd 1947; Postgate 1977). As yet Iraq has not demanded the return of the Assyrian reliefs from Nineveh, but such a request could generate a problem for the British Museum similar to that caused by the Greek request for the return of the Elgin marbles.

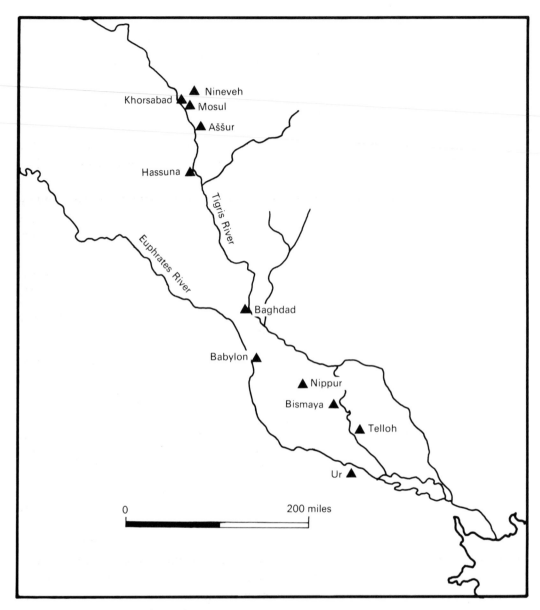

1 Early explorations in Mesopotamia (after Seton Lloyd)

Each country began to stake out an archaeological territory for itself, the Germans at Assur and Babylon, the French under Botta at Khorsabad, and the British under Layard at Nineveh (Map 1). Although the acquisition of fine museum pieces remained a high priority, as it had to do in order to ensure future funding, more scientific methods of exploration and higher standards of recording began to gain ground towards the end of the century. The Germans led the way in the development of techniques for the tracing of unbaked mud-brick walls, which earlier excavators had failed to recognise, and, by training workmen from the village of Shergat to use these techniques, founded a tradition and a 'closed shop' which lasted to the present decade!

Early explorations in the south of the country produced fewer spectacular finds and conditions were more difficult as the fragile and elusive unbaked mud-brick was the main building material; but the great classic sites of Sumer attracted a steady flow of explorers from the middle of the nineteenth century; Taylor, the British Resident, dug at Ur in 1853; in 1877 de Sarzec, the French vice-consul at Basra, began work at Telloh, while the first American expedition to take the field arrived for its disastrous first season at Nippur in 1889. Their camp was attacked and burnt to the ground by feuding tribesmen. Bad luck dogged several of the early American excavations and the following quotation about Banks's expedition to Ur has a fine nineteenth-century flavour to it (Banks 1912).

The work of raising the funds for the support of the expedition rested entirely upon myself. When I had succeeded in obtaining six thousand dollars, half of which had been pledged by Mr Rockefeller, President Morton, the best friend of the expedition, guaranteed six thousand more, making a total of twelve thousand, the sum deemed necessary for the work of the first year. I then purchased an extensive excavating outfit, consisting of everything which I thought could be of service in the desert, and shipped it to Busreh.

One of the most pleasant recollections of those busy days was a Babylonian dinner given by Present Morton to the friends of the expedition. The cards at our plates were written in the language of Nebuchadnezzar; the bread was of the shape of Babylonian bricks; the great tray of ice-cream was the colour of the desert sand over which sweet icy camels bore burdens of other sweet ices; and there was a huge cake, like the Tower of Babel; about it wandered miniature Arabs with miniature picks, and concealed within its several stages was an art treasure for each of the guests. Then and there, as the Director of the Expedition, I opened the excavations, and from the ruins of the huge cake I rescued and distributed its buried treasures – antiquities fresh from Tiffany's. Finally the host proposed a toast to the expedition, but it happened by some chance that no glass was at my plate. Imagine my consternation when the guests were raising their glasses and were expressing wishes for my success, and I could not respond! Did it portend failure? Was it destined that success be denied me?

By the early 1920s the momentum increased and the next step forward was taken when Iraq, with the help and advice of Gertrude Bell, enacted its first antiquities law. This provided that all archaeological exploration had to be licensed; all foreign expeditions had to be staffed to certain standards; unique objects might not be taken out of the country and all other finds were to be divided on an agreed basis between the excavators and the National Museum of Iraq, which opened in 1926 with Gertrude Bell as its first director. She was also one of the driving forces behind the foundation in 1932 (after her death) of the British School of Archaeology in Iraq, a body whose name is associated with many of the major excavations this century and whose fiftieth birthday was celebrated at a special Rencontre Assyriologique in London in 1982. The antiquities laws have now changed again: no antiquities may be exported at all. The

National Museum has expanded and flourishes and a major government department is now responsible for all matters relating to the national heritage, including rescue work, long-term major research projects and the care and restoration of monuments. The success of these measures can be judged by the rate at which new information is coming out of Iraq, making the revision of many of our ideas a recurrent theme. The assimilation of this new information, often available only in specialist journals, sometimes in languages other than English, poses real problems and means that textbooks need frequent updating.

Excavators and field workers are also faced with new problems, notably an astronomical rise in the cost of mounting a field expedition; the mammoth expeditions of the past, employing hundreds of workmen, are now themselves historical curiosities and financially unthinkable, even if enough skilled supervisory staff could be found to meet modern requirements. Today, most expeditions, unless involved in rescue operations, tend to concentrate on the solution of specific, well-defined problems with a much smaller team, including specialists such as photographers, conservators and architects as well as site supervisors. Scientists, such as palaeobotanists, are regularly involved in fieldwork and sampling, as well as in post-excavation analysis, when computers are used with increasing frequency to process large bodies of data. Ethnographers, too, provide valuable data by studies of traditional methods of farming and industrial production, in areas where such information is still accessible.

This emphasis on the solution of particular problems has in turn meant an increasing reliance on survey techniques in order to pinpoint in advance the place where there is the best prospect of solving a particular question. Sadly, it is often impossible for strategic reasons to use aerial photography in the Middle East, a marvellous tool for survey work, but satellite photographs are now providing an interesting new source of information. Some of these photographs can even show remains a short distance below the ground surface in light soil or sand. In spite of the political and practical difficulties much work has been done and the most important contribution to survey work in Mesopotamia has been made by R. McC. Adams and his colleagues. They have refined techniques of surface collection and interpretation so that, in spite of the accepted limitations of the method, it is now possible to begin to map out the distribution and scale of settlement from the earliest times into the historic period. It is possible too, from survey work, to make at least relative estimates of fluctuations in population, even if absolute numbers are still difficult, or even impossible, to assess. Their survey work has also enabled Adams to make valuable attempts to reconstruct some of the physical characteristics of prehistoric Mesopotamia, notably the shifting courses of the major rivers and the controversial matter of the position of the head of the Arabian Gulf. The courses of a number of the major canals can also be traced, linking groups of sites, and thus sometimes helping to define ancient political units (Adams 1981).

THE PHYSICAL BACKGROUND

It is obviously impossible to study the archaeology of Mesopotamia without a thorough knowledge of its physical characteristics. Unfortunately, we cannot assume that the conditions we see today are in every respect the same as those in earlier millennia, and our evidence is not always complete enough to be able to reconstruct past conditions; fluctuations in climate, for example, which have almost certainly occurred in the nine millennia or so since the area was first inhabited, are not always easy to detect. However, there seems to be a measure of agreement among the experts that there have been no drastic or fundamental changes in the physical geography or the weather patterns, although man himself has undoubtedly modified his environment, usually for the worse! Deforestation and overgrazing have both had their effect on precipitation and in marginal areas even a minor shift in the amount of rainfall can have economically disastrous effects. Irrigation, which made much of this area habitable, has, ironically, rendered vast tracts of land today, at least temporarily, uncultivable through salinisation.

In spite of these changes we do now have enough evidence to begin to reconstruct the environment of the first settlers in the area with which this book is primarily concerned.

This region is sometimes called Greater Mesopotamia and is in no way a unit. Its boundaries cover parts of the modern states of Syria and Iran and all of modern Iraq. Climatologically and geographically it divides roughly into three main zones (Map 2). The most northerly of these comprises the foothills of the Taurus and Zagros mountains in the north and east of modern Iraq, an area which has produced the earliest evidence of settlement. It is an area of sheltered intramontane valleys with plenty of water, grazing, game, fruit, nuts and wild cereals, in many ways an ideal spot for the first attempts at settlement in the late Palaeolithic and pre-pottery Neolithic periods. However, winters are harsh and communications are difficult between valleys or across mountains. Some limited cereal cultivation is possible though the soil is not rich, and there are lavish supplies of stone and timber, as well as isolated deposits of resources such as copper and bitumen in the north-east. Various pigments, galena, malachite and ochre also occur.

The second zone covers the plateau which lies between the Tigris and the Euphrates south of the Taurus foothills, and north of a line from Hit to the Tigris at Samarra, as well as the plain east of the Tigris. The former area is roughly similar to the Roman province of Jezirah 'the island' and the name is still used. It includes the range of the Jebel Sinjar and is subdivided into two uneven parts by the 200 mm isoyet, north of which rain-fed agriculture is conventionally said to be possible. At present this line lies south of the Jebel Sinjar, but its exact position in prehistoric times almost certainly

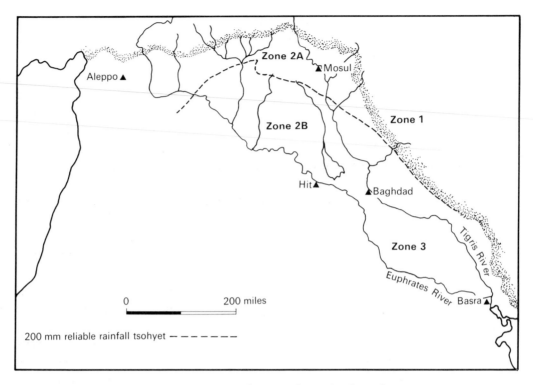

2 Greater Mesopotamia, showing climate/ecological zones

fluctuated and the evidence of heavy settlement in the area south of the Jebel Sinjar in
the Hassuna period, which covered much of the sixth millennium, suggests that at
times it may have run considerably south of its present position. Rain-fed agriculture is
not reliable in this district. Oates and Oates have put forward a persuasive case for the
300 mm isoyet being a much more reliable indicator of the boundaries of rain-fed
cultivation, which would suggest that this is the division, lying considerably north of
the Jebal in modern times, we should look at (Oates and Oates 1976). Wherever the
exact dividing line fell, it is clear that at least half of our second geographic zone lay in
the region where reliable agriculture is only possible with the help of irrigation.

The natural resources of this area are varied but much less extensive than in the
foothills of the mountains. Good alluvial land is limited, but with irrigation yields can
be high and there is relatively plentiful grazing. There is stone; there is some timber;
there were herds of onager in the Jezirah, and wild pig and a number of predators in the
thick scrub on the banks of the rivers. Mineral resources are non-existent except for
important deposits of bitumen at Hit and sulphur in the Wadi Tharthar depression.
Sulphur has important medicinal applications, and was used in tanning, and as a
pigment, from very early periods. As we shall see later, the pattern of early settlement

in the Jezirah contrasts sharply with that in the south and typically consisted of a scatter of villages interspersed with small market towns.

The most productive land in this second zone lies between the Tigris and the Zagros mountains and formed the heartland of the Assyrian empire. It is rich corn-growing country, where irrigation is not necessary to produce heavy yields, and the plain is dotted with the tells of the Assyrian capitals. Some of them have proved to have been inhabited from the earliest prehistoric periods, but the earlier levels are deeply buried and difficult to reach except by sondage; Mallowan's sounding at Nineveh is a classic example of this type of excavation (Thompson and Mallowan 1933). Two rivers, the Greater and Little Zab, bisect the plain and underline its links with the east. The finds from this area dating to a time before *c*.1200 BC often show an individuality which suggests a different range of contacts, with the north and east, as well as with Sumer and Akkad. A major route runs from the north-east corner of this plain up onto the Iranian plateau via the Rowanduz gorge and seems to have been an important artery of communication from Neolithic times on.

South of the Lesser Zab the diagonal range of the Jebel Hamrin interposes itself between the Tigris and the mountains proper, running north-west/south-east and defining the western edge of the Hamrin plain. This area has recently been extensively surveyed and sampled, in advance of a new dam, which will drown large areas of the valley. These explorations have underlined the importance of these more peripheral areas, both agriculturally and as highways linking the major centres of south-western Iran, southern Mesopotamia and Assyria. The southern end of the Hamrin valley is loosely defined by the Diyala valley, another important route onto the Iranian plateau. In much later times this was the route followed by one branch of the Silk Route to Cathay, the great Khorasan road.

The third zone consists of the flat alluvial plain between the two rivers, the Euphrates and the Tigris. It comprises the ancient kingdom of Sumer in the south of the plain, and Akkad in the north, and according to tradition was the site of the Garden of Eden. Looking at it today it is hard to understand why this featureless waste, exposed to every extreme of heat, flood and storm, should ever have been identified with the original land of plenty and ease. Yet, in spite of its apparent inhospitality, the soil is immensely fertile, capable of producing a huge agricultural surplus which under-pinned what is arguably the earliest civilisation in the world. The Sumerian civilisation is in many ways the classic example of the Toynbee theory of 'stimulus and response' or, in less academic terms, of necessity being the mother of invention. Large-scale settlement was impossible in this inhospitable environment without the development of a social system sufficiently complex to provide the co-operation between groups of people which enabled them to produce an economic surplus through irrigation agriculture, which in turn allowed them to trade and to develop the specialist skills necessary for survival. It is not entirely frivolous to suggest that if the region had been more hospitable the Sumerian civilisation might not have developed as early as it did.

Here, in the southern plain, we can provide better evidence for the changes which have taken place in the environment over the six or seven thousand years since the plain was first permanently settled. The most important of these changes is in the course of the rivers. A combination of aerial and ground survey indicates that the Tigris and Euphrates may at one time have formed one stream in the vicinity of modern Baghdad. A number of streams then ran out into the alluvium. Adams (1981) suggests that this may have been the position at the time of the earliest settlement on the plain in the fifth or early sixth millennium. Gradually some of the smaller streams dried up, leaving a forerunner of the modern Euphrates running approximately in the middle of the alluvium, while the Tigris was being edged eastwards into its modern bed. The westward movement of the Euphrates can be traced physically, and by the progressive abandonment of ancient sites, such as the old religious capital of Nippur. The two rivers come together again at the southern end of the alluvium to form the Shatt-el-Arab, which winds its way through the great reed beds described so vividly by Wilfred Thesiger (1964), among others, out into the Arabian Gulf. The position of the head of the Gulf in early times is another matter which still requires further clarification. Early in this century it was generally accepted that it had lain considerably north of its present line and that siltation had pushed it gradually southwards. Then an article was published by Lees and Falcon, putting forward the hypothesis that, thanks to tectonic movements in the floor of the Gulf, which compensated for the build-up of silt, the shoreline had actually moved very little (Lees and Falcon 1952). Ten years later this conclusion was itself under fire, and today there is a growing feeling that perhaps the texts of the third millennium which describe the ancient towns of Ur and Lagash as being on the coast may, in fact, be accurate (Adams 1981: 15–16). There is also evidence from the west coast of the Gulf in the Ubaid period to suggest that the shoreline may have been considerably higher then than it is now, a conclusion which would support a more northerly position for the head of the Gulf too at that time.

Whatever the exact details of the movements of the two great rivers, it is from them that the fertility of the plain is derived. Both were, until very recently, liable to severe flooding, which over the millennia has spread a thick, rich blanket of silt over the area. Sites of the fifth millennium have been found under as much as five metres of deposit. But there has also been severe wind erosion which, according to Adams, is now exposing third- and fourth-millennium land surfaces. Plainly, the process has not been one of straightforward aggradation over the years and this conclusion has immediate implications for the interpretation of the findings from surface survey. The whole of the alluvial plain lies outside the area of rain-fed agriculture: rainfall is as low as 150 mm per annum. Rain is confined to the winter months and summer heat is intense; to add to the problems of the first farmers the rivers flood in the spring at the height of the growing season, washing away the young plants unless measures are taken to hold back the flood waters. If this disaster is avoided, then water must be led into the fields at appropriate intervals to allow the crops to ripen, otherwise they will shrivel and die. If these problems can be overcome, a wide range of cereals, fruits, vegetables and fodder plants can be successfully grown.

Because of the imperatives of irrigation techniques, early settlement tended to concentrate in fairly narrow bands along the river courses, sometimes three or four towns quite close together, sometimes one large city, like Uruk, with a necklace of smaller satellite towns and villages. Villages tend to be underrepresented in the archaeological record, partly because their traces are difficult to find in areas of silt deposition or of wind erosion, and partly because archaeologists have in the past preferred to work on sites which promised richer material pickings, so the picture is inevitably somewhat distorted. Between the settled enclaves were areas of semi-desert, unirrigated, where sheep and goats could be grazed and scrub and thorn bushes collected for fuel. Apart from its agricultural potential, the Sumerian plain has no natural resources of stone or metal. The nearest stone lies in the desert west of the site of Eridu and the nearest supplies of copper are much further afield in Iran, Anatolia and Arabia. Timber, too, was not easily available, though after the introduction of the palm, probably some time during the late fourth millennium, there was a source of rather poor-quality wood for roof timbers and other such purposes. Any other wood had to come from the mountains to the north and east or, in the case of cedars, popular for use in temple buildings, probably from Lebanon. A whole variety of woods was also imported up the Gulf, possibly from as far away as India. Fish was freely available from the rivers and from the great marshes in the south: it was smoked and dried as well as eaten fresh. The shells of river molluscs are found on many sites, together with fish and animal bones, and provided mother-of-pearl for inlay and decoration as well as food. The lush vegetation on the banks of the rivers also provided cover for a variety of game and there was apparently no prohibition on the eating of pig in Sumerian society. The marshes at the southern end of the plain are rich in fish and reeds and the traditional life of the inhabitants seems to have changed little since Sumerian times. Their buildings and their boats can be exactly matched in the art of the third millennium. The earliest inhabitants of this southern plain were physically similar to the modern inhabitants, although the teeth of the skulls from the Royal Cemetery at Ur were said to be unusually large! There are no indications from the skeletal evidence of a mixture of physical types, no evidence for example of brachycephalic Sumerians and dolicho-cephalic Semites, a dichotomy once suggested on the evidence of the art. It must, however, be said that the skeletal evidence from Sumer is usually in a poor condition and exact measurements are often out of the question. Sir Arthur Keith, reporting on the human remains from the Royal cemetery at Ur, notes that all the skulls he was able to measure were big and long and narrow, with a good cranial capacity (Keith 1934).

PASTORALISTS AND FARMERS

Even though it is not possible to distinguish different physical types in early Mesopotamia, there was undoubtedly one very important dichotomy in the population, that between the settled villagers and the nomadic herders. The division between them was not always a clear-cut one: some villagers were probably transhumant, taking their flocks into the hills in search of better grazing in the summer for instance, and according to the texts some nomads in the early second millennium had established permanent camps on the outskirts of large towns, such as Mari and Sippar (Kupper 1957). However, in essence the population can be divided into those people in permanent settlements, who relied primarily on agriculture and stock rearing for their subsistence, and those who wandered between the settlements with their herds of sheep and goats. The two ways of life were in many ways complementary. The pastoralists were able to provide goods and services to the settled farmers in return for supplies of grain, which they seldom produced themselves. In spite of the symbiotic economic relationship, conflicts arose between the groups, and the urban dwellers tended to despise the nomads as uncouth barbarians. Yet the presence of these people on the fringe of the irrigated land was to have a profound effect on the settled population over the course of the third millennium. Observations suggest that there is a natural tendency among pastoralists for the richest and poorest members of the group to drift into permanent settlement. The reasons for this are largely economic. The largest flocks suffer from the law of diminishing returns and profits are better invested in something else, often property, while the poorest members of the group are often forced into towns to look for work. The steady increase in the number of Semitic personal names, often those of nomads, found in the archives of the third millennium towns, where the early names are predominantly Sumerian, suggests that just such a movement was taking place. Some of the immigrants may have originated from Semitic-speaking towns and villages in the north of the Tigris/Euphrates plain rather than from the nomadic tribes. Semitic personal names occur on some of the earliest tablets we have, and by the Early Dynastic period some of the scribes writing in Sumerian at Abu Salabikh had Semitic names. There were only finite numbers of Sumerian speakers representing the first inhabitants of the towns, so that over the years the linguistic balance seems to have tipped against them until by about 2000 BC Sumerian had almost ceased to be spoken (Cooper 1973). By about 1800 it had become a dead language. By extrapolation we may also presume that the urban population now consisted of people for whom a Semitic language was their mother tongue and many of whom may have originated among the pastoral tribes on the fringes of the Sumerian heartland.

Nomadic pastoralists are hard to identify in the archaeological record because of the sparseness of their material possessions and the perishable nature of many of their artefacts, rugs, leather bags and so on. This lack of an archaeological presence has led to

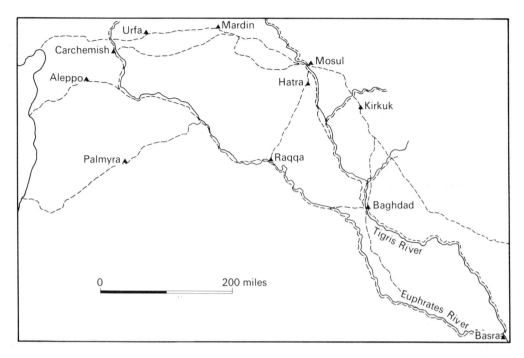

3 The Near East, with routes described in the text

their role in prehistoric times being underestimated until relatively recent times. It is probable that they had an important role to play in the diffusion of both raw materials and ideas, especially in the Neolithic. Their regular cycles of movement, taking their flocks to new grazing, brought them in contact with different groups of people in different ecological niches and seem to have provided a crucial channel of communication through which goods and ideas could flow, linking isolated groups of people over considerable distances. Later, with the development of more complex societies and of writing, this role was to a large extent taken over by urban specialists, merchants, scribes and messengers for instance.

COMMUNICATIONS

We have already seen that Mesopotamia divides into three geographic zones, but these zones together do not in any way form self-contained units. Economically and physically they are part of a much larger entity. There were a number of major routes (Map 3) linking together the Mediterranean and the Mesopotamian plain. The most northerly of these runs from the north-east corner of the Mediterranean, through Turkey, parallel with the modern border, before turning south-east at Mardin, where it was joined by a route from the important copper-producing region to the north around

Ergani Maden. The road then crossed the border and passed close to the important site of Tell Braq, before going through the gap in the Jebel Sinjar, and heading east for the Tigris and the ancient city of Nineveh, modern Mosul. Many of these routes can still be traced today and are followed by modern roads or even railways.

An alternative route ran slightly south of this from Carchemish, more or less directly east to the Sinjar and the Tigris, which, although hazardous, is navigable from Nineveh southwards at certain seasons of the year; at other times an alternative land route was available through the Hamrin valley via Kirkuk. A third route ran still further south, from the Mediterranean via Aleppo across to the Euphrates, approximately in the region of Raqqa, and then had the choice of following the river southwards as far as Falluja before striking east. Alternatively, travellers might head out sooner, probably crossing the Wadi Tharthar in the vicinity of Hatra. This was geographically more difficult but avoided the local inhabitants, who were notorious at certain periods for the extortionate tolls they levied on caravans travelling down the river valley. South of this route and parallel to it ran the route via Palmyra, but we do not know when this was first extensively used. The route across the desert from Amman was not used until the advent of camel traffic and does not concern us here.

Travel from north to south was easier because of the rivers, the Euphrates especially being a crucial link at all periods. Heavy goods were commonly floated on rafts down the Tigris too, as far as Baghdad, but it is a much more uncertain river. As noted before, the land route through the Jebel Hamrin was an alternative. Once in the southern plain, the major canals also provided good means of communications and we known from textual sources that bulk shipments of grain and other commodities travelled by barge. Transport of goods in quantity was easier by water than by land. The gods, too, travelled by boat on their divine progresses to visit their colleagues in other Sumerian cities. Finally, two very important routes ran south from the southern end of the plain to the head of the Gulf, and so out to the sea and the rich lands of Magan, Meluhha and Dilmun. Probably the more important of these routes was again by water up and down the Shatt-el-Arab; we are told in texts of the third millennium that ships from overseas docked at the quays of some of the major cities of the plain, including Akkad, which probably lay at the northern end of the alluvium, and access must have been via the Shatt. There was also a land route running south from the confluence of the two great rivers parallel with the west coast of the Gulf. This is a seasonal route, but one frequently used by nomads in recent times. It may have been in use since the late fourth millennium for the transport of certain types of goods in relatively small quantities.

Here in Mesopotamia we have an area capable of producing a massive agricultural surplus, with excellent links to areas rich in the basic raw materials, especially metals, which it lacked. Trade was the life-blood of the economy and probably a critical factor in the development of urban life in the region and of one of the earliest civilisations the world has seen.

Chapter 2

HISTORY, CHRONOLOGY AND SOCIAL ORGANISATION

The period dealt with in this book covers between 1,500 and 1,800 years. There are, potentially, two major ways of dividing this long span of time up in order to identify the main phases and to pinpoint the changes which took place. The first is the purely archaeological method, which provides a relative system only, while the second, using scientific methods such as radiocarbon dating, gives us absolute dates. In some cases the absolute dates obtained by scientific methods can be cross-checked against the dates obtained from historical or quasi-historical inscriptions. The archaeological or relative sequence begins with the Uruk period, called after the site at which the distinctive plain pottery was first identified and we will look first at the other archaeologically recognisable characteristics of this and the succeeding periods. These can then be used to establish the relative dating of sites.

The Uruk period was characterised by a rapid increase in the amount of settlement and the emergence of a four-tiered settlement hierarchy. That is to say, for the first time there were settlements large enough to be called cities, as well as towns, villages and hamlets.

It is not surprising that the period also sees the development of a more complex administrative system and a more stratified society with the appearance of what may be the first secular leaders. Sadly, it also seems to see the emergence of armies and of organised warfare. All these characteristics are, to some extent, identifiable in the archaeological record.

Technologically, it was a time of rapid and important changes. In metallurgy we see the use of sophisticated casting processes for the first time; in pottery we see the use of the fast wheel; perhaps most significantly of all, we see the introduction of the first pictographic writing on clay tablets. This was accompanied by the introduction of the cylinder seal. The Uruk period was arguably the most innovative and important of any in the history of Mesopotamia and its influence was felt as far as the Mediterranean and the Anatolian plateau.

An enormous amount has been written over the last twenty years about the causes of this so-called urban revolution which distinguishes the Uruk period and it is not necessary here to do more than outline some of the more generally accepted ideas. One point on which most scholars are now agreed is that the term 'revolution' is an inappropriate one. The results were certainly revolutionary, but the process itself was long and slow. It is also agreed that it is no longer possible to pinpoint a single stimulus

13

or cause which brought these changes about. It used to be thought that population pressure, or trade, or irrigation, could be invoked to explain everything, but today a more sophisticated systems-oriented view prevails, which prefers to call on a number of interrelated factors. These are seen as acting on each other to produce an effect which is far greater than the sum of the individual parts. The favoured 'prime movers', as they are sometimes called, still include the old favourites of increased population, the development of both external and internal trade and the increasing sophistication of the irrigation system. There is room for other possible factors too which are less easy to identify in the archaeological record, such as minor fluctuations of climate and even the presence of charismatic individuals who may have gathered people to them.

These stimuli could operate in Mesopotamia only when there was an agricultural surplus. This surplus enabled a number of other developments to take place. It provided grain for export so that the country could trade for the raw materials it so clearly lacked; it also made it possible for full-time specialists to emerge who were not themselves primary producers. These people had other technical skills and provided the administrative expertise necessary to co-ordinate the much more complex society which began to emerge. Specialisation of this sort led in its turn to a more stratified society with an unequal distribution of wealth and status, a development which can be traced both in the architecture and in the graves. There also seems to have been an increase in the scale of warfare as the concentration of resources led some communities to become noticeably richer than their neighbours. The beginnings of this complex process, which is still not fully understood, can be seen in the preceding Ubaid period, but it is only in the Uruk period that a fully urban settlement pattern, with the four levels of settlement referred to above, can be detected in the south Mesopotamian plain. The north of Mesopotamia does not seem to have developed quite so fast (Redman 1978 still provides a valuable introduction to the study of urbanism; see also Haas 1982; Maisels 1990).

The next period, the Jemdat Nasr, again called after the site where the pottery was first located, is less easy to define. It certainly lasted a much shorter time and lacked the innovative quality of the Uruk, but its relationship to the periods which came before and after it is still under discussion (Finkbeiner 1986). There are few, if any, well excavated, fully reported, stratified sequences which cover the end of the Uruk, the Jemdat Nasr and the succeeding Early Dynastic I periods. It used to be thought that the Jemdat Nasr period could be identified by the presence of a certain type of cylinder seal with heavily drilled designs, often showing squatting pigtailed figures apparently engaged in various household tasks. Recently these seals have been found together with seals typical of the classic Uruk style and so can no longer be regarded as chronological indicators. This has given rise to the suggestion that the Jemdat Nasr has no independent chronological existence. However, the other type-fossil of the period, a painted ware with a distinctive purple slip, still continues to be found stratified

I Scarlet ware vase from Tell Gubba

between Uruk and Early Dynastic wares at sites like Abu Salabikh and less distinctive pot types can also now be assigned to this phase (J. Killick in Finkbeiner 1986). It is also possible to isolate a particular style of semi-pictographic tablets which belong exclusively to this timespan (Nissen 1986). The Jemdat Nasr has been reprieved as a period, but its geographical extent is still not properly defined and it may have had a fairly limited local distribution in the Diyala valley and the Sumerian plain. Vases of the same style have also been found along the Gulf coast and in Oman, where they are not indigenous, which seems to indicate trading contacts of some sort between the two areas.

The Early Dynastic period which followed is very much more substantial in terms of both time and material. Excavations in the Diyala valley in the 1930s under the direction of the great scholar Henri Frankfort established a sequence of phases within the Early Dynastic period (or ED), and determined their archaeological characteristics (Frankfort 1934). There are three major subdivisions and the third has now been further divided into IIIa and IIIb. Each phase is marked by stylistic changes in pottery and cylinder seals. For example, ED I is characterised by scarlet-washed pots with both geometric and figurative designs, which do not occur in later phases. ED II has a little scarlet-washed pottery, but after this painted pottery disappears from the repertoire and a certain type of plain jar with an upright handle becomes the most typical pot. In other areas there is an increasing mastery of the technology, but no major innovations. There are of course exceptions to this generalisation and in architecture the period is distinguished by the use of the plano-convex brick. This brick is a rectangle, but the upper surface is humped up into a curve. It is typically laid in a herring-bone pattern and, although it is found in the early part of the succeeding Agade period, its use is much more common in the ED. One new architectural form can also be attributed to the end of the ED and this is the famous ziggurat or stepped tower, which may have been the origin of the biblical story of the Tower of Babel. The earliest of these staged towers have been found at a number of sites in the ED III period (see chapter 4).

Apart from its physical characteristics, the ED period is usually regarded as the period during which the political concept of the city-state first took shape. The history of the time, in so far as it is possible to reconstruct it, is marked by the shifting of political power from one to another of the major cities on the Sumerian plain. The cities seem to have been ruled by governors or princes, possibly with the help of some sort of assembly of citizens. The ruler had military, judicial and religious duties and the power of the temple is apparently less than it had been in the Uruk, though the temple continued to be a major landowner and a vital part of the economy. The secular and religious aspects of the state seem to have been in some sort of balance. In the Agade period which followed, it was, for the first time, the secular power which was the dominant influence; for the first time, too, the whole of the Sumerian plain was united under one conqueror, the great Sargon of Agade.

The archaeological remains of the Agade period are very thin on the ground, for reasons which will be examined in the next chapter, but some magnificent pieces of statuary in both stone and copper have survived and provide us with a tantalising glimpse of the material culture of the period. The craftsmanship is even better than in the ED period and the style becomes progressively more naturalistic. Many of the pieces which have survived portray the kings of the dynasty carved in hard black diorite and the great stele of the penultimate king, Sargon's grandson Naram-Sin, shows the victorious king with the attributes of divinity (Fig. 2.1). He is wearing a horned helmet which previously had been worn only by gods. In the contemporary texts his name is written with the sign for a god, another important break with tradition. Here is more evidence for the triumph of the king, who now assumed divine status and so combined both sectors of the state – palace and temple – in his own

2.1 Naram-Sin wearing the horns of divinity

person. The Agade kings seem to have seen themselves as military commanders first and foremost. Much emphasis is laid on their victories in the surviving royal inscriptions, but they were also very active in the administrative field, centralising government and giving conquered territory as grants of land to their own largely Semitic followers. This activity is reflected in both the monumental art and the seals of the period. It is clear, however, that some of the old Sumerian city governors remained in office and served under Agade kings. There does not seem to have been any victimisation of the old order (Glassner 1987).

In spite of the military prowess of the Agade kings, the last one was overthrown by an enemy horde from the east led by the Guti, a conglomerate of tribesmen from the Zagros mountains, presumably drawn down onto the plain by its evident prosperity.

The Guti dominated Sumer for a period estimated to have lasted anything between forty and ninety years, but the lower figure is now generally preferred. They left few archaeological traces and were finally ejected by a Sumerian coalition led by the governor of Uruk (Hallo 1971). He in his turn was quickly ousted by one of his officers, Ur-Nammu of Ur, who founded what was to be the last of the great Sumerian dynasties, the third dynasty of Ur.

The Ur III period was one of great prosperity, with a booming economy allowing great reconstruction programmes to be initiated at all the major religious sites, most notably at Ur itself. The art of the period is very accomplished, but lacks the fire of the Agade examples. The exception to this generalisation is perhaps to be found in the large numbers of clay plaques and figurines depicting many aspects of everyday life as well as apotropaic figures of gods and demons. There are delightful figures of animals as well as rather stereotyped goddess and guardian-angel types. Even furniture, such as beds and chairs of clay, is found, though its significance is not really known. Archaeologically speaking, the most significant feature of the Ur III period is the magnificent monumental architecture.

By the end of the dynasty, Sumerian political power was virtually exterminated, with only two cities, Isin and Larsa, surviving as independent entities for a few more years. Political power was never to revive again, but the break in the material culture is much less marked.

ABSOLUTE DATING

We have looked at the relative dating of the periods which interest us and will now try to put them into some kind of framework of absolute dates based largely on figures derived from the technique of carbon-14 analysis. Such dates, especially when they are based on samples from a single archaeological horizon, and not on a stratified sequence, should not be regarded as anything more than an indication of a possible calendar date, especially as real problems still remain in calibrating radiocarbon dates with what might be called real, historical time. Radiocarbon dates can, in some instances, be cross-checked against dates derived from the historical evidence. The Uruk period is conventionally said to have begun about 3500 BC (Cambridge Ancient History 1971) but as new, revised radiocarbon dates become available a strong case can be made for suggesting that this date may have to be pushed back four or even five hundred years. This case rests on two new sets of dates, one from late Uruk sites in north Syria and the other from late Predynastic Egypt, a period broadly contemporary with the late Uruk in Mesopotamia (Moorey 1987). On the basis of these dates a timespan of 3400–3200 BC could be suggested for the late Uruk (Nissen 1987). The beginning of the period is difficult to pinpoint, but the excavations at the type-site of Uruk identified eleven major levels, some of them with substantial sub-periods so that a span of 600 to 800 years does not seem ridiculous, especially if we remember how many remarkable innovations are to be attributed to the period. More dates from the early part of the period would be valuable.

Very little direct evidence is available for the date of the Jemdat Nasr period, which, as we have already suggested, seems to have been of relatively short duration. Dates for the beginning of ED I cluster around 2900 BC, which would indicate a maximum of 300 years for the Jemdat Nasr from around 3200 to 2900 BC. On the basis of the archaeology alone, this might seem a rather generous allocation of time and could perhaps be compressed by as much as a hundred years. A number of radiocarbon dates are now becoming available from the later ED, mainly from Nippur and Abu Salabikh. These indicate dates of about 2800 for the end of ED I and of around 2600 for the beginning of ED IIIa (Wright 1980). Radiocarbon dates for the latest ED IIIb and the succeeding Agade periods are not available and we are forced to rely on quasi-historical dates derived from the King Lists and other inscriptions for this timespan. The position in Ur III is slightly better and a date for the beginning of the period from Ur is calculated at 2230 ± 85 BC, and another from Nippur for the end of the dynasty gives 2303 ± 109, which on historical grounds looks much too high and should be discounted.

We have already mentioned that, at least for the Agade and Ur III dynasties, it is possible to crosscheck the radiocarbon dates against the dates derived from the historical sources. Earlier than this the historical records are so incomplete that checking becomes extremely difficult. The most important of the historical sources is the Sumerian King List, a document actually compiled after the fall of the Ur III dynasty and whose interpretation is fraught with difficulty. As our knowledge has increased, its shortcomings as a genuine historical work have become more and more obvious. Some dynasties, such as those of Lagash for which we have incontrovertible evidence in the shape of inscriptions of the actual rulers, are omitted entirely; other dynasties which we know to have been contemporary with each other, again from royal inscriptions which establish the synchronisms, are shown as sequential; the regnal years of the earliest dynasties are fantastic, crediting individual kings with reigns of thousands of years and, finally, there are many lacunae in the record (Jacobsen 1939). A strong case can be made for suggesting that the King List is actually a piece of political polemic, but even so much of the evidence in it is of considerable value (Michalowski 1983).

Additional information can be gained from royal inscriptions, which sometimes provide regnal years as well as the name of the ruler. Occasionally, such inscriptions also include information on momentous events of the time such as victorious campaigns or major building projects. From the Agade period onwards, when the dating system was revised, such information is also to be found in the year-names from which the calendar was compiled. Each year was called after some important event which had taken place in the previous one. The absolute dates derived from these sources for the

Agade and Ur III periods, during which the King List is reasonably complete, are achieved by working backwards from the dates proposed on astronomical grounds for Hammurabi of Babylon, whose dynasty succeeded that of Ur III after an unsettled period of indeterminate length. Five possible dates for Hammurabi's accession are proposed on the basis of observations of the planet Venus, recorded in the reign of one of Hammurabi's successors. Most scholars now favour the middle date of 1792 for this event and, by counting backwards from this year, dates of 2112–2006 BC are given for the Ur III dynasty and of 2317–2191 BC for the Agade rulers (Cambridge Ancient History 1971). However, recently, a reassessment of the astronomical evidence favours a date of 1848 BC for the accession of Hammurabi and if this is accepted the dates for the earlier periods will have to be readjusted accordingly (Huber 1982). It has to be said that at a distance of four thousand years, a discrepancy of fifty years does not seem of fundamental importance. Even this modest amount of extrapolation is bedevilled by uncertainties, and attempts to date the ED by similar methods have not proved useful.

In summary, it can be seen that both the scientific and historical methods, neither of them entirely satisfactory, suggest that the period from the early Uruk to the end of the Ur III period covered a span of about 1,800 years. The Uruk period probably began about 3800 BC and the Ur III dynasty came to an end just before 2000 BC.

HISTORY AND SOCIAL ORGANISATION

Details of the history can be found in a number of textbooks, most of which are somewhat out of date, such as the Cambridge Ancient History and Hallo and Simpson 1971.

This section deals with a period during which Sumerian was one of the languages spoken in the area between the Tigris and the Euphrates, south of the Hit–Samarra line. It was not the only language spoken there; Semitic dialects were also in use. The adjective Sumerian is now loosely used to describe not only the language but also the people and the culture which evolved on the plain of southern Mesopotamia at this time. The southern part of the plain also became known as the land of Sumer. It is not possible to tell how much of this culture should be attributed to the Sumerian speakers and how much to those speaking a Semitic language, but the question hardly matters as it seems to have been the fusion of all the elements in the population which produced the distinctive civilisation which will be described in the rest of this book.

People with both Sumerian and Semitic names were present in the area from the time of the earliest written records at the end of the Uruk period. Initially the people with Semitic names seem to have been concentrated in the north of the plain, in the area which became known as Akkad, in the vicinity of the city of Kish. There is nothing to suggest that either group was a recent arrival at the end of the fourth millennium. The population may well have been mixed from the time of the earliest hunter-gatherers, of whom no archaeological traces remain. From a study of the personal names in the documents of the next 500 years, it is possible to trace a steady increase in the number of Semitic names in the population during the third millennium and, apparently, a corresponding decrease in the use of the Sumerian language. Cooper has suggested that as early as the mid-third millennium spoken Sumerian was in decline (Cooper 1973). By about 1800 BC the process was complete and Sumerian ceased to be spoken at all. It became a liturgical and scholarly language, just as Latin did in medieval Europe.

We do not know for certain where the Semites who came to make up the majority of the inhabitants of the plain came from. It has been suggested that some probably originated from amongst the nomadic groups who lived on the northern and western fringes of the Sumerian plain. Others may have entered the plain from the Zagros mountains to the east. It used in the past to be thought that this influx of Semitic speakers must have caused conflict and even genocide, but there is little evidence for conflict and none for genocide. It seems that the change took place by a gradual process of infiltration over a long period of time, perhaps as long as a thousand years.

Within the span of time during which the Sumerian language was used, we can, for the first time, begin to identify changes in the social and political structures and even to identify specific events of historical significance. In one or two rare cases individuals begin to emerge from their background, though the ordinary 'man in the street' is still virtually unknown. We have already indicated that in the Uruk period the temple seems to have been the dominant institution, but the period may have seen the emergence of the first secular rulers. The evidence is scanty, but we have the depictions in the art of a bearded figure who is not a priest, wearing a type of Pathan hat. We also probably have the word *sharru*, the Akkadian word for king, in a syllabary of the late Uruk period. From the Jemdat Nasr period until the end of the ED period the political scene on the Mesopotamian plain was characterised by a pattern of city-states which dominated it in turn, forming alliances and breaking them in an ever-changing kaleidoscope. Not all of the cities were ruled by Sumerian princes: Kish in the north of the plain was apparently the home of a Semitic dynasty from the earliest times, judging from the names of the rulers of its first dynasty as listed in the King List. Other important cities included Adab, Lagash, Larsa, Ur and Uruk. Eridu, although regarded in Sumerian mythology as the oldest city on the plain, originally founded by the god Ea when he established civilisation, was never apparently the home of a ruling dynasty. Nippur, too, enjoyed a special status as the religious capital of the plain and home of the patron god of Sumer, the father of the gods, Enlil.

Each of these cities, together with its hinterland of satellite settlements, was regarded as the home of one of the major gods of the pantheon. Ur belonged to Nannar/Sin, the moon god, while Ishtar/Inanna, goddess of love and war, had her home at Uruk, which also housed the sky god Anu. These patrons were expected to defend the interests of their own cities in the council of the gods where all major decisions on the future of mankind were discussed. It was in this council that the decision was taken to

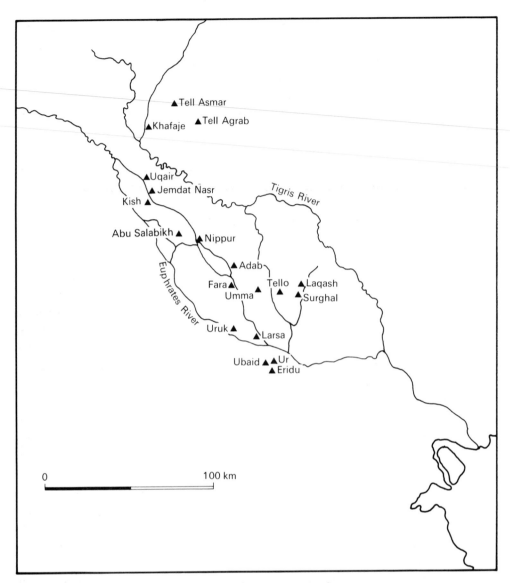

4 The cities of the Sumerian plain

flood the earth because man was becoming altogether too noisy and was disturbing the repose of the great gods. Ea crept out of the council, warned Utnapishtim in Shurrupak/ Fara of the impending disaster and so enabled him to escape on the ark and perpetuate the human race. Given the totalitarian power of the gods and their somewhat capricious exercise of it, it was natural that the first duty of the ruler of a Sumerian city was to keep his patron deity well disposed by observing all the proper forms of worship, and by frequent presents when the economic state of the nation allowed. The ruler seems to have been regarded as the deputy and servant of the city-god and if he failed in his duty towards that god the prosperity of the state would inevitably suffer.

It seems probable that initially power resided with the priests and we do not know how the earliest secular rulers emerged. It has been suggested that they may originally have been temporary war leaders, drawn from the best warriors, whose posts became institutionalised. Possibly they were, in some cases, charismatic men with special powers of some sort, or merely the seniors of group of elders or the heads of the most prosperous extended family in a locality (Maisels 1987). What we do know is that by ED III the office of ruler had become largely hereditary, passing from father to eldest son. The inscriptions from Lagash, for instance, show a continuous descent for at least six generations. Sometimes the ruler would record that he had been specifically chosen for the job by the city's god, but this was frequently a device used by usurpers to justify their seizure of power. Sargon of Agade claimed to have been specially selected by the goddess Ishtar, though his origins were obscure and later tradition said he was illegitimate.

A number of different words for ruler are known in Sumerian and each seems to have had a specific meaning which it is not always easy for us to determine. The most commonly used of these are En, Ensi and Lugal (Hallo 1957). The first may indicate priestly status, the second seems to be slightly less important and to equate roughly with our term governor (Fig. 2.2), while the third is perhaps closest to king in its implication. The word *sharru* or king is probably also known from the Uruk IV period onwards and may perhaps be the Semitic equivalent of Lugal. Glassner has suggested that this title is primarily a military one (Glassner 1987). Various other titles are also found such as King of the Four Quarters, which seems to have been assumed at a slightly later date by rulers who made substantial conquests outside Sumer itself. The title King of Kish also seems to have had special significance and was adopted by the rulers of other cities as an extra feather in their caps. It seems to imply some wider authority, perhaps over the whole plain. In the dispute which raged for years between the towns of Umma and Lagash it was a king of Kish called Mesilim who brought about the initial settlement of the dispute, possibly in his capacity of overlord of both cities, though he may just have been an honest broker (Cooper 1983).

The city rulers of the Early Dynastic period do not seem to have had absolute power; there are indications that there may have been assemblies of citizens in some cities which had to ratify major decisions taken by the ruler. For example, when Gilgamesh wanted to go to war, he was unable to do so until he had obtained the approval of the people. There seem to have been two assemblies in Uruk at the time of Gilgamesh and, having failed to obtain the approval of the council of elders, he then went to the council of young men, who enthusiastically endorsed his proposal (For an alternative interpretation see Katz 1987). It is clear that the priesthood too exercised considerable political control, having as they did a 'hot line' to the gods. This hot line enabled them

2.2 Ur-Nanshe, governor of Lagash, carrying bricks to build a temple

to interpret the omens, which had a powerful influence on every sphere of activity in Sumerian society. Omens could be found in many natural phenomena such as the flight of birds, but the most popular method was the study of the entrails of sacrificial animals. The observation of the configurations of the guts and of any abnormalities were minutely studied, compared with records of past observations and the events which had followed them, and then used to predict the future. Dreams were also important in foretelling events and there were special classes of priests who were expert in each of these different types of divination.

There were economic constraints too on the ruler's freedom of action. The palace was an important landowner, but its power was balanced, at least until the Agade period, by that of the temple. Both institutions controlled large numbers of men and women who worked for them for wages of food and other necessities and who do not seem to have been free to move away, nor did they own any land of their own. They seem to have held a position in society very broadly similar to that of a serf in medieval Europe but the analogy cannot be pushed too far. As well as working the land, these people were also used in the manufacturing industries run by the public institutions which are discussed in more detail in chapter 7. During the third millennium there was also a growth in the private ownership of land. The earliest records we have suggest that land was held by families rather than by individuals and all male members of the family had to give their consent to a sale (Diakonoff 1982). Gradually, this practice ceased, and property seems to have passed into the hands of private individuals. Women could hold land and the wives of the city rulers frequently administered very large estates on their own behalf, but the land more usually belonged to the males of the family. By the Agade period, large parcels of land were being given to his followers by the king as a reward for their services (Foster 1982) and the amount of land in private hands seems to have increased, while there is little evidence for the large temple holdings of earlier times. The amount of wealth in private hands also increased, and by the end of our period private individuals seem to have been involved in long-distance trading and other commercial activities which previously had been the prerogative of the state (Foster 1981). The evidence is still very limited and it may be necessary to reassess our conclusions as more information is collected.

As we have already said, the Early Dynastic period saw the shifting of political power from one to another of the cities on the plain. The power of the city-states seems to have been largely confined to the southern plain, although individual rulers made successful sorties outside it. The end of the ED period saw important changes in this pattern with the emergence of Lugalzagesi of Uruk, a Sumerian governor of Umma who rose to control the whole of the plain and who then pushed as far as the Mediterranean Sea. In an inscription he claimed that Enlil, the patron god of Sumer, had given him all the lands between the upper and the lower seas, that is between the Mediterranean and the head of the Gulf. It seems likely that this conquest was not much more than a successful raiding party, but it marks the first time that a Sumerian prince claimed to have reached what was, for them, the western edge of the world. Lugalzagesi's triumph was short-lived and he was rapidly defeated by a rival from much nearer home.

Sargon of Agade, the successful rival and founder of a new, Semitic dynasty, had apparently begun his political career as the cup-bearer to Ur-Zababa, king of Kish. He broke away from Kish to found the new city of Agade which became the base from which he launched his campaign to subdue all the cities of the plain. Sargon was a formidable soldier and a considerable administrator. He became one of the great heroic prototypes on whom later monarchs modelled themselves and many legends and stories accumulated round his name. This makes it more difficult to establish the true extent of his conquests, but like Lugalzagesi he claims to have reached the Mediterranean and may even have penetrated central Anatolia. A later story tells how merchants at the town of Purushkanda in central Anatolia appealed to him for help against an oppressive local ruler. Sargon also seems to have destroyed a number of north Syrian cities, including, very probably, the recently discovered city of Ebla/Mardikh (Matthiae 1980). He also attacked Elam in the south-east and controlled the waterways down to the head of the Gulf. As well as these military exploits, he seems to have centralised the administration, reformed the dating system, and clipped the wings of the old city-states. He also went out of his way to abide by the old customs and, like many of his Sumerian predecessors, built a temple at Nippur, the home of the national god. In spite of this, his long reign ended in a general uprising which was eventually suppressed by his successor.

It was Sargon's third successor, his grandson Naram-Sin, who was the other outstanding figure of the dynasty. He seems to have followed in his grandfather's footsteps and reasserted some sort of control as far as the Anatolian plateau. His stelae have been found in the Zagros mountains at sites such as Darbend-i-Gawr, commemorating his victories over the hill people and especially over the Lullubi, who figure as the defeated enemy in his most famous victory stele which is described in chapter 8. He and his predecessors were also active east of the Tigris and especially in Elam, the area near the ancient capital of Susa, which seems to have become a vassal state at this time. Naram-Sin campaigned even further afield, and claimed to have conquered the land of Magan, now usually thought to be in the Arabian Gulf, probably an area roughly equivalent to modern Oman.

Like Sargon, he introduced political changes too, of which the most important was his assumption of divine status late in his reign after these outstandingly successful campaigns. They also led him to take the title King of the Four Quarters of the World. It is difficult for us to tell how this break with tradition appeared to his contemporaries, but it may not have seemed too outrageous. It is interesting that later tradition maintained that the dynasty had fallen because of gross impiety by both Sargon and Naram-Sin, but this seems to have been connected with the building of temples at Nippur and not with the assumption of divinity, which passes without comment. All but the first of the Ur III kings also adopted the same status and once again the move seems to have attracted no adverse reaction. As we have said before, by declaring himself a god, Naram-Sin succeeded in uniting the two major powers in the kingdom in his own person.

The empire of Agade was destroyed by attacks from a group of tribesmen from the mountains, known collectively as the hordes of Gutium. They descended into the plain, looting and pillaging, and established themselves there for a period of about fifty years, though the extent of their political control was probably very limited. Several further kings of Agade are listed after the fall of the empire who seem to have continued to rule a rump kingdom in the north of the plain. It also seems likely that the city of Lagash under its prince/governor Gudea and his son continued as an independent state. The Guti were finally ejected by a coalition of the old city-states led by Utuhegal of Uruk, but he did not enjoy his success for long. He in turn was defeated by one of his former lieutenants, Ur-Nammu of Ur, who may also have been his son and who founded the last of the important Sumerian dynasties, the Third Dynasty of Ur.

Ur-Nammu seems to have been a traditionalist and in all his inscriptions refers to himself in traditional terms as the servant of his god Sin. He built widely, not only at Ur itself, where he rebuilt the sacred area and the great ziggurat of which the remains are still standing today, but also at all the other major sanctuaries in his kingdom. We do not know whether his rule extended beyond the plain itself, though a typical foundation nail of this date, now in the museum in Copenhagen, is said to have come from near Mosul and there may be traces of Ur III activity at the site of Tell Brak in the Habur region of north Syria. Ur-Nammu's successor, Shulgi, certainly had to fight a series of battles east of the Tigris, and his successor was worshipped at the town of Eshnunna in the Diyala valley, which may already have been under the control of Ur. Even if not part of the kingdom of Ur, the area east of the Tigris seems to have come firmly within the sphere of influence of the Ur rulers.

It was Shulgi who was to consolidate and reorganise the kingdom of Ur. He introduced new weights and measures, set up scribal schools and apparently presided over a huge expansion of the civil service (Gibson and Biggs 1987). In the later part of his reign Shulgi reverted to the Akkadian habit and declared himself divine, a custom which was continued by the last three kings of the dynasty. Shulgi's reign was marked by a period of great prosperity which lasted into the reign of his successor Shu-Sin, who built a great wall to keep out the Amorites of the west. This ran across where the Tigris and Euphrates are closest together, perhaps suggesting that this marked the northern extent of his kingdom. Ibbi-Sin, the last king, was less fortunate. Agricultural yields seem to have begun to decline, leading to serious economic problems.

The view that this decline was the result of over-irrigation has been challenged recently by Powell, who questions much of the evidence on which the hypothesis was based (Powell 1985). More evidence is needed before this question can be settled, but it does seem as if too much emphasis may have been placed on the economic effects of over-irrigation and attendant salinisation of the soil. Decreasing yields, a series of bad harvests, over-centralisation, treacherous subordinates and another wave of invaders from the east brought the Ur III period to an inglorious close and Ibbi-San was carried off in chains. Two laments (Pritchard 1969) record the impact which the fall of the city of Ur and of its kings had on future generations. Sumer as an entity disappeared from history, never to reappear, the Sumerian language ceased to be used, and a great civilisation was irretrievably damaged, even though two cities, Isin and Larsa, survived the devastation to hand on some of the old traditions.

Many changes took place at about the time that Sumerian ceased to be spoken. Political power, after a period of fragmentation and confusion, seems to have been briefly focussed to the north of Mesopotamia under the first king of the Old Assyrian kingdom, Shamshi-Adad, and then, on his death, Hammurabi of Babylon became the dominant figure. Both of these kings were of Semitic origin. The virtual extinction of the Sumerian language, together with these political changes, makes a convenient break in the history of the area. It must be remembered, however, that the break is more of a convenience for scholars than an actual cataclysmic event.

In spite of the passing of almost five millennia, it is still possible to trace remnants of Sumerian culture in the world today. Perhaps the best-known example of this is the biblical story of the flood, which is similar in many details to the legend of Gilgamesh and his visit to Ziusudra, the Sumerian Noah, who tells him of the great flood and of his escape from it in words which the Bible echoes. The Sumerians may also have been the first people to have used the wheel and in building they probably invented the true arch as well as the corbel vault and the dome. Their counting system, the so-called sexagesimal system, also survives today in the measurement of time with sixty minutes in the hour, and in the measurements of degrees in a circle. The study of the Sumerians can be said to have immediate, if limited, relevance for the development of our own civilisation.

Chapter 3

PATTERNS OF SETTLEMENT AND
AGRICULTURE

PATTERNS OF SETTLEMENT

Archaeologists have always been interested in the way in which people used their environment, but the value of the systematic study of patterns of settlement only became apparent to them in the early 1960s. Archaeological interest resulted from the work being done by geographers like Chorley and Haggett, following in the footsteps of earlier scholars like Christaller and Losch, who attempted to identify the regularities of patterning which could be detected in many different parts of the world. These seemed, at least in part, to determine the position, size and status of each settlement and its relationship to its neighbours. Obviously such theories had immediate and important applications in archaeology and were especially relevant to the attempts then in progress to recognise the earliest urban centres and to define the processes which led to their appearance. In order to achieve this aim and to identify these early urban centres archaeologists borrowed wholesale from the geographers their concepts of the ranking of settlements, of central-place function and of ideal patterns of settlement forming hexagonal territories in an undifferentiated landscape.

The only way in which the archaeological evidence needed for these studies could be collected was by survey, and the sixties also saw the development of new techniques for survey and prospecting, as well as a refinement of existing ones. These were coupled with an increasing sophistication in their application and interpretation. Old-fashioned distribution maps, which were often said to provide more information on the distribution of archaeologists than anything else, gave way to sophisticated statistical analyses and computer modelling.

The first survey work to apply some of these new, improved methods in Mesopotamia was carried out in the early sixties by Robert Adams, first in the Diyala valley and then on the plain itself. It quickly became apparent that there were special problems involved in working on the plain, in addition to those more generally acknowledged in other parts of the world. It is important to consider these problems in order to be able to assess the evidence and the conclusions drawn from it. Robert Adams, himself the foremost proponent of the method, is also its most rigorous critic and would be the last person to put more weight on the evidence than it will bear. All the points made in the succeeding paragraphs are drawn from Adams's own work and reference should be made to his books for further details (Adams 1965, 1981; Adams and Nissen 1972). The problems fall into two main groups, those involved in the retrieval of the material and those involved in interpreting it. Those in the first category are caused by the distinctive physical characteristics of the Mesopotamian plain. Today, the plain is broken up by innumerable wadis and canals, some with few, if any, bridges capable of bearing the weight of a landrover, and much of it heavily cultivated, so that the survey of even a fairly limited area is extremely difficult in the time available for any such enterprise.

In addition, the process of siltation, which has been going on for thousands of years, has wiped some sites, particularly the smaller ones, completely off the map, and covered them with a heavy overburden of redeposited material. Sites like this are only discovered by accident, usually in the course of construction or drainage works. Ras al Amiya, an important Ubaid site near Kish, was discovered in the course of excavations for a canal under 1.2 m of silt (Stronach 1961). Even when the whole site is not hidden, the actual dimensions of a low-lying site may be artificially reduced by silt, or by erosion, thus making it difficult to attribute it to its correct place in the settlement hierarchy.

The possibility that the position of the head of the Arab Gulf may have fluctuated during the period we are dealing with raises the problem that sites in the extreme south of the plain may have been totally destroyed. Survey is today extremely difficult in the unique conditions prevailing in the southern marshes. There are reports of major prehistoric sites in this area, but they have not been substantiated. Taken together, these considerations suggest a considerable underrepresentation of sites in the region.

It is ironical that survey work suffers from the opposite problem as well. Once the soil dries, it becomes extremely friable and wind erosion poses more problems. Whole sites seem to have been blown out in some places and the areas of others drastically altered. Redeposition can further confuse the record, whether the agents are wind and water, or man. Many ancient sites have been used as sources of fertiliser for fields or of ballast for construction work. More recently, illicit excavations have been a problem. Any of these activities are also cumulatively destructive, as once a site has been dug into it is even more vulnerable to erosion by natural agents. A further important destructive force is the salt which permeates the soil over most of the plain and which is capable of destroying all but the toughest materials. At Abu Salabikh, for instance, almost the only evidence for post-Early Dynastic settlement is found in the sherds packed round drains which were sunk from higher levels, now totally destroyed by erosion and the action of salts. In a few places, however, later rubbish tips have been sealed by sedimentation. From surface collection it has been possible to detect Agade settlement, but not that of the early second millennium, which the pottery from the drains proves was also present.

Even once the measurements have been taken and material gathered in as objective and uniform a manner as possible, there still remain major theoretical and practical

problems to identifying hierarchies of settlement at any given period in time. The areas
of sites are often difficult or impossible to assess; the areas of the site at periods earlier
than the surface deposits are even more problematic. The relationship of surface finds
to what lies within a multi-period tell is still far from clear and little systematic work
has been done in this area (Redman and Watson 1970); the dating of many of the type-
fossils is crude, and at some periods very crude, making the recognition of short-term
contemporaneity between sites difficult, and it has yet to be shown that the area of a
site has a direct relationship to its position in the settlement hierarchy. To use a modern
analogy, who, on the survey evidence, would suppose that Washington, not New
York, was the political capital of the USA? Some preliminary work by Adams
comparing the occurrence of prestige artefacts between sites of different sizes shows no
direct correlation between area and the presence of such artefacts (Adams 1981).

Finally, there are the practical problems of transferring such large quantities of
information for storage and analysis. Even with the aid of modern technology there are
inevitably plenty of opportunities for human error to creep in, as a detailed comparison
between Adams's maps and catalogue entries shows.

In spite of all these caveats, and of the real limitations on the evidence, it is quite clear
that it is possible to discern *major* changes in settlement patterns, which seem to reflect
major social and political developments. It is also possible to show that these patterns
vary from one part of Mesopotamia to another, giving us some idea of their relative
importance at different periods. The earliest evidence of settlement in the Sumerian
plain dates from the Ubaid period, which immediately preceded our first identifiably
Sumerian period, the Uruk. The Ubaid period was characterised by a relatively small
number of sites, some of which were already appreciably larger than others, with
evidence for monumental architecture and some degree of site planning, as at Tell Uqair
(Lloyd and Safar 1943). As one might expect, there was already some evidence for the
clustering of sites in certain areas, notably around Ur and Eridu, and the bulk of the
settlements were identified in the southern half of the plain. (This distribution
undoubtedly reflects, at least in part, the patchy nature of the survey material from the
north of the plain, and the fact that the north-eastern area was not included in the
survey.) There is also a focus of Ubaid settlement in the Diyala and Hamrin valleys to
the east, two more areas where a thorough survey was possible. It must be a real
possibility that the absence of small sites in the north of the plain is more apparent than
real. Adams has suggested that, in the Ubaid period, the population was not yet totally
dependent on irrigation agriculture, a considerable section still being at least semi-
nomadic; these groups would be very difficult to recognise from settlement survey. On
the other hand there is convincing evidence from Choga Mami, a site to the east of
Baghdad, in the foothills of the Zagros, for a simple irrigation system from the early
Ubaid. Certainly from the Uruk period onwards the availability of irrigation water was

the decisive factor in the location of sites and this constraint produces patterns of
settlement far removed from the classical hexagon shapes mentioned earlier in this
chapter.

There is a considerable increase in the total number of sites identified for the early
and middle Uruk periods and a greater range in the size of settlements found; there is
again a difference in pattern between the north and south of the Sumerian plain. The
north is characterised by fewer, larger sites, well dispersed over the landscape, while in
the south there are only two sites of more than 20 ha, one of which is, of course, Uruk
itself. To compensate there are a larger number of sites in the 5–10 ha range which show
a tendency to cluster round the larger foci. It would seem that about the same total area
of land, around 2,100 km^2, was under cultivation in both north and south. By the late
Uruk the picture has altered considerably and the area under cultivation in the south
exceeds that in the north by an estimated 600 km^2. Four ranks of settlement can be
identified, with Uruk dominating the region in terms of size, having apparently
reached an area of about 100 ha, well ahead of anything in the north. The presence of
this one large settlement in the south seems to have had an inhibiting effect on the
development of middle-ranking sites in its vicinity. None has been identified within a
radius of 30 km.

In a recent paper Postgate has noted an important discontinuity in settlements at the
end of the Uruk period (Postgate in Finkbeiner 1986). On the southern plain there was
widespread abandonment at the end of the Uruk, and again at the end of the Jemdat
Nasr. In two peripheral regions, which will be more fully discussed later, the Er/Eridu
area and the Diyala valley, 'a substantial proportion of smaller sites were abandoned'
(*ibid.*). These were not resettled, but the Jemdat Nasr saw a larger number of new
villages founded, which continued in use until the end of ED I. This change in pattern
at the end of the Uruk period, coupled with the simultaneous dramatic cutback in
external contacts with Syria and Iran, does suggest a major political and economic
upheaval. On the other hand, the abandonment at the end of the Jemdat Nasr, which
was not apparently accompanied by any other signs of dislocation, may be attributable
to the centripetal effect of the expansion of large urban centres like Uruk, which
reached its maximum size at this time.

The evidence for Jemdat Nasr and ED I is best treated together as it is sometimes
difficult to distinguish them on the grounds of survey alone. The evidence indicates the
possibility of a further decrease in population in the north in the Jemdat Nasr and Early
Dynastic I periods; this may be accounted for by a considerable drift of people to the
south of the plain where it is estimated that there was a large increase in population.
Uruk continued to expand rapidly, and by the end of this time seems to have covered
something in the region of 400 ha; the inhibiting effect mentioned above is still
noticeable and no middle ranking sites have been found within a 15 km radius.
However, further to the north-east, there is a new cluster of medium-sized settlements

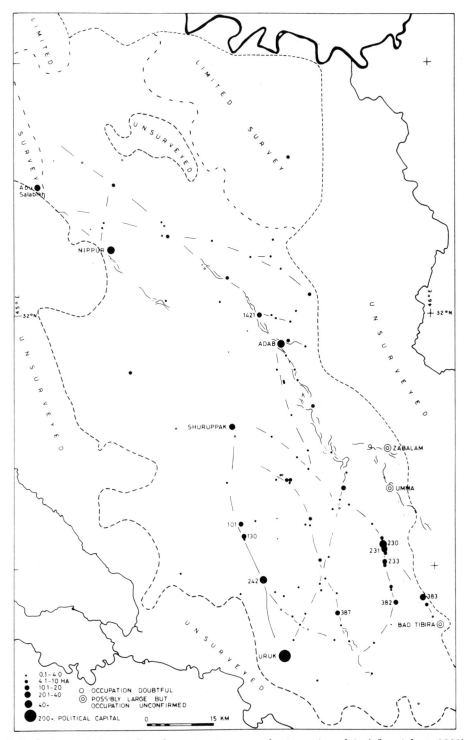

5 Early Dynastic I period settlement patterns on the Sumerian plain (after Adams 1981)

all apparently lying on the same waterway, either an old Euphrates channel or a large canal. In the centre of the plain, away from the inhibiting effect of Uruk, a number of the towns which were to become politically important later in the Early Dynastic period, now appear on the map. Adab covers about 50 ha and Shurrapak 25 (Martin 1983). Throughout the decline in population noted for the northern plain, Nippur seems to have remained fairly stable in size, perhaps reflecting what seems to have been its special function as a religious centre; by the end of ED I it was about 50 ha in extent while Abu Salabikh to the north-west was about 25 ha; the trend towards depopulation in the north began to reverse itself.

The later Early Dynastic period presents a considerable contrast with the patterns of settlement observed for earlier periods in a number of respects. Looking at the distribution maps one is instantly struck by the linear distribution of the later ED sites and by the disappearance of many of the smaller sites. Adams estimates that 78 per cent of the greatly increased population lived in sites larger than 10 ha in area and these sites lie, often quite close together, on the major waterways, underlining the crucial importance of access to water for irrigation as well as for ordinary domestic purposes. The most heavily populated of these ancient waterways seems to have been the more easterly of the now dry Euphrates channels which linked cities like Adab and Umma. Uruk lost its former pre-eminence and other major cities like Larsa and Bad Tibira appeared at the southern end of the plain. The geographic distribution, with no one dominant site, fits well with what we know of the political development of the period, which was characterised by a pattern of loosely knit city-states (see chapter 2). The proximity of some of the middle-ranking towns, all lying on the same waterway, so that the one furthest upstream exercised a measure of control over the supply of water to the others lower down the stream, seems to have been a potent source of conflict most vividly illustrated by the long-running saga of battles between the cities of Umma and Lagash in the ED III period (Cooper 1983). Unfortunately, Lagash lies outside the area of Adams's survey, but a preliminary survey of the area was carred out by Jacobsen (Jacobsen 1969), and it appears that some of the area is covered with a heavy overburden of silt. In any case details of the temporary abandonment of towns in the course of the ebb and flow of local power politics are impossible to identify from the sort of survey data at our disposal.

The later ED period was a highly urban society. Adams estimates that a higher proportion of the population lived in towns or cities than at any other time before 2000 BC. As a result of this, there was also a noticeable decline in the number of small settlements. A total of 1,659 sites is listed for the later ED period. The succeeding Agade period shows a decrease in the number of sites identified to 1,416, and there is a marked falling-off in the number of large sites. No sites over 200 ha in area are reported and the number in the bracket 40–200 ha also decreases. To balance this trend, the total number of small sites increases, evidence in Adams's view for the unsettled political

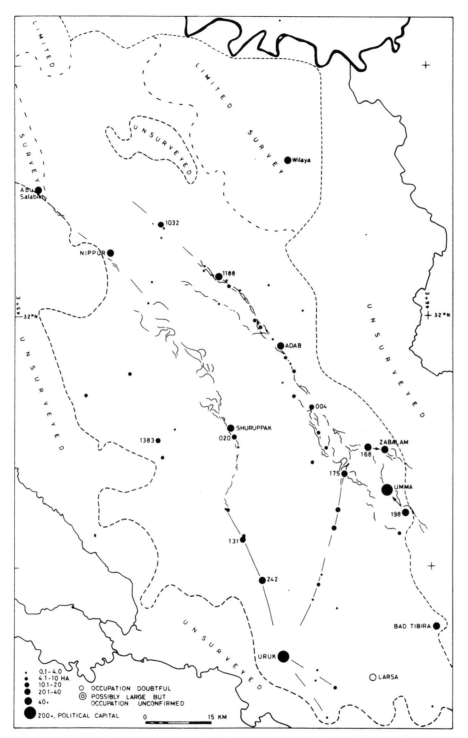

6 Late Early Dynastic period settlement patterns (after Adams 1981)

situation which drove people out into the country away from the major cities, which were the first targets for attackers.

This scenario is a somewhat puzzling one for a period which was, at least in Mesopotamian terms, a relatively stable and prosperous one. The old idea that the accession of Sargon of Agade represented a traumatic break with the traditions of the Early Dynastic period and a period of genocidal conflict can almost certainly be abandoned (see chapter 2), particularly in the light of the evidence of the monumental and glyptic art, while Naram-Sin of Agade reigned almost fifty years, a most unusual achievement. There is also documentary evidence for a flourishing overseas trade network.

Perhaps we should look elsewhere for the reason for the decrease in the number of sites and the absence of any settlements in the 200 ha bracket. We might consider the possibility that the decrease is more apparent than real. A possible explanation is provided by a number of factors which illustrate some of the problems mentioned earlier in reconstructing settlement patterns from survey evidence alone. The pottery of the Agade period is more difficult to recognise than that of earlier periods: it has relatively few unique and distinctive characteristics, much of it is undecorated, all of it is unpainted, so that sherds can easily be misattributed. The Agade period ended in a series of very destructive raids, followed on many sites by a period of abandonment, witness the evidence of the lamentation texts (Pritchard 1969). Mudbrick is a notoriously fragile building material and disintegrates rapidly if walls are not plastered and roofs are not repaired regularly. After this period of abandonment, lasting perhaps as long as fifty years in some cases, came a period of extensive rebuilding and renovation under the Ur III dynasty, which involved levelling the battered remains of earlier periods to provide stable foundations for new public buildings. Finally, as mentioned before, the heartland of the Agade empire has only been partially surveyed. These four factors, the difficulty of identifying type-fossils, the destruction at the end of the period and the extensive renovation fifty years later, coupled with incomplete survey data, may go some way to explaining the underrepresentation of Agade sites in the survey.

It might be expected that evidence for Agade settlement would be found in the Lagash region, where the political continuity remained relatively unbroken under Gudea and his successors, but, as noted before, the survey for the area is only preliminary. Finally, Adams's identification of a high proportion of smaller, rural sites, which led him to suggest a flight from the urban centres because of the unrest prevailing, is open to another interpretation. It could be said that it is only in well-ordered and stable conditions that people are prepared to leave the safety of a walled city and risk their lives, and those of their families, out in the open countryside. Some of the increased rural settlement may also be attributed to the settlement of nomadic groups attracted by the evident prosperity of the villages. The evidence which we have can at best be seen as ambiguous on this point.

There is no ambiguity about the obvious increases in settlement in the succeeding Ur III period. The Adab branch of the Euphrates was again the most heavily settled, and it seems to have been linked by canals with the Nippur/Uruk waterway, which also supported an increased number of settlements. The largest sites on the plain include Isin, Umma and Larsa with Adab, Nippur and a number of unnamed sites in the next rank. A large number of new canals was constructed to support the new settlements, new land being brought into cultivation and intensively irrigated. Royal inscriptions underline the importance attached to these hydraulic activities; considerable efforts in terms of manpower and resources were invested in upkeep and maintenance. Large bodies of men were required for periodic cleaning and repairwork and both the army and prisoners of war seem to have been drafted in as required. The initial result of this increase in the amount of water available was a corresponding increase in agricultural production with the emphasis on cereals. Yet, ironically, this intensification of agriculture seems to have been self-destructive. The presence of salt in the soil has been mentioned before, but the third millennium appears to have seen a considerable increase in the amount present, to the levels where the soil was rendered increasingly barren, at least in some areas (see chapter 2).

The reasons for this man-induced problem are to be found largely in the curious physical characteristics of the Mesopotamian plain. There is hardly any natural fall in the land from the latitude of Baghdad to the head of the Gulf, which means there is little natural drainage. Repeated applications of irrigation water to the fields do not drain off but lie on the surface. The water contains salts in solution, as almost all water does, and the hot sun causes evaporation of the water, leaving a crust of salt behind. The frequent flooding advocated by Sumerian agriculturalists (Kramer 1963) made matters worse. The situation is further exacerbated by more salts carried in the ground water, which, as the water-table is high, tends to be drawn to the surface by hygroscopic action when the soil is damp. Again the water evaporates, leaving more salty deposits to compound the problem. Over a period of years this process leads to dramatic drops in yields, a shift to salt-tolerant plants and eventually to the land being abandoned for cultivation. Adams has pointed out that salinisation is not entirely the result of human activity, but that 'It is endemic on semi-arid, sub-tropical alluviums where high evaporation and slow drainage gradually concentrate even the low salt levels that are present in rivers like the Tigris and Euphrates' (Adams 1981: 20).

The problem has been a recurrent one in Iraq and other parts of the world ever since the third millennium, but both the archaeological evidence and recent schemes by the Iraqi government have shown that it is not an irreversible one. Fallow periods, good drainage schemes and the planting of deep-rooted plants like prosopis, which help to lower the water-table, can return the land to its former fertility.

So far we have looked at patterns of settlement only on the southern plain. No systematic survey has been carried out between the two rivers north of Baghdad, but evidence is available from two areas to the north-east, the Hamrin and Diyala valleys.

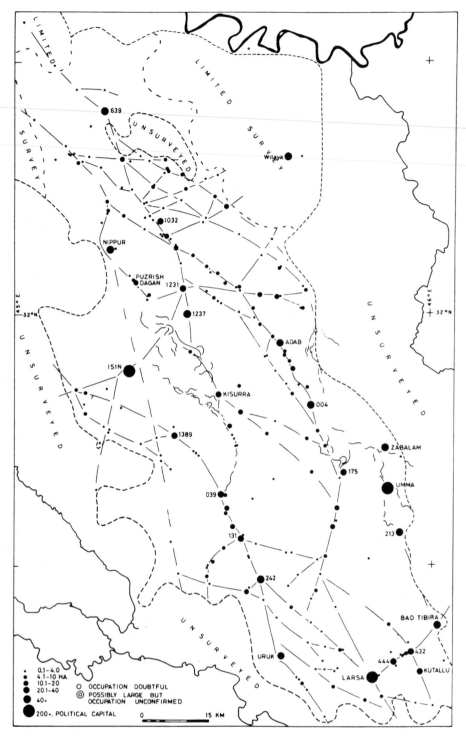

7 Ur III–Isin–Larsa period settlement patterns (after Adams 1981)

There is also a survey of the Ur area, south-west of the plain. This work was carried out by H.T. Wright (Wright 1981), who notes first that physically the area has changed dramatically since it was first inhabited in the early fifth millennium. Then the southernmost course of the Euphrates provided water for both the Ur region and a fresh-water lake on whose banks stood a number of sites including the town of Eridu, reputed in mythology to be the earliest city of all, home of the god Enki who saved mankind from the flood. The area has been subject to extreme environmental changes relating to shifts in the course of the river, which have caused rapid swings from agriculture to desertion. These sudden changes have obviously had an immediate effect on the settlement patterns, which as a result are considerably distorted when compared with the patterns observed on the plain, and so of relatively little use in confirming or modifying the conclusions drawn from them.

However, as on the plain, the early Ubaid period is characterised by a scatter of small sites, but by the later Ubaid there is evidence for at least a two-tier hierarchy of settlement, Ur and Eridu both ranking as small towns. The distribution of the settlements, and of a scatter of clay sickles which Wright takes to indicate the extent of the cultivated land, suggests small-scale irrigation with small canals branching off slightly larger ones. In essence this would be the sort of system which could be organised and maintained on a village network. Wright estimates a total cultivated area for the late Ubaid of *c.* 200 km². The early Uruk, by contrast, was identified at only two sites, Ur and Eridu. Eridu is known to have had a number of substantial buildings and to have covered a total area of between 40 and 45 ha; nothing is known of the total area of Ur, but Wright supposes some slight increase in population over the previous period. There is nothing comparable to the dramatic increase seen on the plain. The contrast is heightened in the late Uruk, when the plain saw further expansion, but Eridu seems to have been deserted, presumably because of water problems, while Ur remained small. A number of satellite villages do appear in the Ur hinterland, apparently all lying on the same waterway. Another canal seems to have branched off this and to have run south towards Eridu, without apparently reaching it. After a discontinuity, also observed on the plain, at the end of the Uruk, the Ur area continued to expand and prosper in a modest way into the ED III period, when it became the home of two ruling dynasties in fairly quick succession and reached a maximum size of *c.* 50 ha, still small by the standards prevailing on the plain. By the end of the period Eridu seems to have been reoccupied, perhaps reflecting a further shift in the Euphrates channel which brought water back to the site; two so-called palaces or administrative buildings belonging to this phase are known.

During the Agade period the region again deteriorated, Eridu was once more deserted, and Ur returned to being a smallish provincial town with fewer dependent settlements, a situation which was to change once more with the advent of the Ur III dynasty and its return to prosperity and political eminence. It seems possible that this part of the country may have escaped fairly lightly from the ravages of the Gutian hordes which brought about the collapse of the Agade empire, simply by virtue of its relative geographic isolation, and so was well placed to profit from their eventual expulsion by the Sumerian confederation under Utuhegal. Under the Ur III rulers the whole area seems to have flourished and the population to have doubled.

The evidence from the Diyala survey (Adams 1965) agrees better with that from the plain, although there are important divergences. The Ubaid settlements lie on natural waterways or on simple gravity-feed canals with little differentiation in size. In the south-east of the valley there is a cluster of five sites close enough together to suggest some sort of inter-village co-operation, at any rate in water management. In the Uruk period the number of settlements almost doubles, and a two-tier settlement pattern is clearly present. There are, by contrast with the plain, no major urban centres and this perhaps reflects the politically and geographically peripheral nature of the region. It was, however, important as a major route up onto the Iranian plateau, where evidence for Uruk contacts was found at Godin Tepe, a site controlling the access to the plateau near Hamadan (Weiss and Young 1975). This route seems to have been cut at the end of the Uruk, which may help explain the desertion of settlements at that time.

As on the plain, the Jemdat Nasr and Early Dynastic periods were clearly a time of important and rapid expansion, with the number of sites more than doubling and now falling into three size categories. Ten of the largest now covered more than 10 ha, still small by the standards of the south, and as much as 400 ha of land seems to have been under cultivation. As on the plain most of the settlement, 77 per cent, was in urban centres. In contrast to the position on the plain in the Agade period, the Diyala saw no diminution of settlement. Some of the ED sites were abandoned, but new ones were founded to compensate. The number of large towns drops slightly from ten to eight but the total area under cultivation seems to increase slightly. This perhaps tends to support our contention that the contraction of settlement seen on the plain is more apparent than real. The Ur III period saw a further expansion in total numbers of sites, but the area under cultivation remains much the same. For the first time we have historical, documentary evidence for the existence, by the middle of the Ur III period, of an independent kingdom, centred on the Diyala town of Eshnunna, which must have influenced the settlement pattern.

The patterns in the Diyala region diverge in two important respects from those on the plain. Full urbanisation does not arrive until the ED period, and the Agade is apparently as populous and as urban in character as its predecessor. The differences may perhaps be explained in part by the geographical position of the area; for instance, the emphasis in Sumer, in the Uruk period, seems to have been on westward connections with Syria, where fully urban centres like Habuba Kabira were certainly present by the late Uruk, leaving the Diyala relatively unexploited. The prosperity of the Diyala in the Agade and Guti periods is more difficult to explain. Except at Eshnunna, there does not seem to have been the massive rebuilding during Ur III which appears to have been so destructive on the plain. Perhaps the area's provincialism saved the Agade evidence for us, which the prosperity on the plain destroyed.

The evidence from the Hamrin is a by-product of a massive salvage operation by an international team in advance of the construction of a new dam and has not been as thoroughly examined, or as systematically presented, as the rest of the material dealt with in this chapter. The Hamrin basin is traversed by three important trade routes and differs in one important respect from two of the other areas looked at: in the Hamrin some cereal cultivation is possible without irrigation. This and the presence of the north–south trade route have affected settlement patterns in the region. The patterns which emerge, although incomplete, are extremely interesting and again diverge in a number of ways from those in the other regions (Postgate 1979; Postgate and Watson 1979; Roaf and Postgate 1981). The Ubaid period is well represented, and up to sixteen sites are scattered over the basin, both north and south of the Diyala. Several of these sites have been excavated and were found to be villages with sophisticated domestic architecture, one house being typically larger and more elaborate than the others. There is also evidence for manufacturing activities and one or two of the sites seem already to have had central-place functions (Jasim 1985).

Surprisingly, this prosperous picture is totally upset in the Uruk period. Only three sites have been identified for this period in the valley, none of significant size. This would seem to support the evidence from the Diyala for the essentially westward connections of Sumer at this time. In the ED the basin was better provided with settlement, though the total number of sites is still smaller than in the Ubaid. Excavation enables us to say something about the character of these sites, which, in at least four cases, seems to be that of a fortified farmhouse or manor, with subsidiary houses. Perhaps this is an indication of the fact that this was essentially a border area with all that that implies in terms of unsettled conditions and of the need for special types of building. The best published example of this sort of fortified house is from the site of Uch Tepe (Gibson 1981). None of the ED sites can be described as fully urban.

The number of sites is approximately halved in the Agade period, again at odds with the situation in the Diyala, and the few sites where the nature of the settlement can be established indicates that they too may have been fortified manors. Unfortunately, separate figures are not given for the Ur III period, but settlement seems gradually to have increased to rival numbers in the Ubaid for the first time.

In contrast to all the other areas we have looked at there is no real evidence for urban settlement in the Hamrin during the Sumerian period. Small defensible enclaves seem to have been much better suited to the geographical and political nature of the area.

The lesson that emerges clearly from this comparison of the data from these four different surveys is the importance of recognising that there are local patterns of development, just as there are local stylistic developments in the field of material culture. As is so often the case, the accumulation of new evidence tends initially to blur the simplistic picture with which we all begin, but the hope is that yet more facts will allow the construction of a model which, though complex, more nearly approaches reality. The danger of sweeping generalisations is evident.

So far we have been considering the relationships of settlements to the landscape and to each other, but each of these settlements was supported by its own agricultural hinterland separating it from its neighbours and providing the vital foodstuffs and fuel on which its survival depended. The utilised land can be divided into three categories: the intensively cultivated gardens, which often lay within the boundaries of the settlement, the irrigated fields lying in a band parallel to the waterways and producing the bulk of the staple crops, and the land further from the water supply which was used as grazing, for collecting fuel, for hunting, and occasionally for catch crops when conditions were favourable.

The most important crop produced by the garden plots south of the Hit–Samarra line in the third millennium was almost certainly dates, although the archaeological and textual evidence for the production of dates at this time is surprisingly flimsy. Date stones are reported in a late Ubaid context at Eridu (Wright 1981: 324) and at Tell Ouelli, but an isolated find like this cannot be taken as evidence for cultivation. A plant thought to be a date palm is shown on a stone plaque of ED IIIa from Lagash and on a soft stone vase now in the Louvre (Fig. 3.1). More date stones were found in the grave of queen Puabi in the Royal Cemetery at Ur, which is approximately contemporaneous (Ellison *et al.* 1978). The textual evidence from pre-Sargonic Lagash mentions dates, and after the Agade period we have economic texts dealing with date gardens and reports of imports of special sorts of date from Dilmun. In one version of the story of the birth of Sargon of Agade his adoptive father is described as a labourer in a palm garden, who spotted the basket containing the remarkable child caught in the rushes on the banks of the river where his garden lay. It seems that we can be reasonably sure that the date palm was cultivated by the middle of the period we are dealing with, but we still cannot say when it was introduced into Mesopotamia. Some wild species have been reported from the Gulf and this seems the most likely source.

The date palm is ideally suited to the conditions in south Mesopotamia: it flourishes with its roots in stagnant, salty water and, as long as it is kept wet, pollinated and pruned, can be relied on to produce heavy crops south of the 35th parallel. As far north as Qurna it is not even necessary to irrigate because of the backup from the tidal regime on the head of the Gulf. The trees not only produce a highly nutritious food which is a staple part of the diet, but the sap provides a useful sweetener and can also be used to make a sort of fermented date wine. Even the stones can be used as fuel, while the leaves provide fibre, and the trunk wood.

The other plants grown in the garden plots were vegetables such as onions and

3.1 Soft stone vase showing date palm

cucumbers, which, although gastronomically very desirable, were probably not of major nutritional or economic importance. Some fruit trees were also grown, including vines, figs and even perhaps apples.

The irrigated arable land formed by far the most important category of land in terms of both area and productivity. The soil is extremely fertile if watered, although we have already discussed the problems posed by salinisation of the soil and the resulting drop in yields. The regimes of the two rivers, unlike that of the Nile, are not well adapted to cereal cultivation. Their floods come in the early spring when the snow melts in the mountains where the rivers rise, just as the crops are ripening. The flood water must be kept back, or diverted, to prevent the total loss of the harvest. This seems to have been achieved by leading flood waters off into swampy, unused land where it could do little damage, but it was a fairly inefficient method of control, as the repeated floods of Baghdad until the 1950s illustrate. It was really only with the recent construction of a great dam on the Diyala to control the flow of this major Tigris tributary that the problem was solved. When water was needed, on the other hand, before sowing in the autumn, the rivers were at their lowest after the long dry summer. Seeds could often not be sown until the first rains had fallen in November or even December, though the preliminary ploughing and harrowing could be done well in advance of this. After planting, water had to be led into the fields to supplement the meagre rainfall in the south, and even in the north irrigation improved yields dramatically. The Sumerian Farmer's Almanac directs the farmer on the ideal number of times that water should be led into the fields to secure a good harvest. Four applications seems to have been considered suitable, but when sheep were allowed onto the young barley shoots to graze, an additional application was advised. Such grazing presumably produced shorter stemmed, thicker crops less liable to wind damage, and of course provided instant manuring, a thoroughly labour-saving device.

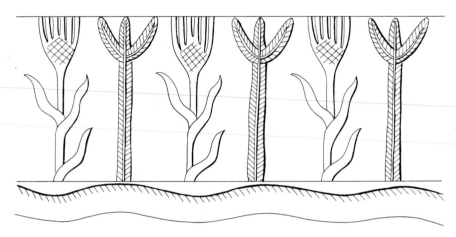

3.2 The vegetation on the Uruk vase: corn and (?) flax

Curiously, there is no evidence for deliberate manuring of the fields, other than by grazing of the young shoots, or of the stubble after the harvest. The importance of crop rotation and of fallow periods was apparently understood and followed.

The crops were ready for harvesting in April and the harvest was usually complete by early May, though exact times varied slightly, depending on the part of the country, and the weather in any particular growing season. Threshing and winnowing went on in a leisurely manner through the summer on a household basis. Barley and wheat were the most important cereals, with the amount of wheat declining throughout the third millennium, probably as a result of increasing salinity (Fig. 3.2). Millet occurs occasionally, but the evidence for its cultivation is very slight as early as this. Another important range of crops was the pulses – lentils, beans, peas – all of which have a high protein content, and fodder plants like the vetches. Flax was grown, probably for fibre rather than oil, to judge from the fragmentary representational and textual evidence. It is also possible that sesame was being grown by the later third millennium after its introduction from India as a result of the trading contacts established during the ED III. This trade expanded and flourished under the Agade kings and continued into the second millennium. Sesame, and millet as well, are summer crops and so, with a good water supply, can be grown as a second crop in the same ground as the main winter crops of cereals and pulses, so providing a useful way of intensifying agricultural production without having to bring new land into cultivation. (For discussion on sesame and flax see Postgate 1985).

Our evidence for the tools used by the early farmers is not extensive, but two of the pictograms found on the Uruk IV tablets, dating to the end of the fourth millennium, clearly represent ploughs, one with a seed funnel. Another type is shown on a cylinder seal of similar date. A two-register seal from ED III levels in the Hamrin shows a plough

3.3 Cylinder seal of ED III date with a plough and seeder funnel

which clearly has a seed funnel attached, being drawn by two animals (Fig. 3.3) (al Gailani-Werr 1982). These must be some of the earliest examples of a plough with seed funnel in the world, and it is a motif which appears regularly in the glyptic repertoire of succeeding periods. The texts of the Ur III period detail quantities of seed to area of land and thus allow estimates of the yield to be made. This seems to have been as high as 30-fold (Postgate 1985). Undoubtedly stone hoes were used for turning the soil, especially in the garden plots, while copper ones became increasingly common. There is a triangular object on the end of a long handle, which is shown on many seals as an attribute of the god Marduk and which is usually described as a hoe, but it looks very like the long-handled spade widely used in Iraq today.

Metal and stone are used alongside each other for other types of tools as well; flint sickles continue in use throughout the third millennium to judge from the frequent occurrence of serrated blades at sites such as Abu Salabikh which span this period of time. Yet copper was widely available by ED III; one suspects that the copper tools may not have been as effective as the older flint ones because relatively pure copper was being used in many cases. This produces a rather soft blade, which would not have kept its cutting edge well. By Ur III, however, copper tools predominate. In the Uruk period, and even earlier in the Ubaid, hard overfired clay sickles were widely used. Many agricultural tools would have been made of wood, and even of reeds, which were widely used for baskets and mats, so that all traces of them have vanished. The more elaborate types of equipment, such as the ploughs, were presumably owned by only the richer farmers. Smaller men hired them, with the draught animals, from the temples when they were needed. On the other hand, no doubt every peasant owned his own spade or hoe, and flint sickle. The extent of private ownership of the land itself is unclear, but it seems that the biggest landowners were the public institutions, the temples and palaces. Some land was held by groups of individuals as well, probably on a kinship basis. Some rulers also seem to have made grants of large tracts of land to important officials, apparently for their own upkeep. It is not known whether the land reverted to the crown on the death of the official, or whether it passed to his family in perpetuity.

It seems that the land was farmed by a number of different categories of people, under a number of different arrangements. The big institutions let land out to officials for their own upkeep, they rented land on a commercial basis to tenant farmers and they employed large numbers of men and women, many of whom seem to have been landless, to work the land for the benefit of the institution itself. Seasonal labour was also drafted in at harvest time. It is to these labourers that the rations of basic foodstuffs and other commodities itemised in the ration lists were issued. Other temple servants benefited in this way as well. There is some textual evidence for slaves, but they do not seem to have formed a significant part of the labour force at this period.

The third category of land which we listed at the beginning of this section was the unirrigated land, which lay furthest from the waterways, and which merged into the unused land referred to in the texts as the Edin. This empty land formed a buffer between one settled enclave and another. This unirrigated land also had a considerable economic role. For much of the year it provided valuable grazing for the sheep and goats, who supplied both meat and dairy produce, as well as wool for the important textile industry. In the summer months the land yielded nothing more than a little scrub, but plants with deep roots, such as prosopis, survive on very little moisture and not only provide a little meagre grazing but also small quantities of fuel, as does the dung dropped by the animals. This is mixed with chopped straw and dried and today provides a major source of fuel in a virtually treeless environment. The hunting of both large and small game has always been an important additional source of protein and gazelle in particular were a valuable food supply. Judging from the animal figurines and amulets, hares and other small rodents were hunted too, and various birds also supplemented the diet. Herds of wild onagers which roamed the steppe were a valuable resource in prehistoric times when they were hunted for their hides, and by the third millennium wild stallions were apparently being brought in to cross with donkeys in order to produce an animal which had some of the spirit of the onager but was easier to train than the pure-bred wild species. It is suggested that it was these crossbreeds which drew the Sumerian war chariots shown, for instance, on the Royal Standard of Ur (Zarins 1978).

Stock rearing in general was an important element in the economy. Very large flocks of sheep and goats were kept by the temples – an aggregate of 350,000 is mentioned in a single year of King Shulgi of the Third Ur Dynasty. As we described above, they were used for many different purposes. It seems likely that the smaller peasant farmers also

3.4 Saluki hunting dogs on a seal from Tepe Gawra

kept small numbers of animals, as they do today, and the resources of the settled community could be augmented from the flocks of the nomadic and semi-nomadic people on the borders of the agricultural land, especially in the foothills of the mountains. Cattle were also kept, though in smaller numbers than sheep and goats. They too seem to have been used for a number of purposes, as draught animals and as dairy cattle; a frieze from the temple at Al Ubaid shows the temple herds being milked and butter being churned. The herds also supplied the important leather industry, which is particularly well documented at Isin (Van de Mieroop 1987). The provision of animals for sacrifice in the temples and for divination was an important responsibility of the temple herdsmen. The animals for these purposes had to be of the highest quality and very large numbers could be involved in a single year. Various other creatures were also probably kept, pigs, ducks and geese for example, as well as the ubiquitous cur, which still terrorises visitors to many villages and towns in the Middle East. As well as being guard dogs, many of them seem to have been hunting dogs like the modern saluki (Fig. 3.4). Horses are not attested till the later third millennium, nor are camels; the donkey and various hybrids were the major draught animals, together with oxen, as mentioned above.

Agriculture was the major industry in Sumer and large numbers of townspeople, as well as peasants in the villages, were primarily involved in agricultural production, a fact which had a considerable impact on both the size of settlements and their relationship to each other. The nature of the agriculture, heavily reliant on irrigation, was, as we have seen, another crucial parameter in determining patterns of settlement and land usage.

✹ Chapter 4 ✹

TOWN PLANNING AND TEMPLE
ARCHITECTURE

We began by looking at the patterns made by settlements in the landscape. It is logical to look next at the patterning within some of these settlements, at some of the earliest evidence we have for town planning. This evidence is very incomplete: the cost of excavating an entire site has always been prohibitive, even in the comparatively wealthy days before the Second World War. An American expedition had to abandon the attempt in the 1930s to excavate the relatively small tell of Tepe Gawra in its entirety. About half-way down the scale of the undertaking became apparent and funds began to run short. This means that, especially when dealing with large urban sites, such as Uruk, we are forced to deduce overall patterns from a number of small, disjointed scraps of evidence, a thoroughly unsatisfactory situation. However, by using evidence from survey, from ethnography and from the texts, as well as from excavation, it is possible to make some general observations on the use of space in Sumerian towns and cities. Descriptions of smaller settlements, villages and hamlets are even more difficult to formulate as so few sites of this type have been excavated or surveyed. There seems to be some evidence for widely scattered compounds, loosely grouped together at the site of Sakheri Saghir (Wright 1969), while other villages such as Raidau Sharqi in the south (Heinrich and Falkenstein 1938) and Qualinj Agha in the north (Es-Soof 1969) seem to be more tightly knit together, with houses packed fairly close together in blocks round a central space. As in Iraq today, there was probably a considerable variety in the layout in the smaller communities, much of it entirely haphazard. This is an area where the ethnographic evidence can be of considerable help in amplifying the archaeological record by providing comparative material. Frankfort, working on the Diyala sites in the 1930s, compared the ecology of the Early Dynastic towns of Khafaje and Tell Asmar with the present-day city of Erbil, and was also able to match specific architectural details such as the window grilles found in both Khafaje and Erbil (Frankfort 1934).

The best examples we have of town planning from the Uruk period come from the north Syrian sites of Habuba Kabira and Jebel Aruda. Both these towns seem to be similar to the less fully excavated sites on the Sumerian plain from where their inhabitants probably originated. Both sites lie on the banks of the Euphrates river, but while Jebel Aruda is undefended, Habuba Kabira is protected on three sides by a massive buttressed wall, with the river giving protection on the fourth. The area enclosed by the wall is about 18 ha and there is access through two well-defended gates. Inside the walls, there is a main road, paved with sherds, running parallel with the long axis of the walls, while smaller alleys run off it, giving access to blocks of buildings. There are a number of areas with different characters, each apparently with a different function; the town is dominated by an acropolis on which are the temples; a harbour area appears to lie on the river margin, though this has not been excavated; there is also an area of gardens or orchards and finally a domestic quarter with some evidence for cottage industries like pottery making. A separate administrative centre was not identified at either site, but the temples may have fulfilled this role too (Strommenger 1980; Van Driel 1979) (Fig. 4.1).

This sort of urban land usage seems to be found throughout the third millennium; it occurs again writ large in the city of Ur under the kings of the Ur III dynasty (Fig. 4.2). By this time Ur covered *c.* 100 ha and boasted two harbours, one on the Euphrates and one on the major canal; it had a great acropolis with its own defensive wall, on which stood temples, palaces and the great ziggurat; beyond this inner wall lay the various quarters of the city, each on its own smaller tell, separated by roads and canals from each other, but all within the outer perimeter wall, which probably defended the city from flood as well as from attackers (Woolley 1976). A group of smaller tells within the inhabited area is a feature of many sites and it is easy to see how such a configuration could arise. The area of a site can expand or contract with time, independent suburbs can be assimilated or new settlement extend beyond the original line of the walls, as at Khafaje for instance; or the focus of habitation can shift from one part of the site to another, as at Abu Salabikh, where one area settled in the Uruk period was apparently left empty thereafter and settlement concentrated in adjacent tells. There is also the suggestion that different areas of settlement within the towns were lived in by specific groups of people, or had specific affiliations. There is the so-called scribal quarter at Nippur; there is a walled area adjacent to the Temple Oval at Khafaje which probably housed the temple personnel, and a group of houses at Abu Salabikh with elaborate two-storey ovens may have been a bakers' quarter (Crawford 1983).

This division into different functional areas was not rigorous. Excavations at Ur at the very end of our period show small shops, chapels and a school among the houses, which range from the extremely commodious merchants' houses to small, cramped rooms squashed into any available corner (Fig. 4.3). Space in the towns seems to have been at a premium and there are few public spaces within the walls, though examples are found at both Ur and Mari on the Euphrates, where an open 'square' with a colonnade on one side was excavated in the late Early Dynastic town (Woolley 1976; Parrot 1936). It is often suggested that large markets and public gatherings may have taken place at the city gates, where there was more space.

One of the most completely surveyed towns of the later third millennium is Tell Taya, close to the Jebel Sinjar in northern Iraq, where the stone footings of Early Dynastic and Agade buildings have survived on the present ground surface, covering

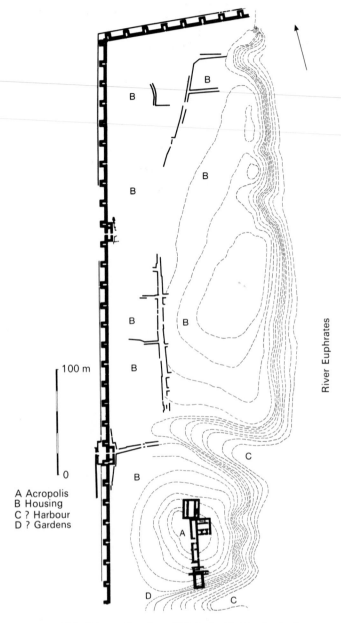

4.1 Schematic plan of Habuba Kabira in Syria

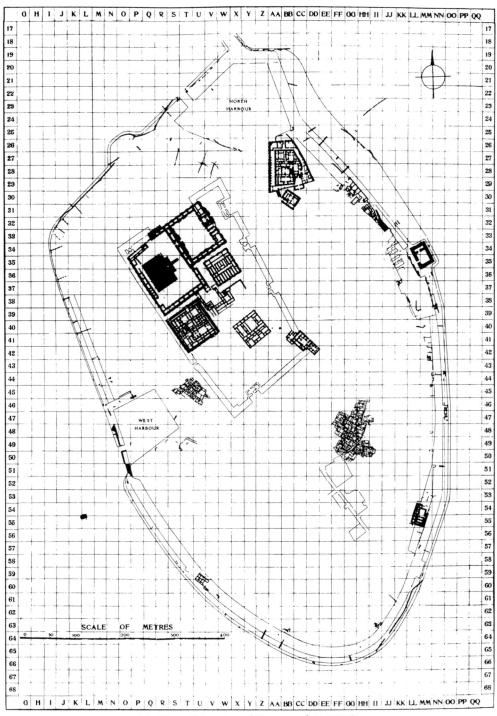

4.2 Plan of the city of Ur around 2100 BC

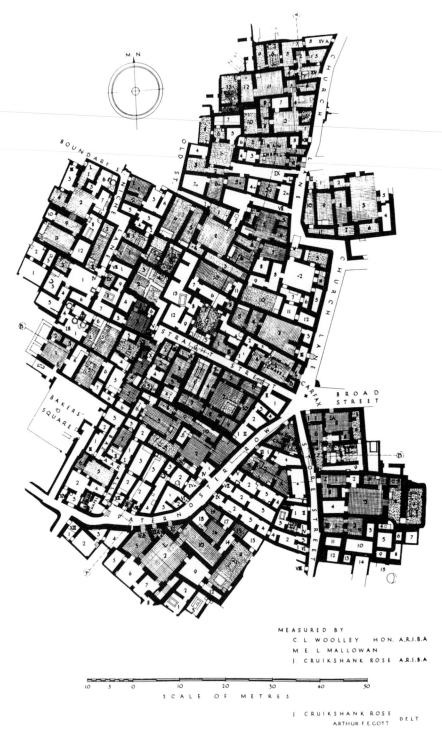

MN

BOUNDARY STREET

CHURCH LANE

OLD STREET

CHURCH LANE

STRAIGHT STREET

CAREFAX

BROAD STREET

BAKERS' SQUARE

STORE STREET

PATERNOSTER ROW

MEASURED BY
C. L. WOOLLEY   HON. A.R.I.B.A
M. E. L. MALLOWAN
J. CRUIKSHANK ROSE A.R.I.B.A

10   5   0   10   20   30   40   50

SCALE OF METRES

J. CRUIKSHANK ROSE
ARTHUR F. E. GOTT   DELT

4.3 Sketch plan of part of Ur around 2100 BC

an area of about 155 ha in all. The town stood on either side of a stream, and was divided into a number of differentiated areas of which the focus was a fortified acropolis, or citadel (Fig. 4.4), on which all the major roads converged to form a star-shaped plan. Around the acropolis lay the inner town with its own wall, only partly recovered. Adjacent to this enclosure on the south-west was a third one with small rooms on two sides, which the excavator suggests may have been a barracks. Alternatively, it may have been something like a caravanserai where merchants brought and stored their goods. Further from the centre of the town, there was a semi-organised sprawl of largely domestic buildings which may originally have been protected by an outer town wall. One of the main roads into the town seems to have been guarded by a tower of some sort, which supports the idea of an outer defensive wall. The survey shows clearly that there were a number of different types of building in the outer town, including the standard courtyard house, large compounds with smaller units opening onto them and some more formal buildings which are intepreted as neighbourhood chapels. On the outskirts there are areas with potters' workshops and kilns, as well as flint-working areas. Unfortunately, little excavation has taken place outside the citadel area, so that the dating and interpretation of the surface remains is sometimes difficult, but the pattern agrees well with what we have seen elsewhere (Reade 1982).

Many of these third-millenium towns show evidence of public works, the most striking usually being the perimeter walls, but major streets are often surfaced with sherds or bricks, and some have drains to carry off effluent and surface water. The provision of fresh water was also of crucial importance and we find wells and cisterns, often in the temple precincts, but sometimes, as at Tepe Gawra, in among the houses (Speiser 1935).

BUILDING MATERIALS AND TECHNIQUES

The characteristic tell formation of many settlements in Mesopotamia is a by-product of the main building material used. Unbaked mudbrick is cheap and convenient, it is easy to produce, but unless a mudbrick building is kept in good repair with a sound roof and plastered outer walls it deteriorates very quickly and the bricks crumble back into a low heap of earth. This heap will often form the basis of later buildings and so, over a period of years, a miniature tell is formed. This process, repeated on the grand scale, augmented by domestic and industrial debris, together with the products of the occasional disaster, leads eventually to the formation of the tells which represent ancient settlements in much of the Near East today.

These mudbricks are most conveniently made by digging earth from close to the banks of a canal and puddling it with water drawn from the canal, through a small breach in the banks. Chopped straw is usually added to improve the consistency and then the mixture is shaped, usually by means of a wooden frame in the shape of a

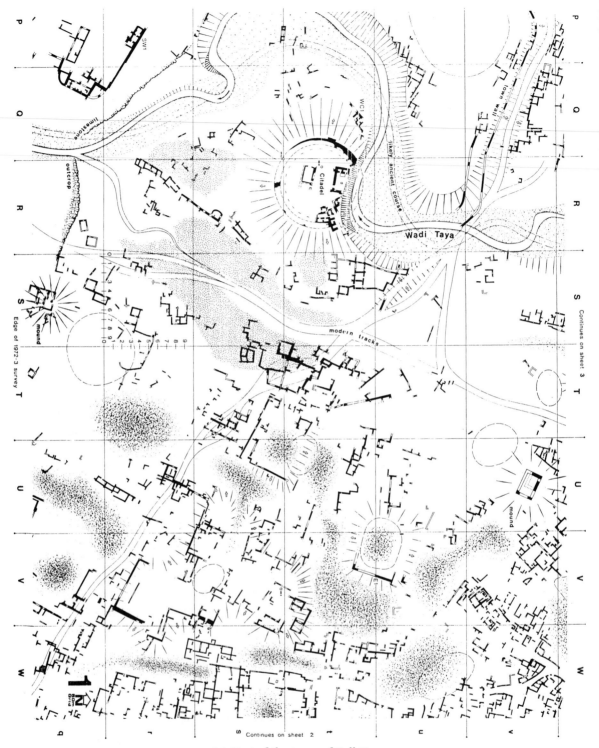

4.4 Part of the town of Tell Taya

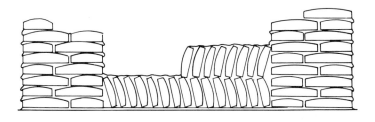

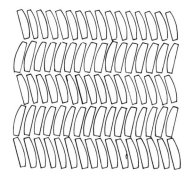

4.5 Plano-convex bricks and how they were laid (after Delougaz)

rectangle and left to dry in the sun. Sometimes the mud is just shaped randomly by hand to what is known as tauf, an inferior product often used for building animal shelters and more temporary buildings. The size and shape of bricks changes through time and can sometimes be a useful guide to the age of the building. For example, the Early Dynastic period is characterised by the use of the so-called plano-convex brick, a curious object, rectangular in plan with a humped top often with a depression on top. This odd shape seems to have been achieved by rounding off each brick made by the wooden frame by hand, instead of striking off all the surplus mud to make a flat surface (Delougaz 1933). These bricks were often laid in a distinctive herring-bone fashion, although they were also used in more conventional bondings of which the builders had a good understanding (Fig. 4.5). Although these bricks are so distinctive and are found mostly in the Early Dynastic period, they are not an ideal type-fossil as they do not occur in the north and have recently been found in Agade contexts as well.

A more durable baked brick was used as well, but it was produced in much more limited quantities, as it is a relatively expensive commodity in areas where fuel of any sort is at a premium. Until the Third Dynasty of Ur, the use of baked bricks was restricted to areas of maximum wear and tear like thresholds, and to the more important or prosperous buildings. Ur-Nammu, however, used them in large quantities in his building operations on the temenos at Ur, as did his successors. The ziggurat is encased in a skin of baked brick, one of the reasons for its relatively good state of preservation today, and the royal tombs were built throughout with baked bricks stamped with the names of Shulgi and his successor Bur-Sin.

The mortar used with both types of brick is usually mud, though bitumen is also used in a few cases. Bitumen is more usually reserved for waterproofing drains, cisterns, bathrooms and external areas like courtyards. The importance of protecting outside walls from the weather has already been mentioned, and mud or lime plaster is usually used to achieve this. The lime plaster could be smoothed and polished to give a high-quality finish, while the mud plaster was considerably rougher. Interior walls were normally also plastered, and in the Royal Tombs of the Third Dynasty there are traces of elaborate inlays of gold leaf and semi-precious stones, a decoration undoubtedly reserved for only the most prestigious buildings. Floors could also be plastered, but usually they were just of tamped earth.

Roofs were usually flat and were made much as they are today, the rafters of palm trunks being covered with mats and layers of mud, each being carefully rolled to ensure a watertight finish. Royal inscriptions tell us that major buildings were roofed with imported timbers from Lebanon and Elam, cedar being the most prized wood. Ur-Nanshe of Lagash in ED IIIa boasted that he had wood imported from Dilmun by boat (Sollberger and Kupper 1971) for this purpose and Gudea used woods from the mountains of Magan and Meluhha as well (Thureau-Dangin 1907). In the north of Mesopotamia, where the rainfall is much higher than in the south, and where timber is more easily available, it is very probable that there were pitched roofs as well. Stone was more freely used here too, particularly for foundations, while the superstructure was of mudbrick. Tell Taya provides examples of this construction technique.

With this limited range of materials at their disposal, the Sumerian builders mastered all the construction techniques which were in use in the West before the advent of modern materials like steel and concrete. We know little about the tools they used, and their surveying equipment was probably limited to sighting rods and measuring lines, while their building tools consisted of mattocks, spades, trowels and simple lifting gear (Fig. 4.6). With this minimal equipment they were able to lay out large-scale buildings with accuracy, providing right-angles for the corners and orienting them to the cardinal points as tradition seemed to demand, while decorating the external walls with a regular display of buttresses and recesses. The mathematics needed may not have been very sophisticated, but an understanding of basic engineering principles and of the properties of mudbrick must have been essential. It has recently been claimed (Beale and Carter 1983) that there is some evidence for the use of a standard unit of measurement at Tepe Yahya in the Uruk period and it will be interesting to see whether this standardisation extends to other sites as well. Standard units of measurement from the mid-third millennium have been recognised for many years. From the Agade period onwards we have clay tablets with plans of buildings on them,

4.6 Builders' tools carried by Ur-Nammu of Ur

but the evidence for professional architects is slight (Fig. 4.7). Gelb suggests that the word 'Itinnu' found on an old Akkadian tablet may mean architect, but it is more usually translated as builder (*CAD* 1960, vol. 7). There are other specific designations for canal builders and for brick makers from Early Dynastic times on, so we can be reasonably sure that there were professional builders by then. The evidence of the buildings themselves strongly suggests their presence as early as the Uruk period. Possibly, scribes or priests with a particular expertise took overall charge, rather than having a separate profession of architect. We know that surveying was part of the curriculum in the scribal schools by the Ur III period (Sjöberg 1976). The ethnographic evidence suggests the presence then, as now, of skilled local craftsmen, whose expertise was passed on to others by an apprenticeship system (Fathy 1973). Among the techniques employed by these early builders were barrel- and corbel-vaulting, while both the true arch and the dome are found in the Early Dynastic period. Engaged and free-standing pillars are found in the great temples of the Uruk period and occur again throughout the third millennium. Skill, experience, unlimited supplies of the essential raw material, mud, and a great reservoir of manpower, which probably included the army and prisoners of war if required, allowed the Sumerians to produce monumental buildings on a scale unprecedented in Mesopotamia.

THE URUK TEMPLES

In the Uruk period, our evidence relates mainly to temples and to other apparently religious buildings. (For an exhaustive analysis of religious architecture, see Tunça 1984.) Most of it comes from the great precinct of Eanna at Uruk, dedicated to the goddess Inanna, and from the adjacent areas. Two of the oldest temples from Eanna, which are well enough preserved to allow us to discuss them, are the Mosaic temple,

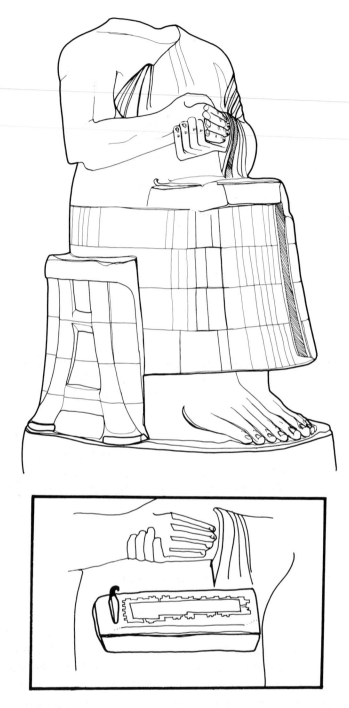

4.7 Gudea, governor of Lagash, with architect's plan (inset)

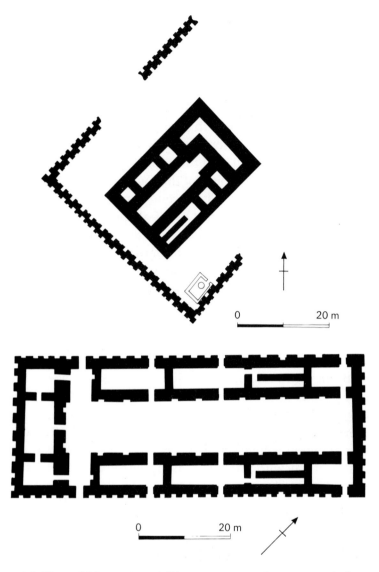

0   20 m

4.8 Plans of (a) Mosaic and (b) Limestone temples, Eanna V/IVb

just north-west of the main terrace and the Limestone temple upon it (Fig. 4.8). Both buildings are unusual in having limestone and bitumen as their main building materials, which must be an indication of their importance, an indication confirmed by the fact that both temples survive from level V into level IVb. The Mosaic temple is decorated with stone cones of different colours, black, red and white, arranged in geometric patterns, and lies within its own elaborately recessed and decorated enclosure wall. The Limestone temple also has cone mosaic, but its most remarkable feature is its huge size 76 × 30 m. Two standard temple plans have been recognised in the Uruk period. One is the tripartite plan, already well known from the Ubaid period at Eridu, for instance. This type has a rectangular central hall flanked on either side with rows of subsidiary rooms, and is normally entered from one of the long walls. As the altar lies on one of the short walls, this gives a so-called bent axis approach. The walls on either side of the altar are frequently elaborately decorated with recesses and the interior is carefully plastered; a hearth or offering place in the centre of the hall is also a standard feature. On the exterior, the walls are again buttressed and recessed, sometimes with cone mosaic as well, and the corners, which may project beyond the line of the walls, are oriented to the points of the compass. The whole complex usually stands on a plinth or low platform. The second type of temple plan has much in common with the first, but is distinguished by a T-shaped central hall, sometimes with an additional range of rooms running parallel with the head of the T, a plan not found as yet in a temple of the Ubaid period, but well known from the houses of the period, especially those in the Jebel Hamrin (Jasim 1985). Both the Limestone and the Mosaic temples seem to belong to the second group with T-shaped halls, though the plans of each are damaged at crucial points. If they do in fact belong to this group, they are the earliest examples we have at present.

In the late Uruk level IVb, the Eanna precinct seems to have consisted of three separate terraces, each with its own temple buildings (Fig. 4.9). Nearest to the Mosaic temple was a platform with a roughly north–south orientation on which stood Temple B with a tripartite plan; to the south, on another platform, was the fragmentary plan of Temple A. Between them, and lying approximately at right angles, lay the third terrace, on which were the most impressive remains of the period. These were a double row of eight free-standing columns, decorated with cone mosaic in red, black and white. The cones are of clay with painted heads to give the same effect as the differently coloured stones used in the Mosaic temple. The row of pillars apparently gave access to another temple whose plan was not recovered. The portico itself was approached up stairs from a great courtyard decorated on the east side with engaged columns with mosaics on them, while the double main staircase had its supporting wall covered in mosaic representing the façade of a shrine.

In spite of all this colour and magnificence, the temple precinct was extensively remodelled in the final phase of the Uruk period, level IVa, and one large platform was built to enclose the remains of all the earlier temples except the Mosaic temple, which went out of use. On this much larger terrace were erected at least two major temples, temples C and D, the fragmentary remains of what is possibly a third one, the Red temple, and a number of other buildings whose functions are not always clear. These include a barrel-vaulted hall, an elaborate courtyard with cistern, and traces of an outer wall and gate. Temple D is again large, 54 × 35 m, and is reconstructed as having a T-shaped hall, though the evidence is fragmentary. It has the usual orientation and the

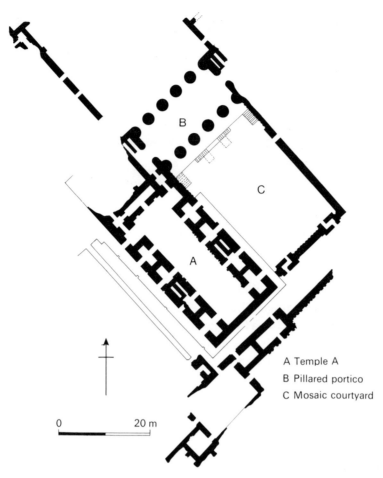

A Temple A
B Pillared portico
C Mosaic courtyard

0   20 m

4.9 Plan of Eanna IVb, central area

usual treatment of the walls. Temple C, however, is rather different, and combines both the standard plans in one entity (Fig. 4.10). The NW/SE axis had the T-shaped hall plan, while a second unit running NE/SW across the head of the T has the old tripartite plan. The southern range of rooms in the Tripartite temple also housed the sanctuary at the head of the T-shaped hall. There was access from one unit to the other on either side of this sanctuary. The plan of this temple is unique in the way it combines both types in one.

At the end of level IVa the whole area was again levelled and apparently left empty for a while before remodelling began. It is possibly to this period, when Eanna was being reconstructed, that another remarkable temple should be attributed. This is the White temple, which stands on a twin terrace thought to have been dedicated to Anu, the

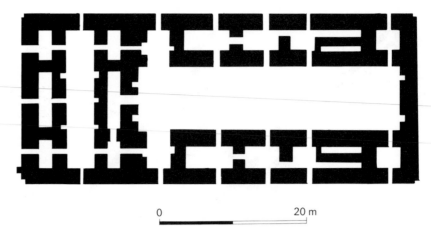

0   20 m

4.10 Plan of Temple C, Eanna IVa

father of the gods. This terrace, like the Eanna terrace, contained within it the remains of a number of earlier buildings. The White temple survives today in a remarkable state of preservation, approached by a fine flight of stairs and standing on a low plinth. It has the classic tripartite plan and is plastered throughout with fine gypsum plaster, which must originally have been of dazzling whiteness in the bright sun. Its date is not entirely certain, but it probably belongs to the end of level IVa or the beginning of level III on the Eanna precinct, that is to say to the end of the Uruk, or to the succeeding Jemdat Nasr phase. The city was obviously flourishing in both phases and the general prosperity is reflected in the care lavished upon the buildings dedicated to the city's gods and especially to its patron Inanna. (Information on the Uruk temples is summarised in Eliot 1950; Lenzen 1964; and Heinrich 1982. For details consult Vorläufige Berichte über die Ausgrabungen in Uruk-Warka *passim*.)

The use of cone mosaics to produce technicolour designs, primarily on the exteriors of buildings, has been described, but there is also evidence for another form of wall decoration in the Uruk period. The Tripartite temple excavated at Tell Uqair (Lloyd and Safar 1943) was painted inside with elaborate frescoes of which only parts survive (Fig. 4.11). Enough remains to reconstruct a red dado about 1 m high, above which were geometric patterns and a frieze of men and animals in procession. The front of the altar podium is decorated with a painted representation of a temple façade, very similar to the one in the mosaic courtyard of Eanna IVb. The sides of the altar are painted with spotted beasts, probably leopards, one couchant, the other sitting upright, which recall the foundation deposit of the bones of big cats, a leopard and a lion, found below the White temple at Uruk. A variety of vivid colours was used, although no blues or greens were found, and in the dim light of the interior the effect must have been overpowering.

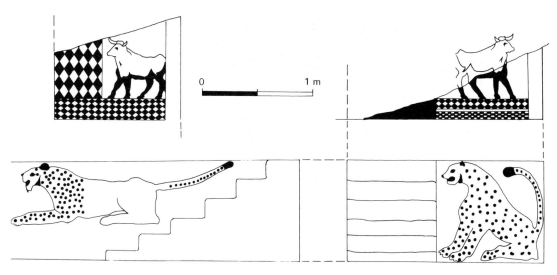

4.11 Animal figures from the frescoes at Tell Uqair

When we turn to the north of Mesopotamia, a group of buildings from Tepe Gawra, which were regarded as temples by their excavators, seem to show another independent architectural tradition. The earliest example of this type of temple comes from level XI, where only part of the plan was recovered. The best-preserved examples come from level VIII, and the earliest phase of this level, VIIIc, produced two buildings of the type, the Western and Eastern shrines. The plan is basically tripartite, as in the south, with a large central room with an elaborate hearth, flanked on either side by smaller rooms. The Gawra examples are distinguished by the fact that auxiliary rooms extend beyond the central room to form a deep porch or liwan. This plan, often described as a megaron plan, is unmatched in Mesopotamia and may well be more at home in Anatolia (Fig. 4.12). It is interesting to note that some of the associated pottery with moulded and impressed decoration may also have Anatolian connections (Voigt, pers. comm.) while links with the south are generally much less pronounced than they were in the preceding Ubaid period.

Two more major problems are raised by these megaron buildings – one is their true function and the other is their exact dating. J.-D. Forest has recently suggested (Forest 1983) that these buildings are not temples at all, but represent instead the houses of an élite ruling group. The original identificatiron was based on their scale and the sophistication of their construction, on the number of infant and other burials associated with them, and on the presence of elaborate hearths. Recent excavations in the Jebel Hamrin have clearly shown that even in the Ubaid period domestic architecture was complex and sophisticated in design and that large numbers of infant burials might be found associated with the so-called headmen's houses. The hearth

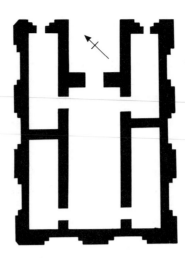

4.12 Plan of megaron building from Tepe Gawra

alone can hardly be seen as sufficient justification for regarding these buildings as religious and serious consideration should now be given to reclassifying them as secular.

Although the earliest of the megaron buildings belong to the Uruk period, it seems probable that level VIII actually continues into the Early Dynastic period. It was finally destroyed by a savage fire and the succeeding level shows much closer ties with the south and ED II/III.

JEMDAT NASR TEMPLES

Evidence for the temple architecture of the succeeding Jemdat Nasr phase is limited to the White temple, which has already been described, the Eye temple from Tell Braq (Mallowan 1947) and two temples from the Diyala valley, one from Tell Asmar, the other from Khafaje (Delougaz and Lloyd 1942). The last two differ fundamentally from the White temple in that they are more in the nature of neighbourhood chapels and lack the sophistication and sumptuousness of the Uruk examples. The Eye shrine, part of a larger building, has a T-shaped central room and is decorated with cone mosaic. It has an altar on the short wall decorated with gold strips, white limestone and grey shale and seems to be the latest example of a T-shaped shrine we have. It is the last in a long series of buildings on this site which are visible only in fragments in the sides of robber pits so we cannot trace the first occurrence here of this plan.

The early levels of the Sin temple at Khafaje are interesting as the latest appearance, on present evidence, of the tripartite plan, which then seems to disappear from the record. The Archaic shrine at Tell Asmar, on the other hand, is a single room, squashed in a lopsided way into a pre-existing space. Possibly because of the constricted space, there is an entrance facing the altar, rather than on the side wall, which we have seen is more usual.

It seems, on the small amount of evidence available, that the Jemdat Nasr phase sees the end of both the classic Uruk temple plans, which date back at least to the middle of the Ubaid period, but which do not survive into the Early Dynastic period.

EARLY DYNASTIC TEMPLES

The Early Dynastic period is remarkable for the lack of a standardised religious building plan after the apparent disappearance of the two classic earlier plans. It is a period which sees much variety in temple planning, although certain elements remain constant and provide links with the earlier traditions. These are the orientation, the treatment of the facade, a bent-axis approach in the majority of cases, and the presence of certain standard fittings like an altar, a hearth and offering tables. Not all the temples stand on a platform, but the tradition of enclosing earlier shrines, too holy to be destroyed, within a platform is still found. New foundations, like the Temple Oval at Khafaje, stand instead on elaborately prepared and purified foundations, which in some cases may include a mirror-image temple filled in to floor level with earth. The true shrine was then built on top. An example of this was found at al Hiba, ancient Lagash, during the excavation of the Ibgal of Inanna (Hansen 1978).

The apparent lack of standardisation in the temple plans may to some extent be explained by the accident that much of our evidence for this period comes from shrines situated in the middle of domestic quarters, parish churches rather than major cathedrals. The plans may reflect local taste rather than strictly canonical practice. The exception to this is of course the evidence from Ur, but even here we have not recovered the plans of any major Early Dynastic temples, just of subsidiary, service temples. This contrasts with our evidence from the Uruk period, in which all the plans we have come from major religious centres and from the central religious precinct, which may explain the more standardised nature of both plans and decoration. It is possible that the fact that the Early Dynastic period was a time of political fragmentation may also have had an effect on the architecture, encouraging diversity, with small city-states asserting their independence, and vying with each other for supremacy. We also have to remember that our evidence for the ED period is more than usually skewed, with much of it coming from the peripheral, and possibly provincial, Diyala region. If we ever do retrieve the plans of major temples from a large city centre, we may find that the classic plans continue to occur in that more formal setting.

In spite of the variety of temple plans, one general trend does become apparent in the Early Dynastic and this is the development of the temple into a self-contained unit with all the offices and facilities necessary for the cult present within a perimeter wall. The development of the Sin temple at Khafaje illustrates this well. The earliest levels, dated

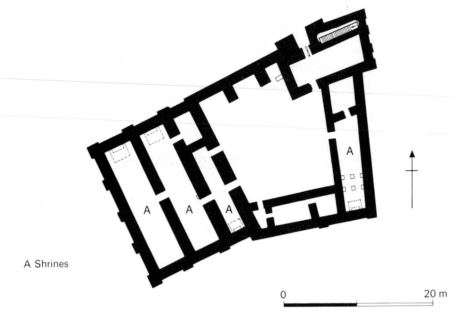

A Shrines

0   20 m

4.13 Multiple shrines, Sin X, Khafaje

to the Jemdat Nasr phase, represent a tripartite plan with only a vestigial courtyard; in levels IV and V the courtyard increases in importance and in level VI, dated to the ED I period, it becomes an integral part of the plan, with rooms on three sides and the perimeter wall on the fourth. One of these rooms, room 12, contains a kitchen range, presumably for the preparation of the god's meals, and perhaps for those of the priests as well. These priests may have lived in other auxiliary rooms. The later levels of the temple see this pattern continue and a second new trend can also be isolated. The number of shrines within an enclave tends to increase; in level X of the Sin temple (Fig. 4.13) there are four and in the Shara temple at Tepe Agrab, three in the half of the building which has been excavated. The same type of multiple, self-contained units can be seen at Mari in the Ninni-Zaza and Ishtarat temples, and possibly also in the Inanna temple at Nippur which has twin shrines. These self-contained temple units have been compared with the plans of contemporary domestic buildings, to which they bear a strong resemblance. This resemblance is especially strong in the Square temple at Tell Asmar (Delougaz 1942), dedicated to the god Abu. The plan of this temple, with rooms grouped round a central court and in a number of other temples such as the Ishtar temple at Mari (Fig. 4.14) can be matched in many contemporary private houses. There are three shrines, an ablution room and a room with a baking oven and storage jars; these latter rooms probably served as living accommodation for the priest. A large number of statues of both men and women were found in the shrines, all with their hands clasped before them in an attitude of supplication. They probably represent

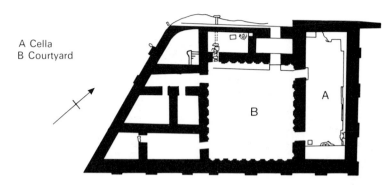

A Cella
B Courtyard

4.14 A house-plan temple with courtyard, Ishtarat temple, Mari

worshippers and petitioners who left their statues in the shrines as surrogates. In some temples they seem to have stood on low benches round the walls, much as live petitioners must have sat or stood round the walls of the audience chambers of the rulers, waiting for their turn to speak (Fig. 4.15).

A pair of statues, one male, one female, from the earliest Square shrine, are thought likely to represent the god and his consort. They may have stood originally on top of the stepped altar. In the contemporary Ishtar temple at Ashur a highly painted bas-relief of a bejewelled woman is thought by the excavator to represent the goddess herself and he suggests it may have stood originally in a niche behind the altar (Andrae 1938). Apart from a few fragments of large-scale statues, the shell inlay of an eye and copper fragments from various sites, we have little evidence for the statues of the gods. The concept of the temple as the home of the god and of his physical presence there makes the adoption of the house plan for temples an eminently logical one and the idea continued to hold sway throughout the rest of the Sumerian period.

There is one type of religious enclosure which is at the moment unique to the Early Dynastic period in Mesopotamia and that is the oval enclosure with a central platform to support the shrine. Subsidiary service and storage rooms are found round the enclosure. The best preserved of these is the Temple Oval at Khafaje (Delougaz 1940), which at its most prosperous had a double perimeter wall with the so-called House D lying between the two walls at the north-west end of the Oval (Fig. 4.16). The house is thought to have been for the chief priest who served the temple, of which, sadly, no trace remains. The great courtyard was recovered, with its basins and offering places flanking the rectangular platform on which the shrine must have stood. The rooms round the court yielded traces of the wealth of the temple in both grain and offerings. Some of the activities which took place within the compound could also be identified.

The perimeter wall of another Oval was found at Tell al Ubaid, again with a rectangular platform in its centre. In front of this platform, on the floor of the courtyard, lay pieces of elaborate decorations, thought by Woolley to have fallen from

4.15 Reconstruction of the interior of a shrine with statues of worshippers and offering stands

the facade of the temple which had originally stood on the platform (Fig. 4.17). These pieces included part of an inlaid frieze depicting the milking of the temple herds, elements of geometric inlay originally from copper and bitumen pillars, stone flowers set into the heads of clay cones, with the petals of contrasting colours of white, pink and grey, and some magnificent copper figures of animals. The finest of these is the so-called Imdugud relief, a plaque with three figures, in very high relief (the heads of the animals are actually three-dimensional), showing the lion-headed eagle, Imdugud, between two stags with splendid antlers. The excavator suggested that this plaque had originally stood over the main entrance to the shrine. There are also the remains of four lions with staring shell eyes, fierce white teeth and red jasper tongues. At least two of these heads were attached to fragmentary forepaws, which suggest that the beasts crouched as guardians on either side of the entrance. There are also parts of several figures of cattle, bulls and birds, all of copper, some hammered, some cast, some, like the lions, moulded on a core of bitumen. Here is evidence for decoration far more

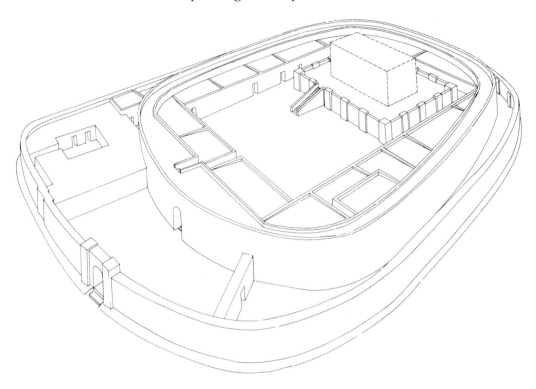

4.16 The Temple Oval at Khafaje

elaborate and varied than anything which has survived from the Uruk period, but the
use of clay cones, now with flower heads, instead of painted ones, and of felines as
guardians both underline the links with the older tradition, and the recurrence of
familiar motifs (Hall and Woolley 1927).

As well as the plans already mentioned, a number of small, single- or double-roomed
shrines has been found, including an unusual example from Tell Chuera in north Syria.
The Kleine Antentempel, as it is called, has a very unMesopotamian forecourt in front
of a simple, direct-axis shrine. This atypical shrine yielded some instantly recognisable
Sumerian votive statues, and so should perhaps be included in this survey. The plan,
however, seems to have closer links with the west and the megaron buildings of
Anatolia than with Sumer (Mallowan 1966) and perhaps with the megaron buildings at
Tepe Gawra mentioned above.

AGADE AND UR III TEMPLES

Unequivocal evidence from the Agade period in Sumer itself is limited to patches of
mudbrick stamped with the names of Sargon and Naram-Sin at some of the major sites
like Adab and Nippur, and to the North temple from the same city. This unimpressive

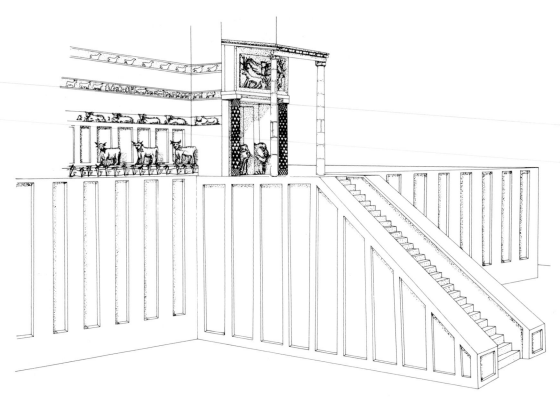

4.17 The decoration of the temple at Tell Ubaid

building probably falls in the house-plan category, to judge from the better-preserved
remains of the Early Dynastic levels. Further north, in the Diyala valley, the Nintu and
Oval temples at Khafaje may have survived into the early Agade period, but the only
shrine which is firmly attributable to the period is the single-shrine Abu temple. This
building, as its name suggests, began as a simple, single-roomed shrine with a bent-axis
approach and a service room complete with oven. In its final period the shrine was
subdivided into two. From the north there come two single shrines, one from Nuzi and
one from Tell Taya. The Nuzi example is approached by a courtyard and in its second
phase has a second room adjacent to it which may have been either a service room or a
second shrine. The Taya shrine stands on the citadel and is distinguished by two small
rooms which flank the altar on either side. The excavator suggests that these may have
been stores in which the ornaments of the divine statue were kept. It is possible that
there may have been a second simple shrine on the citadel, but only part of the plan was
recovered (Reade 1982; Starr 1938).

There is, as we have said, no clear example of a house-plan temple from the Agade
period, but then the evidence is scrappy in the extreme. In the succeeding Ur III period

this is the standard temple plan, so it would be surprising if examples from the previous period were not found in the future. The evidence from the Ur III period can hardly be called representative. It consists of the 'Royal' mortuary chapels at Ur, two chapels included in the Gigparku, or palace of the priestesses at the same site, and a shrine to the deified Shu-Sin at the provincial town of Eshnunna. Apart from these house-plan temples, there is the enigmatic Enunmah at Ur, and the Enlil temple at Nippur, of which only the foundations were recovered. Both these temples seem to have had special functions, the first possibly as a treasury, and the second as a kitchen, or service temple.

It is perhaps facile to equate the return of a unified political rule under the kings of the Third Ur dynasty with the return to a standard temple plan, but it is an attractive parallel to draw. This new orthodoxy certainly contrasts sharply with the architectural and political diversity of the Early Dynastic period. The advent of the deified rulers of Ur III brought church and state together into one integrated system, administered from one centre and controlling all the Sumerian plain. This same move towards standardisation can be seen in other areas too, in the introduction of a single system of weights and measures, in the development of a standardised script and grammar and even perhaps in the formal and repetitive designs of the cylinder seals of the period.

The earliest of the Ur III house-plan temples is the mausoleum built by Shulgi at Ur, either for himself or for his father Ur-Nammu. In essence it is similar to the earlier house-plan temples like the Square temple at Tell Asmar. It has an altar or offering table in the court and the shrines are reached from the courtyard and have a bent-axis approach. There is also a kitchen or living-room, as in the Square temple, though of course the presence of the two tombs below the Shulgi mausoleum is unmatched in the Early Dynastic examples. However, in the second mausoleum, built by Shulgi's successor Bur-Sin, the main shrine, identified by its wide doorway, can have had the altar only on the wall opposite the door, as there are further doors on each of the short walls (Woolley 1974). This direct access to the altar now becomes standard for the rest of the Sumerian period. It has been suggested that this change in the method of approach may reflect a philosophical change of attitude which allowed men to approach their god directly without the intervention of an intermediary, the priest. This theme may also be illustrated in a different way in the most common motif on the cylinder seals of the period, which show mortals being led directly into the presence of the deity by their own personal god. For the first time we also find chapels in some of the richer private houses, where family burial vaults are found. Taken together, all these factors may well reflect a shift in religious thinking.

The two shrines in the Gigparku, the home since the time of Sargon of the Entu priestesses, are also interesting in that the smaller, domestic chapel looks as if it may span the switch from bent- to direct-axis approach. The altar now stands on the long wall opposite one of the entrances, but the plan, which features a large niche or small

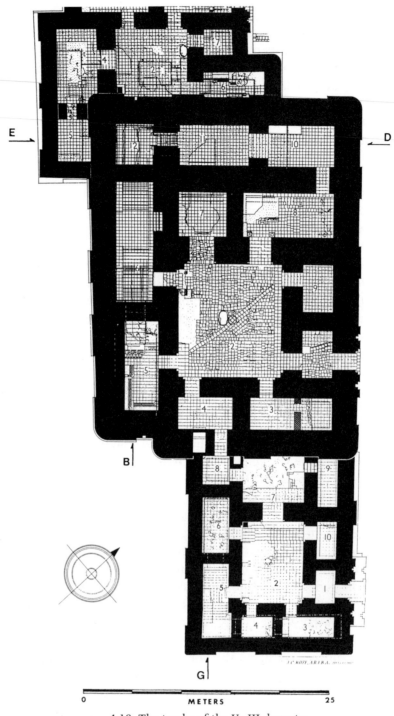

4.18 The tombs of the Ur III dynasty

room at the north end of the cella, suggests that the divine statue may originally have stood there. The more important temple, which forms the south-eastern block of the building, is more formally laid out with the new direct-axis shrine and antechamber opening off the main court. The statue stood in a niche on the back wall (Woolley 1974). The temple at Eshunna dedicated to the divine Shu-Sin, penultimate ruler of the dynasty, has the same arrangement without the antechapel, which reappears in the domestic chapel attached to the palace of the governors (Frankfort *et al.* 1940). In essentials this plan survives into the Assyrian period.

ZIGGURATS

The best known of the Sumerian religious monuments must be the great ziggurats or staged towers, which dominated the major cities. It seems that the ziggurat developed as a logical extension of the long-established tradition of raising temples on platforms or terraces above the surrounding buildings. This tradition can be traced back to the Ubaid period (Busink 1970). The platforms, and later the ziggurats, both seem to have served the same purpose, to raise the home of the god even closer to the heavens. Scholars have debated for many years the purpose of these constructions. Their proposals cover a wide range of possibilities, from the suggestion that the ziggurat reflects a folk memory of the mountainous country from which the Sumerians may, or may not, have originated, to the theory that it was a giant sacrificial altar. The names of the ziggurats certainly include the word mountain in many cases, but this may be no more than a reference to their size and shape. High places are often regarded as holy places. Moses went up onto the mountain to receive the Ten Commandments and the Lord of the Old Testament often refers to his Holy Mountain.

It is usually assumed that the ziggurats supported a shrine, though the only evidence for this comes from Herodotus, and physical evidence is non-existent. It has also been suggested by a number of scholars that this shrine was the scene of the sacred marriage, the central rite of the great new year festival. Herodotus describes the furnishing of the shrine on top of the ziggurat at Babylon and says it contained a great golden couch on which a woman spent the night alone. The god Marduk was also said to come and sleep in his shrine. The likelihood of such a shrine ever being found is sadly remote. Erosion has usually reduced the surviving ziggurats to a fraction of their original height, but textual evidence may yet provide more facts about the purpose of these shrines. In the present state of our knowledge it seems reasonable to adopt as a working hypothesis the suggestion that the ziggurats developed out of the earlier temples on platforms and that small shrines stood on the highest stages, although we must not forget the very inadequate nature of our evidence. Assuming the presence of the shrine, which in common with other ground-level temples, was certainly seen as the home of the god, the sacred marriage may well have been one of many ceremonies enacted here. It may

4.19 Ziggurat on a cylinder seal of ED III date

also have taken place in a special room in the temple of the Gigparku at Ur, the home of the priestesses of Nannar. The ethnographic evidence would suggest that the marriage was more likely to have taken place in the home of the husband, than in the home of the woman, that is to say in the temple of the moon god, rather than the Gigparku. Where a goddess was involved the situation may have been different.

The date of the earliest ziggurats has also been a matter of dispute, but the evidence now points to the Early Dynastic period, and probably to the later part of that period, for their first appearance. There are a number of cylinder seals (Amiet 1980) which show staged constructions of various kinds, some of which may be taken as representing ziggurats, or possibly altars built in the shape of miniature ziggurats (Fig. 4.19). There is one fine seal from the Agade period which shows a stepped altar or ziggurat with a possible shrine on top. The best archaeological evidence comes from the site of Kish, where, according to the very scrappy reports, two ziggurats of plano-convex bricks were found, the larger of which measured 84 m square and had apparently had four receding stages. At Nippur too, the early excavators claim to have found a massive structure which dated to the end of the Early Dynastic period and has 'Several receding stages'. At Ur there is strong circumstantial evidence for the presence of an Early Dynastic ziggurat enclosed in the later construction of the Third Dynasty. This may be the case at other sites too, where excavation has not taken place. On the other hand, the German excavations at Uruk show that there was no proper ziggurat here before the Ur III period. The earlier constructions seem to have been high terraces, not staged towers.

The greatest of the ziggurat builders was undoubtedly Ur-Nammu of Ur, the first ruler of the Ur III dynasty, and the best preserved of his ziggurats is the one excavated by Woolley at Ur itself (Woolley 1939). Woolley's reconstruction shows three great receding rectangular platforms (Fig. 4.20), the lowest measuring 62.5 m × 43 m; he assumed the presence of quite a modest shrine on the top stage. The whole construction is built of unbaked mudbrick with a skin of baked brick and the sides are slightly bowed both horizontally and vertically in order to give the illusion of being straight.

4.20 Reconstruction of the ziggurat at Ur by Sir Leonard Woolley

The walls are decorated with niches and recesses to break the monotony of blank brickwork and were originally plastered. They are also pierced by a number of so-called weeper holes, whose function is uncertain, but which may have been connected with drainage; Woolley's suggestion that drainage was necessary because groves of sacred trees were planted on the platform of the first stage has little to support it.

Access to the first stage, which stood 11 m above the ground in the centre, though it was lower at the outer edges, was by a triple stair. Two flights ran parallel with the north-east facade, one from each corner, and the third ran between them, and at right angles to them. All three stairs met under an arched canopy below the level of the first stage and continued up as a single flight to the level of the platform. Further single flights gave access to each of the higher stages. The second stage, which was reasonably preserved, stood 5 m above the first, and the third, of which very little remained, seems to have stood about 2.9 m above the second. No trace of the shrine itself was recovered. Two rooms, presumably shrines, were found on the ground, in the angles of the stairs, one on either side of the central flight, while another small room was found on the first stage, built against the south-east wall of the second stage. This room contained a number of small 'charms' of copper and gold in the shape of crescents, boats and bees. We can only speculate that it may have been a treasury for the deposit of ex-votos, or even a subsidiary shrine.

It has already been suggested that the Ur III ziggurat was built round an earlier one, possibly dating to the Early Dynastic period; buildings of that date have been found on the ziggurat terrace, but could have been associated with a high terrace rather than a proper ziggurat. If an earlier one does exist, it is piously enclosed in the heart of the later building. The idea of the ziggurat spread beyond Sumer, and by the Old Babylonian period examples are known from the north as well. A recently excavated example comes from the site of Tell Rimah in the Jebel Sinjar. Here the ziggurat backs onto the main temple and access seems to have been from the roof of the terrace to the platform of the first stage (Oates 1982). It is not possible to determine how many stages there were originally. The concept is found beyond Mesopotamia as well; in south-west Iran a fine complex, probably dating to the second half of the second millennium, was excavated at Tchoga Zambil, near Susa, where the method of construction was entirely different, although the final appearance was similar. At Tchoga Zambil the lowest stage was built first as a hollow square, having shrines and storage rooms within the walls, entered by stairs within the thickness of the building. The higher stages were then built inside the lowest one like a series of Chinese boxes. Access to the higher stages was again by internal stairs, rather than external ones as in Mesopotamia.

Somewhat similar constructions are known from even further afield, at Altyn Tepe in Turkmenia, for instance, and at Mundigak in Afghanistan. There is no reason to suppose that these multiple platforms, about whose construction we only have limited information, are derived from Mesopotamian originals, but their presence may suggest contacts, possibly indirect, between these widely separated areas. Alternatively, they may represent a universal desire by man to reach ever nearer to the gods, a theme found again in the Bible and the story of the Tower of Babel.

Chapter 5

PUBLIC BUILDINGS AND PRIVATE HOUSING

PUBLIC BUILDINGS

Although, as we have seen in the previous chapter, the temples and ziggurats were the dominant features of Sumerian towns and cities, there is a good deal of evidence for other important buildings, some genuinely monumental, some merely larger and more imposing than their neighbours. It is often difficult to identify the purpose of these buildings and as a convenience, rather than for any more objective reason, they are sometimes labelled as palaces. This nomenclature is misleading. Many of the buildings in question seem to have been multi-purpose; some of them may have housed officials of either temple or state; some may have been industrial units; many seem to have shared several of these functions.

More significantly, the use of the word 'palace' implies a whole political system which may well not have existed until the later part of the third millennium. We must be cautious about assuming the presence of a king earlier than this. Evidence for a dichotomy of 'church' and 'state' in the organisation of the Sumerian city before ED III is slight. The ruler was after all high priest, and, at a later stage, a god himself, so that the secular and religious halves of the state seem to have been closely interwoven and inextricably intertwined. It seems arguable that there was in theory, if not in practice, one unified system where the division into 'temple' and 'palace' was primarily an administrative convenience. There was, on the other hand, friction from time to time between the interests of the priests and the ruler. A situation of this kind is probably reflected in the so-called Reforms of Urukagina, which list a number of abuses by the priests which the ruler, Urukagina, had apparently stamped out. Under a weak or corrupt ruler the priests could increase their power, and with a powerful one the economic and moral power of the temple could, as we have already suggested, act as a useful counterbalance and restraint on the power of a divine ruler. Although, then, we talk for convenience of palaces and temples, of religious and secular, it is important to remember that our knowledge of the workings of the Sumerian state is still very scanty and we may be implying a type of government and a separation of powers which did not in fact exist.

The Uruk period

The construction and design of the non-temple public buildings has much in common with the temple architecture. The building materials and construction techniques are

77

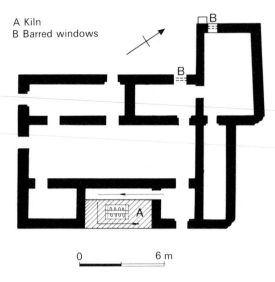

A Kiln
B Barred windows

0   6 m

5.1 Priests'(?) house at Eridu

in general much the same, though the decoration which survives is less elaborate; there are very few mosaic inlays; there are no frescoes on the internal walls either, but we cannot say with certainty that these were never present, especially as two of the earliest buildings in this category show traces of paint on the walls. Walls may also have been decorated with carpets or hangings of some sort, as they were in historic times.

There is a number of non-temple buildings from the Uruk period, which by virtue of their size and location can be assumed to be something more than private houses. The most impressive of these were found in the Eanna precinct at Uruk in level IV, but details are not easily available and it is difficult to say more than that they seem to include a barrel-vaulted hall near Temple C, another hall, adjacent to the first, with square pillars decorated with cone mosaic, and an elaborate square building built round an open court with a cistern or bath in one corner (Lenzen 1974). There are no clues to the functions of these buildings, the finds from them are largely unpublished and we have no comparative data from other sites to help us to interpret them. Eridu is the only other site, in the south, to have yielded non-temple buildings with any claim to be monumental; both examples, like those at Uruk, lie in the immediate vicinity of the temples and are probably connected with them. The more fully excavated of them, the house in H5 (Fig. 5.1), seems to be a wing of a larger unit (Safar *et al.* 1981). It has a central room or court, 12 m long by 3.5 m wide, with two rows of flanking rooms, one on either of the long sides. One room on the east side contains a kiln raised on a sloping platform, possibly used for melting bitumen, as the upper chamber of the kiln was found coated with it. The building was very well preserved, with window and door lintels still intact, and three coats of reddish plaster on walls and floors. It seems possible that this unit was part of the priests' residence. Bearing in mind the slightly later evidence from House D at Khafaje, where a lime kiln was found (Delougaz 1940), running repairs to the temple seem to have been part of the duties of the priests. Supplies of lime for plastering, and bitumen for waterproofing and for use as mortar, would have been essential to keep the temples in decent repair. The second building at Eridu is called the Portico building and is not fully described, but is said to consist of three interconnecting rooms, parallel to each other, in which votive offerings were deposited (Safar *et al.* 1981). With so little information available, we can do no more than note its presence.

Although none of the buildings described so far are temples, it is difficult to divorce them from their settings and to see them as truly secular; more realistically, they all seem to be part of large religious complexes and give no support to the idea of a secular administrative system existing alongside the temple. In the north, however, the position is different and the case for secular buildings of some importance is stronger. As we have already mentioned, north Mesopotamia seems to have been less urbanised than the south in the Uruk period, although the survey evidence from the north is still very patchy. A dispersed pattern of smaller sites, often on important trade routes in areas where rain-fed agriculture is possible, appears to be typical. Tepe Gawra, east of Mosul, is at present the only site to have yielded monumental architecture prior to the Uruk period and even in this period there are only three sites with any claim to possess public buildings, Gawra itself, Grai Resh and Qualinj Agha. Grai Resh lies on the Sinjar to Tell Afar road, and Qualinji Agha close to Erbil. All three sites have fine buildings, which may be interpreted, with due caution, as headmen's houses, though in earlier publications they have sometimes been referred to as shrines. The case for seeing them as headmen's houses has been strengthened by the recent excavations in the Jebel Hamrin, especially at Abada and Kheit Qasim, where somewhat similar buildings have been found in the Ubaid period, which almost certainly fulfilled this function (Jasim 1985). The house in level II at Grai Resh and the so-called Western shrine in level III at Qualinj Agha are the outstanding buildings in the contemporary settlement by virtue of their positions and their plans; each has outer walls thicker and stronger than normal, presumably for defence; each has a modified form of the T-shaped central hall found in the Hamrin; each is associated with manufacturing debris, obsidian blades and cores, suggesting the redistributive and central-place function, deduced at Abada from the presence of counters. The hall of the house at Qualinj Agha is painted, but this in itself does not distinguish it from another, less well planned building to the south, which also has traces of paint in the main room (Lloyd 1940; es-Soof 1969).

The third of these possible headmen's houses is at Tepe Gawra and is entirely different from the ones which have already been described. In level XIa, which marks the beginning of the Uruk period, a remarkable round building was found in the centre of the mound (Fig. 5.2). It too has features in common with Hamrin, Grai Resh and Qualinj Agha examples, in function if not in form. It too is the dominant building in the settlement: the walls are thick enough for defence and are strengthened by buttresses

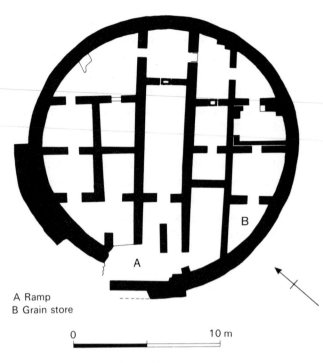

A Ramp
B Grain store

0   10 m

5.2 Plan of round house at Tepe Gawra

of a sort on either side of the entrance; access is by a ramp downwards to a series of
rooms, one of which was certanly used for storage of grain. This may again suggest a
redistributive function. The ramp apparently then turns upwards, suggesting that
there was an upper floor, which presumably housed the living quarters (Speiser 1935).
The building is 18 m in diameter, a span which would not have been impossible to roof,
given that there are load-bearing internal walls.

It can be suggested, then, that the position in the north is almost the mirror image of
that in the south where all the important buildings seem to be, broadly speaking,
associated with the temples. In the north, we have no firm evidence for temple
buildings of this date, and what few more formal buildings there are seem to have a
secular administrative role as well as their domestic functions. Their scale is smaller,
too, providing no evidence for the large economic surpluses accumulated in the south
and expended, at least in part, on the huge temple complexes.

The Jemdat Nasr phase

In the Jemdat Nasr phase, the evidence is still extremely limited, but we have another
possible headman's house in the Hamrin at Tell Gubba, and what is probably an

administrative building in the south at the type-site of Jemdat Nasr itself. This latter is not the earliest example of its kind as a large non-temple building of Ubaid date was partially uncovered during the excavations at Tell Uqair (Lloyd and Safar 1943). It does, however, seem to be the case that from this period onwards the number of such administrative buildings increases, and this may reflect not only the increasing complexity of the social and economic systems, but also the growing power of the ruler at the expense of the temple. The complex of buildings at Jemdat Nasr was only partially excavated, and inadequately published, so that its exact nature is difficult to determine. Its extent, and even its orientation, are uncertain; the excavated area covers approximately 275 m × 200 m of ground. A heavy casemate wall with internal rooms has been identified on three sides and seems to enclose a number of structures, including a platform, 1 m high, approached by a flight of three steps. Moorey has compared the complex with the Eanna III compound at Uruk (Moorey 1976), and has suggested that it should be seen as an administrative complex belonging to the temple estate. The finds are poor, with little metal and few exotic materials such as carnelian and lapis, items which one would expect to find in a palace; on the other hand, there are storage jars associated with carbonised remains of wheat and barley; agricultural tools; kilns; a number of economic tablets, and both stamp and cylinder seals and sealings. One of these sealings from the neck of a large jar has the names of a number of towns on it, a so-called collective seal, evidence, it has been suggested, for inter-city co-operation. As there is no evidence for a temple or shrine within the excavated area, there is no means of knowing whether the administration housed in this building was connected with a temple or with a palace. Excavation is currently being carried out on the site by the British Archaeological Expedition to Iraq and it is hoped that many of these questions will soon be answered.

We return now to the headman's house at Tell Gubba in the Hamrin (Fig. 5.3) (Fujii 1981). This is another circular building, where once again we seem to have only the substructure, or basement, of a complex building whose plan is far more sophisticated than that of the Gawra round house. It would seem that the basic building in Gubba level VII is a unit of five concentric walls enclosing four concentric passages with a core of masonry in the centre. The whole complex is about 20 m in diameter from east to west, but nearly 30 m from north to south, as there is a protuberance at the northern end which housed a well and an entrance. This gives the structure an ovoid plan. The central core of masonry has a fireplace and a shallow trench cut into its top surface, but it is not possible to say whether these features are contemporary with the construction, or whether they were dug into the ruins at a slightly later stage. The circular building was obviously still visible for some time after it went out of use, as the later level V houses form a circle around its circumference. There is also a tunnel with a corbelled roof running into the central core of masonry which, sadly, it proved impossible to excavate in its entirety. Bag-shaped pits and carbonised grains were found in the

II The circular building at Tell Gubba

passages, together with large coarse-ware storage jars; several staircases were found, presumably giving access to the upper living area. There are two more, slightly later concentric walls, outside the main structure, a moat and an eighth wall with intramural rooms and stairs beyond the moat, the whole creating a formidable defence unit to which a considerable proportion of the population could retreat if necessary. It is interesting to note a mass grave containing sixteen bodies, including children, within the walls, so the place may not have been impregnable. The remains of grain, storage jars and pits may again suggest a redistributive function (Fujii 1981). In spite of the difference in date, there are obvious similarities with the building at Gawra and although neither settlement was fully excavated, it is tempting to deduce something of the same frontier/trading-post function for each.

It seems useful to look here at two more of these massive circular buildings, although

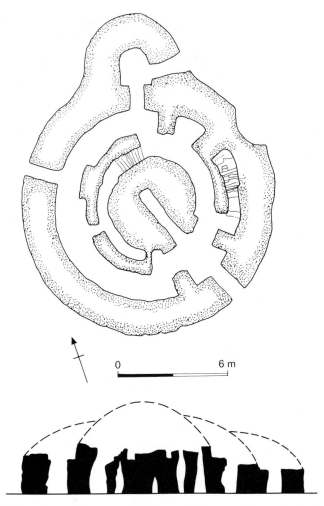

5.3 (a) Plan of round house at Gubba and (b) a possible method of roofing

they date to the succeeding ED I period. The site of Uch Tepe is in the Hamrin valley, some 18 km north of Gubba, so sharing with that site some of the characteristics of a frontier post and overlapping in time with it too. The round building at Uch Tepe was founded on virgin soil, probably shortly before the building at Gubba was deserted (Fig. 5.4). The plan of the two buildings is very different and the building techniques at Uch Tepe are more sophisticated, but Gibson (1981) sees a similarity of function between them and suggests that both were strongholds with administrative functions. The Uch Tepe building also lies in the middle of the settlement, it has a diameter of 27 m and consists of two concentric walls with a courtyard in the centre. The space between the two concentric walls is divided into five rooms, each of which connects with the

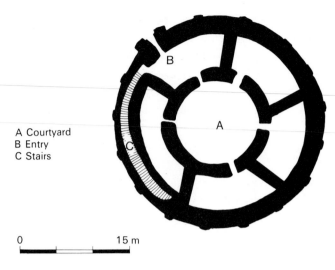

A Courtyard
B Entry
C Stairs

0   15 m

5.4 Plan of round building at Uch Tepe

central courtyard, but not with the neighbouring rooms. The external wall is buttressed, and may have stood as much as 5 m high, presenting a formidable barrier, especially as there was only one entrance. This door, protected by the buttresses, opened into a large room giving access to the central court, and on the right, or south-west wall, to a stair apparently leading to the roof. One of the most remarkable features of this building was the roofing, sections of which were recovered intact over the stairs and parts of the rooms. The ceilings were corbelled and a flat roof had been laid above the corbelling, an engineering feat of considerable sophistication. The central court-yard contained a large bin, perhaps for storing grain, and a series of ovens. The finds have not yet been fully analysed, but they appear to be predominantly domestic in character, with only a few seals and sealings presenting shreds of evidence for an administrative role for the building. As stated earlier, the parallels for this building, though not exact, seem to lie in the preceding Jemdat Nasr phase in the north, rather than in the Early Dynastic of Sumer. The second example is reported from Kheit Qasim, also in the Diyala, but no details of this circular building, surrounded by a cemetery have yet been published (Forest 1982). A final, unpublished, example was found at Sleimah in the Hamrin.

The Early Dynastic period

The Jemdat Nasr and ED I phases are closely linked in both cultural and temporal terms, as we have just seen in the case of Uch Tepe, but by ED II a number of distinctive new features can be identified. One of these is the recognition of large public buildings at various sites. These buildings have a number of traits in common, though it is by no means certain that they also shared a common function. The buildings are usually referred to in the literature as palaces and examples have been found at Kish, Eridu, Wilaya and Mari. Of these the Eridu, Mari and Kish A, examples probably date to ED II in their early phases. The so-called Stampflehmgebäude at Uruk is now also thought to date to the Early Dynastic period and has some similar features (Finkbeiner 1986). With the exception of the Uruk example, which lay within the Eanna precinct, the others are all divorced from the religious enclaves and are sometimes placed on a small tell of their own like the Kish A palace. Sadly, the plans of these buildings are all incomplete, so it is impossible to make definitive statements on their size, orientation or overall planning. However, by comparing the various incomplete plans which are available, it is possible to make some generalisations. These 'palaces' typically have a heavy buttressed external wall and the interior is divided into a number of different sectors, often by means of long, narrow passages. Each sector seems to have had a specific function, some of which can be determined with a degree of confidence. The main entrance to one of these complexes has been recovered at the Kish A palace, where the approach to the first stage of the building is up a flight of steps flanked by monumental towers with buttressed and recessed walls. Elsewhere only side doors, or 'tradesmen's entrances', have been found so we cannot be sure that all examples had such fine entrances.

Until recently, it was considered that these were single-storey buildings, built around courtyards, with the insulating passages providing access, protection, and perhaps acting as cooling devices as well. However, Margueron (1982) has now put forward a case for there being an upper storey over part, or all, of each of these buildings. He bases his case on a number of factors: on the thickness of interior walls, on recognition of rooms whose shape suggests to him the presence of staircases, although no traces of stairs were found, and on his judgement that the rooms excavated could not have accommodated all the purposes for which the buildings seem to have been designed. The arguments are not wholly convincing; remains of stairways have, as Margueron rightly says, been identified, notably at Mari, so it is hard to accept that so many more have totally disappeared. We also know that, in many cases where stairs are present, they led to the flat roof and not to an upper storey. At Kish another objection arises as, to uphold his proposal, Margueron also has to interpret the pillared hall in the annexe of the A palace (Mackay 1929) as a store-room and postulate the presence of a reception suite on the first floor. The principle of Occam's razor makes this interpretation unattractive, and such a fine room seems likely to have had a more visible function. We must also remember that in no case do we have a complete 'palace' plan, so that the argument based on lack of accommodation also loses some of its force. The possibility of a second storey cannot be ruled out altogether, but the evidence, to this author, seems to be weighted against it.

The problem of identifying the functions of the different sections of the 'palaces' has

A ? Throne room
B Enceinte Sacrée
C Domestic area

5.5 The palace at Mari at the end of ED III

already been mentioned; the possibility of a reception suite in the annexe to the A palace at Kish has already been referred to and the presence of fragments of ivory inlay from wall plaques in Room 61 would support this interpretation; both Kish A and the Plano-Convex Brick building at Kish have rooms which appear to be ordinary domestic units, with other possible examples from Eridu, Wilaya and Mari; storage areas, identified by rows of long, thin rooms, are found at Uruk, Kish and Eridu. Traces of industrial activities were found at Kish A and at the PCB building; the former had a forge and metal ingots, while three large circular installations in the latter are thought to have been ovens or kilns (Moorey 1978: 38). At Mari there was an important ritual sector with a shrine, a number of altars and other ritual installations in an adjacent courtyard (Fig. 5.5). This has led Margueron to suggest that this whole building should be reclassified as a temple. Perhaps this question too should be left open for the time being as there seems to be no inherent contradiction in these multi-purpose units having a sacred sector amongst their other functions.

The earliest of these buildings is perhaps the Stampflehmgebäude at Uruk, though the dating evidence is not yet fully published. Some Jemdat Nasr objects have been found associated with the building, but it is now thought that these belong to earlier levels into which the foundations were sunk. It has been suggested that the Eridu palace may have been founded in the ED II on the basis of pottery forms (Safar *et al.*

1981), but the majority of these buildings seem to belong in ED III. It is also probable that the Wilaya example continued in use in an attenuated form into the Agade period, when half the rooms seem to have been sealed off (Rashid 1963).

The textual evidence is not helpful on the question of the contemporary designations or functions of these buildings. We know from the later King List that Kish and Mari were both the seats of ruling dynasties in the ED period, but Kish has produced two contemporary palaces. This is not an insurmountable obstacle as we know from archives at Lagash that the governor's wife there had her own establishment. On the other hand, neither Wilaya nor Eridu is mentioned in the King Lists and, as already noted, the building at Uruk lies within the Eanna precinct and so would appear to be closely allied to the temple administration. Margueron has wisely pointed out that there is no objective justification for calling any of these buildings palaces. Bearing in mind their distribution in both capital and provincial cities, and their location in both religious and secular surroundings, the less emotive term 'administrative building' seems more appropriate, if less romantic. As we have already seen, both the En/Lugal and the priests had wide-ranging administrative responsibilities which included agriculture, manufacturing industry and trade, as well as their more formal functions. Whatever the precise status of these complex buildings, their presence serves to underline once more the increasing sophistication of life in the ED period and the concomitant increase in bureaucracy.

There is one more building which should perhaps be included in this section, though its nature is also somewhat unclear. This is the earliest Northern palace at Tell Asmar. It is built of plano-convex bricks and lies east and north of the Abu temple in what seems to be an area of well-planned private houses. It is the size of this building rather than any single feature which suggests that the Northern palace may have been a public building of some sort, though its layout is quite unlike that of the other 'palaces' we have been looking at (Delougaz *et al.* 1967). The eastern wall is almost 40 m long and the building has an irregular, L-shaped outline, being built round three courtyards or large rooms. The complex has a number of unusual features, including an elaborate drain running from the north court out through the entrance of the building, a deep cistern in a side room with a funnel-shaped bitumen cover, a well, and two elaborate 'lavatories' of the seat rather than the more usual slit-trench variety. A lot of charred grain was found in the south-east unit and a more spectacular find was made in the south-west unit where a large pot was found within the walls at the south-east corner of room 35. This contained a considerable number of copper artefacts, including a bowl inscribed with the name of the god Abu, copper drinking tubes and a copper dagger handle with an iron blade. The wall had been carefully plastered over after the pot had been put in position. There seem to have been two periods of occupation, the second of which was confined to the south-east unit, the rest of the building being already in ruins. This period of time may perhaps equate with the gap in the sequence between stages 2 and 3 of the adjaent Abu shrine and should probably be dated to the end of the ED or the first part of the Agade period, when there seems to have been a certain amount of political upheaval. A discussion of the possible function of this building will be left till the consideration of the later Northern palace in the next section.

The Agade period

With the exception of the later phase of the 'palace' at Tell Wilaya, there is no coherent evidence for public buildings in Sumer itself. The two outstanding examples come from Tell Asmar on the Diyala and Tell Brak in the north. As we saw when dealing with religious architecture and with settlement patterns, a combination of factors has left this important period vastly underrepresented in the archaeological record.

To return to the evidence from Tell Asmar, following the destruction of the earlier Northern palace, another more extensive, better planned complex was erected in the same area, using the flat bricks associated with the early Agade period (Fig. 5.6). The walls were much thicker, the eastern one being strengthened with buttresses and its length being almost double that of its predecessor. Three large courtyards, or rooms, survive as the nucleus of the new plan, but on different alignments and with more rooms associated with each. Like its predecessor, this building has an unusually large number of water-related installations including six seat-type 'lavatories', lavish provision of vats, one of which was associated with eighty-five bowls of the same type, and some fine, brick-built drains leading out of the building. There is also a stairwell in the central unit, which suggests the possibility of a second storey over part of the complex, though the stair may have led to the flat roof.

The presence of one, and possibly two kitchens, and the traditional layout of the south-east unit, suggest that this complex had some domestic functions. However, the presence of lumps of iron and copper near the hearth in courtyard 1 and in room 8 of the south-east unit, together with red oxide, and unidentified yellow pigment, and the presence of a mould for making studded-ware bowls, all suggest other, more industrial functions, as well. This suggestion was first made by Delougaz *et al.* in the original publication (1967) and he also proposed the idea that the so-called lavatories were for use in some industrial process such as tanning, which requires a great deal of water. Further support for some non-domestic function can be drawn from the presence of the eighty-five identical bowls found in one place associated with a large vat. No household, however, large, would need so many, but a workforce might, either as part of some industrial process, or for their private use. Margueron (1982) has made the interesting suggestion that the so-called road to the east of the building may in reality be an internal passage and that the 'palace' is actually part of a much larger unit which continues to the east. This suggestion would enhance the likelihood of the building having some industrial functions, as one of the specialist sectors in a large

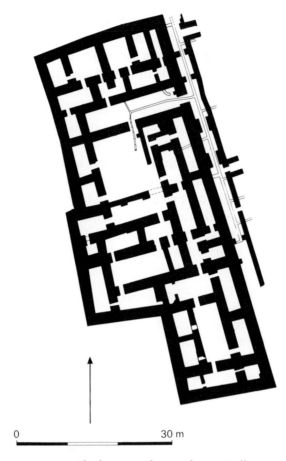

0   30 m

5.6 The later Northern palace at Tell Asmar

administrative complex. We saw evidence of similar activity in both the palaces at Kish. Tablets found in the debris above the Northern palace deal with the activities of a textile workshop and this seems a more likely industry for a residential area as it produces less noxious waste than a tannery.

To sum up, there is a good case to be made for saying that the later Northern palace may be a wing of a larger building that may well have had some manufacturing functions; it is suggested that these are likely to have been in the field of textile working and perhaps metallurgy. The evidence from the earlier building is insufficient to say whether it too had industrial functions, nor is there evidence for its being part of a larger unit. Its status must remain in doubt.

The second public building of the period to be described here is the palace of Naram-Sin at Tell Braq (Mallowan 1947: 63–8). Once again the term palace is a misnomer and this well-planned, well-built, rectangular structure covering almost 10,000 square metres appears to be a great storehouse. The plan consists of one large and five smaller courtyards, each surrounded by long, narrow magazines or store-rooms. The relatively large number of seals, sealings and tablets from the building underlines its commercial function and it seems to have housed goods in transit from the Anatolian plateau en route to the major commercial centres further south on the Sumerian plain. We do not know whether these goods represent tribute or genuine trade; the presence of large quantities of grain in the magazines may perhaps suggest that goods from Anatolia such as timber and copper were being exchanged for locally grown grain. On the other hand, the grain may simply represent local surpluses stored as taxes, or as a cushion against future lean years. At least the date of the building is not in doubt, as the bricks are stamped with the name of Naram-Sin. It may not have been in use for very long, and was destroyed by fire. The finds of flint arrows in the main court suggests the building may have fallen to a military attack, probably as the Agade empire began to crumble under Naram-Sin's successor, Sharkallisharri.

The Ur III period

Two buildings only represent the evidence from this period, one from Ur and one from the Diyala site of Tell Asmar. The Ur building is the 'palace' of Ur-Nammu, the Ehursag, which Woolley in the final publication (Woolley 1974) identified as a minor temple of some sort. The building lay according to Woolley, within the outer wall of the great temenos, south-east of the Gigparku and separated from it by a sloping bank. Margueron (1982: 165–6) has questioned this, and considers that the palace lay just outside the temenos, a suggestion which is supported by the fact that it lies on a slightly different alignment to the major buildings within the enclosure. Its plan, of which only about half was recovered, has been heavily reconstructed by analogy with the plan of the Gigparku, to show a rectangular building with buttressed walls and an entrance in the north-west. The interior is shown as subdivided into three sectors, the largest, thought to be ceremonial in character, occupying the northern half of the building and two smaller sectors in the southern half, which interconnect with the main sector but not with each other. The interpretation of this structure is not easy, but most scholars regard it as a palace or administrative building. Margueron has pointed out that the evidence for Woolley's reconstruction of the north corner of the building is based on one fragment of disconnected masonry, and he therefore suggests the possibility that the surviving building may in fact be a wing of a much larger complex, now destroyed. He would also reconstruct a second storey over part of the area. The south-west unit has the layout typical of many private houses, but as most of the domestic installations recorded seem to be intrusive, it is hard to be certain even about the function of this one sector.

The date of the foundation of the building is reasonably clear as it is built with bricks

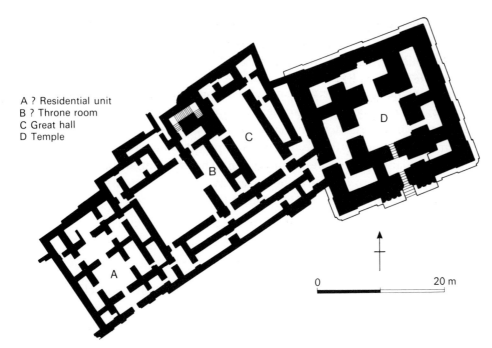

A ? Residential unit
B ? Throne room
C Great hall
D Temple

0   20 m

5.7 The Palace of the Rulers at Tell Asmar

stamped with the name of Ur-Nammu, while some of the pavements are built with the bricks of his successor, Shulgi. It must therefore date to the early part of the Ur III period. However, the finds of tablets of Isin-Larsa date in the debris of the building suggest that it may have continued in use into this period.

The palace of the rulers of Tell Asmar (Frankfort *et al.* 1940), on the other hand, dates to the end of the dynasty and was erected in the main by Ituria, vassal to the penultimate ruler Shu-Sin (Fig. 5.7). The building is in three sections, of which the most easterly is a temple to the deified Shusin (Gimil-Sin in the earlier reports). It is laid out on the classic house-plan lines with direct access to the shrine which lay on the far side of the central court from the entrance. This direct access is what distinguishes the house-plan temples of the Ur III period from those of the ED period, when access was usually indirect (see chapter 4). West of this temple block, with direct access to it, is a ceremonial/administrative block, which may have existed before the temple was erected. It is on a different alignment and has a number of large rooms, one of which seems to have been a vaulted hall with finely plastered walls, and a second room which was identified by the excavators as a throne-room. This identification is not entirely convincing. Its position west of the vaulted hall suggests an anteroom, or waiting-room, and there are no traces of a throne base or any other special fittings. There are two stairs in this block, giving access either to an upper floor or to the roof.

The third and most westerly block communicates with the central unit and its layout mirrors almost exactly that of the royal temple, though it has an anteroom in front of the shrine. This plan led the excavators to suggest that it was the ruler's private chapel, yet there is direct access from the street and in the second phase of occupation it was undoubtedly secular in character. It may be that it was a residential unit; the shrine occupies the same relative position as the private chapel in the better planned houses of the same period in the residential quarter at Ur itself. This may well have been the living quarters of a high official with its own private chapel incorporated. The full extent of the palace at this time is unknown. The residential quarters of the king himself may have lain to the north of the excavated area, or on the putative upper storey, but it is not impossible that he himself lived in this most westerly of the three units of the palace complex.

Summary

The public buildings of the Sumerian period naturally evolve and change over the period from the end of the Uruk to the fall of the Ur III dynasty about 2000 BC. In the southern part of Mesopotamia the early buildings seem to be closely associated with the temple precincts, if the evidence from Uruk and Eridu can be taken as typical. In the north the buildings of comparable date are more modest in character. They seem to share some redistributive, and possibly manufacturing, functions with those in the south, but are divorced from any religious buildings. Their form varies considerably and the group of circular buildings, of which the latest is ED I in date, is a particularly interesting addition to our knowledge of the period.

The evidence from the Jemdat Nasr period in the south is ambiguous, consisting as it does of the large complex at Jamdat Nasr itself. This building may continue the tradition of the Uruk of associating administrative buildings with religious precincts, but the evidence is not available to allow us to make a definitive evaluation. By ED III, however, the situation is clearer, and we have good evidence for the existence of important, multi-purpose buildings, which can convincingly be seen as divorced from religious centres. They seem to have fulfilled ceremonial, administrative and possibly manufacturing functions as well. Here then is solid evidence for another form of authority in addition to that of the temple, an authority which can, with some certainty, be identified as secular. The politically fragmented nature of Sumer in the ED period, which is indicated by the texts too, may explain the number of examples of this sort of building, as each independent city presumably needed its own administrative centre.

It might be expected that in the Agade period when, for the first time, authority over the whole plain was centralised in the hands of one city, there would be fewer such buildings. Certainly one of the ED palaces continued to function, that at Tell Wilaya, and it seems to have operated on a much reduced scale. Sadly, the evidence is too incomplete to make any generalisations with confidence. The evidence from the Ur III period is also tantalisingly fragmentary, but there does seem to be some standardisation of religious, and perhaps secular architecture as well, a trait which would be in keeping with the presence of another strong central authority, this time at Ur itself. There is also some indication that with the deification of the ruler the two halves of the state may have coalesced, bringing all administrative functions together.

PRIVATE HOUSING

The planning and construction of domestic buildings changes little from the fifth millennium to the end of the third. Indeed, many of the features of these early houses can be paralleled in the traditional architecture of today. This continuity means that ethnography is a valuable extra tool for the archaeologist working in this field and modern studies have produced useful evidence on topics like room usage, population density and construction methods; this continuity also suggests that the buildings were admirably adapted to the prevailing climatic and social conditions and that these too may have changed relatively little. There is obviously some variation in the house plans, but this is largely due to practical considerations such as the different levels of rainfall in different parts of the country, and the differential availability of building materials. It is possible to make some broad generalisations about the typical Sumerian house. It was usually built of mudbrick, sometimes with a stone footing if stone was locally available; the plan was usually rectangular and was based round a central court or room. The central area was sometimes covered in areas of higher rainfall, but the courtyard seems to have predominated. The width of the rooms was determined by the length of the timber available, so that rooms were rectangular rather than square. The houses looked inwards; light and air came from the central court rather than from the exterior; doors and windows were small, the latter being closed with grilles or bars to exclude the sun in the summer and conserve heat in the winter. Roofs, at least in the dry south of the country, were flat and served as additional living space in the summer with access by stairs from the court in many cases. The question of an upper storey will be dealt with later in this section.

The type of house just described was essentially urban. We have very little evidence for village housing but there are indications from sites like Umm al-Jir (Gibson 1972a) that the houses were more scattered and may have consisted of a number of rooms round a central compound, a plan which is also found in an urban setting at Tell Taya and which can be found in many contemporary villages (Fig. 5.8). Today, some of the rooms provide living quarters, some are stores and some house animals. The compound serves the same function as the courtyard in an urban house.

The identification of room function is frequently impossible from the archaeological

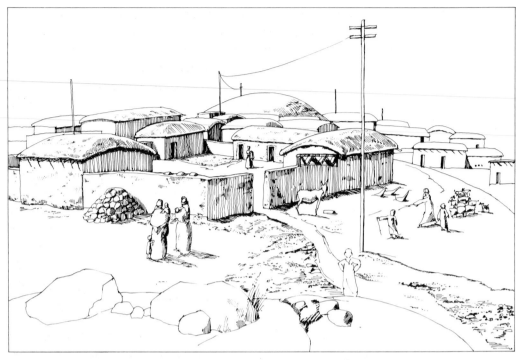

5.8 Compound in a modern Iraqi village

evidence, but here again ethnography suggests some possible answers, even though the conventional tabulation of fittings, and locational analysis of finds, has not proved very productive in Mesopotamia. The reasons for the failure of this technique, which yielded useful results in other parts of the world, are complex. Fixtures are often minimal, sometimes hearths or ovens, less often bins, niches, platforms and benches. Artefacts, too, are usually limited: pottery predominates with occasional fragments of bone, flint and metal. One of the reasons for this relative paucity of evidence is probably the fact that raw materials, such as metals and stones, were precious commodities which were recycled many times rather than being discarded, as all had to be imported over considerable distances. Another factor seems to have been the nature of the use of these rooms. Ethnographic parallels strongly suggest that room usage was not fixed and immutable, but that it was affected by many things such as the changing seasons and fluctuating family size. Tasks which in winter would take place under cover would be performed in the court, or on the roof, in the summer. Rooms also seem to have had a multitude of purposes, as kitchen workshop and sleeping quarters for instance, as well as changing their functions over time. Rooms which at one time housed an elderly relative or pensioner, may later become animal shelters, or store-rooms (Kramer 1979). A byre may be swept out and refurbished to provide a room for a newly married son, but when both have tamped earth floors it is not easy to tell which function the room was performing at the moment the archaeologist is concerned with. As the function of each room is non-specific and frequently transitory, the number of archaeologically identifiable special features is also small, making analysis of usage almost impossible. Obviously there are exceptions to this; it is often possible to identify a kitchen-cum-living-room by its hearth or oven, but we must not forget that the same room may have been used for sleeping as well. Conversely, other rooms may have been reserved for formal functions as guest rooms and so have been untenanted for much of the time.

The transitory and changing nature of room usage gives rise to a further problem if we attempt to estimate prehistoric populations. Such estimates are usually based on the amount of floor space in the living quarters, divided by some fairly crude estimate of the minimum living space required per person. This space seems to be culturally determined and varies widely (Hall 1969). Today Americans top the league table with the Japanese coming somewhere near the bottom (the study of this phenomenon has given rise to a whole new field of study called Proxemics). We do not, and cannot, know how much personal space the Sumerians needed and we do not know how they were using the rooms, roofs and courts of their houses so we cannot be precise about the amount of their floor space at any given moment. This must mean that any attempt at estimating populations during the fourth and third millennia is impressionistic at best. It is perhaps tempting to ask whether this built-in inaccuracy matters, as it is arguable that it is relative, rather than absolute, levels of population which matter from period to period. To obtain relative numbers is perhaps within the capability of the archaeologist and so is a realistic and useful goal. We can study how a specific community expands or contracts through time, or how the total number of settlements in a region changes, but anything more precise than this is usually beyond our reach. Apart from the problems already described in estimating the number of people living in a particular unit, there are further problems in extending that estimate to cover a whole settlement. An archaeologist seldom has more than a small proportion of the total area of a site to work from and must extrapolate, yet he cannot know how much of the town or village was used for non-domestic purposes, for ceremonial buildings, for workshops, or for gardens. When dealing with estimates for a whole area of country, the problems multiply again and there is the additional complication of allowing a figure for the presence of nomadic people, who the texts show to have been present, but who, in most cases, are archaeologically invisible. In the present state of our knowledge absolute numbers are still beyond us. (For a more detailed discussion on these problems, see Kramer 1979.)

The Uruk period

This section began by stressing the continuity in the design and construction of private houses during the Sumerian period and this claim will now be examined in more detail.

Sumer and the Sumerians

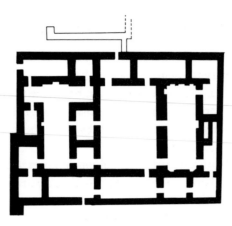

5.9 Plan of house from Jebel Aruda

The best examples of houses from the Uruk period come from the north Syrian sites of Habuba Kabira and Jebel Aruda. Two types of houses predominate in these towns; the first is the rectangular house, built round either an open court or a large room, while the second resembles the plans of the tripartite temples of the Ubaid and Uruk periods. Some have a rectangular central area, others have a T-shaped one which closely resembles those found in the Ubaid period houses in the Hamrin (Fig. 5.9) (Ludwig 1977). The best examples of these T-shaped halls come from the well-planned Ubaid houses at Tell Abada and Kheit Qasim (Jasim 1985). In north Syria (Roaf 1984), however, the two types of plan are sometimes combined into one unit, as we can see in the largest house in the southern area at Jebel Aruda. The northern area at Jebel Aruda has two complexes, NC and NF, where the house opens onto a large compound with kilns, ovens and other quasi-industrial debris including a large number of bevel-rimmed bowls in NF. It is difficult to tell whether we have an industrial unit here or whether we have a self-sufficient domestic unit producing its own household crockery and processing its own agricultural produce (Van Driel 1983). The evidence from Mesopotamia is much more fragmentary, though one fine house was excavated at Grai Resh on the Sinjar–Tell Afar road (Lloyd 1940). This is basically tripartite in plan too. It has a large central room with niches in each of the short walls and a modified form of the T-shaped layout. The walls are finely plastered and it is linked to the street by a long, narrow, passage-type room. There is a certain amount of quasi-industrial debris here too, in this case cores and blades of obsidian and chert (Lloyd 1940). The other houses of Uruk date are at Qualinj Agha and have also been discussed earlier in this chapter. In these houses too there are blades and cores of obsidian, perhaps indicating the self-sufficiency of these communities, where large households produced all their own necessities even if raw materials and luxuries had to be imported.

The Jemdat Nasr and Early Dynastic periods

The evidence for these periods will be treated together and comes mainly from two small provincial towns in the Diyala valley, Tell Asmar and Khafaje (Delougaz *et al.* 1967). More recent evidence comes from another small town actually on the plain, Abu Salabikh, lying within sight of the great religious centre at Nippur. Houses in all these small towns are crammed together in blocks separated by large streets and threaded through with narrow alleys. Space was obviously at a premium and the pressure on land led to a considerable variety of *ad hoc* modifications to the standard courtyard house plan. The tripartite houses of both types do not seem to occur after the Uruk period and it will be remembered that after this time the plan also begins to disappear from the repertoire of religious architecture as well. No examples are known from the ED period. The houses of JN and ED date from the Diyala can all be seen as variations on the courtyard theme, but they are distinguished from the earlier courtyard houses by the presence of brick tombs in many of them from late ED I onwards. Intramural burial is nothing new in Mesopotamia, but the presence of these well-built, often vaulted tombs in many of the houses at the Diyala sites is an innovation. Their presence poses a number of questions – there are not enough of them to have housed all the dead of the settlement and we do not know what the criteria were which determined who was buried in them. The skeletal remains indicate that no single sex or age group accounts for all the remains. Although no brick tombs have yet been found at Abu Salabikh many of the houses there also have graves dug below rooms and courtyards, graves which contain bodies of both sexes and a wide age range. Some of these people were buried with rich grave goods, some with nothing (Martin, Postgate and Moon 1985).

Another feature which distinguishes these ED houses from the earlier ones is the lack of manufacturing debris within the houses, though there are exceptions. It seems that even prosperous households were no longer having to produce their own pottery and basic tools, pointing perhaps to an increasing industrialisation during the third millennium and a shift from the cottage industries of earlier periods. This shift is also suggested by the texts, which frequently deal with the management of large workshops, usually under the control of the temple or palace. The floor areas of these houses vary enormously. In the ED III level Va at Tell Asmar one house covered 248 square metres, while another was only 44 square metres in area (Delougaz *et al.* 1967). Taken together with the variation in the quality and quantity of grave goods, these wide discrepancies underline the increasingly stratified nature of Mesopotamian society.

It would be tedious to describe each of these houses in detail but one, the Arch house, founded in level Vc at Tell Asmar, will serve as a prototype (Fig. 5.10). This house lasted, with a series of modifications, from ED III into the Agade period. The original plan is rectangular, the corners are oriented to the points of the compass and

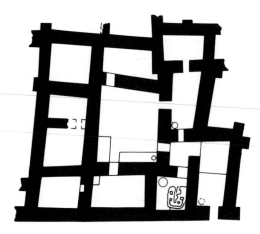

5.10 The Arch house, Tell Asmar

the nucleus of the house is a rectangular courtyard from which four (originally five?) arched doorways give access to the adjacent rooms. There are various illustrations in the court including a bench and an area paved with gypsum, on which a water pot or 'hub' may have stood. The kitchen, identified by a kitchen range and a bread oven, does not communicate directly with the court, but leads to a small anteroom and then to a narrow, rectangular hall which gives access to the street. Two of the rooms have niches in the walls, and probably served as cupboards, but apart from that there are no distinguishing structural features. The house goes through a number of vicissitudes, but the only new feature is the addition of a paved lavatory in the early Agade period. There is no evidence for a second storey at any stage in the occupation of this house.

At Abu Salabikh large areas of the surface of the tell are being scraped down to reveal the walls of buildings just below the surface. Exact dating of the structures is not possible by this method and even relative dating may have to be confirmed by excavation, but a remarkably coherent plan of a considerable area of the third-millennium town has been recovered by this technique at relatively low cost. The scraping of the west mound showed an area of ED I housing which produced an interesting and unusual feature. The mound seems to have been subdivided by heavy perimeter walls into discrete blocks of buildings. Four of these blocks were identified, but the plans of individual buildings within the perimeter walls were rather fragmentary. Enough remained of the buildings in block A, however, to indicate that they were probably of the courtyard type (Postgate 1983). Another group of houses on the main mound of similar date were distinguished by the presence of fine, two-storey ovens (Crawford 1983). By the ED II/III periods the focus of settlement had shifted to the main mound and we again see the familiar pattern of larger streets, paved with sherds, separating blocks of buildings reached by smaller alleyways. Even without excavation, it is obvious that some houses are, as in the Diyala, much larger and better planned than others. Excavation is proceeding in one or two selected houses and, as mentioned earlier, graves are being found in considerable numbers associated with each of these houses. Apart from hearths and ovens, domestic installations are minimal (Postgate 1984).

The Agade period

More evidence, collected by surface survey, comes from the site of Tell Taya, east of the Jebel Sinjar. Extensive surveying revealed a town covering as much as 150 ha in all; the stone footings of the walls provide probably the most comprehensive picture of urban sprawl in Early Dynastic north Mesopotamia we are ever likely to have (Fig. 4.4). The exact date of each unit is again difficult to establish, but Reade would see most of the surveyed walls as dating to levels IX and VIII, that is to say to late ED III and early Agade (Reade 1973). Here, for the first time, we seem to have a new type of housing alongside the ubiquitous courtyard house. This is the compound, which has a number of rooms round a large court, which may be as much as 15 m long. None of these compounds has been excavated so we do not know whether they were domestic, administrative or industrial in character. Reade suggests that they may have served a variety of purposes. Two houses, both outside the area of the survey, were excavated and each showed unusual features. The first, W1, was located within the town wall west of the citadel area and the wadi Taya. It has two courtyards and a large number of flanking rooms arranged in as many as four parallel rows, an unusual arrangement in a relatively small unit. The second, S1, lay east of the wadi and south of the citadel (Fig. 5.11). The rooms here are small and built round a rather cramped courtyard; the excavator suggests that there was originally a second storey, partly because of the absence of any large rooms on the ground floor and partly because several complete pots were found having apparently fallen from above. Two cess-pits were also found opening off the central court and steps led down into an outer and inner cellar; the entrance to a vault or family tomb was found in the north wall of the latter (Reade 1971).

Some of the modifications at Taya of the standard house plan may be merely adaptations to local conditions. The rock-cut tomb is probably in essence the same as the brick tombs of the Diyala, or the graves of Abu Salabikh, but the compounds suggest the possibility of a real difference between north and south. House plans are generally accepted as being linked to family size and social groupings so the compounds raise the possibility that the groupings may have been somewhat different in the two areas. Such a suggestion can be made only in the most tentative terms, but the difference should be noted and an explanation sought. We also have, for the first time, good evidence for the presence of a second storey in a private house.

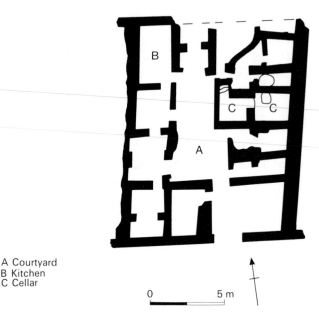

A Courtyard
B Kitchen
C Cellar

0   5 m

5.11 Plan of house from Tell Taya

Another site of Agade date which has produced some atypical house plans is Tepe Gawra, where in level VI the tell was topped by a group of buildings with stone and mudbrick walls built round a central area, which may have housed some sort of public building, although the excavator dated the public building in question to the succeeding period (Speiser 1935). The stone footings form a number of small, square rooms; the largest identifiable unit consists of rooms arranged on either side of a passage with a drain running out of it. The size of the rooms suggests the possiblity that they were for storage rather than for living and that the domestic quarters were located in mudbrick or stone superstructures of which all trace has now disappeared. Given the limited space available on the top of the tell, such buildings could have been several storeys high, thus enabling the maximum number of people to take advantage of the relative safety offered by the (probably defended) top of the tell. Good parallels are to be found for this type of architecture and this sort of use of limited living space in Yemen today and the magnificent tower blocks of towns like Sana'a.

The Ur III period

The residential quarter of Ur is mainly of Larsa and Old Babylonian date, according to the excavator (Woolley 1976) and was destroyed by Shamshu-Iluna of Babylon in 1738 BC (on the usually accepted middle chronology). The foundation of the individual buildings is more difficult to date, but some of them certainly belong to the Ur III

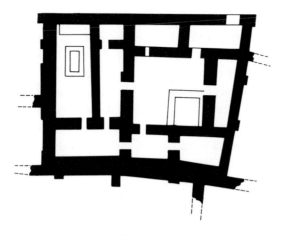

5.12 Plan of house from Ur III Ur

period. 3 Store Street, for instance, produced a number of Ur III tablets. Burnt brick was more widely used in these houses for foundations, thresholds, pavements and arches than in earlier times, but the plan remains essentially the same. There was one important new feature in these Ur III houses, and this was the presence in the more prosperous ones of domestic chapels (Fig. 5.12). These typically lay behind the main room, and parallel to it; the family burials lay below the floor, some in vaulted tombs, the infants in clay pots buried before the altars. The later Larsa chapels had elaborate fittings and fixtures including altars with panelled facades and what Woolley interpreted as incense hearths, which had chimneys or flues built into the wall of the chapel. He also suggested that these chapels were only partly roofed and that the area over the tombs, which usually lay at the end of the room furthest from the altar, remained open to the sky.

The most controversial of Woolley's suggestions was that these later houses, and by inference the Ur III ones as well, had an upper storey, reached by the stairs found in many of the houses and with access to the upper rooms from a wooden balcony running right round the court. The archaeological evidence for this suggestion is extremely slim and consists of a possible base for one of the supports of this putative balcony in 3 Gay Street (Macadam 1981). The rest of the argument is based on his view that there was insufficient space on the ground floor of these houses to accommodate a prosperous family and its servants. Yet he himself records all the necessary domestic equipment in these houses, including a wooden bedstead in 5 New Street, indicating that someone at any rate slept on the ground floor. Woolley suggests it was the servants, but one questions whether they would have had a bedstead. It may perhaps be that the excavator was applying Western values in an area where they are inapposite. On the other hand, his comparison with the architecture of the traditional Arab town house, which is built on several floors, is a seductive one.

From the Uruk houses of Habuba Kabira and Jebel Aruda to those of Third Dynasty Ur is a time-span of more than a thousand years, yet the houses are in many respects similar. The houses are Ur are more sophisticated with their chapels and their paved lavatories, and perhaps their upper floors, but they are still built round their central court or room, looking inwards for light and air with arched internal doors. The living space appears limited by Western standards and it seems fair to guess that then, as now, many tasks were carried out in the open air or on the roof. The domestic architecture of these early periods presents us with one of the few tools we have for attempting to reconstruct daily life and it is frustrating that we are still so far from being able to achieve this goal.

❧ *Chapter 6* ❧

LIFE, DEATH AND THE MEANING
OF THE UNIVERSE

As we have seen in the last chapter, the private houses tell us relatively little about the everyday life of the people who lived in them. They have few distinctive features and, generally speaking, are poor in small finds. This is not because the people who lived in them were poor and unsophisticated, but because objects tended to be reused until they fell apart and furniture and fittings were not widely used. The plans of the houses, which usually focus inwards on a central hall or court, suggest the self-contained nature of these households and their importance as the basic unit in society. The plans sometimes suggest the segregation of certain members of the household, as they are subdivided into a number of discrete units, which do not seem necessarily to be distinguished by differences of function. The position of the house at the centre of family life is emphasised by the presence, from late ED I onwards, of graves below the floors, thus returning to earlier customs. The graves contain the bones of people of both sexes and all ages, in contrast to earlier times when it was normally only children who were buried in this way. The number of graves is not usually large enough to have contained all the postulated inhabitants of a house, so some members of the family seem to have been singled out for this treatment, while the rest were presumably buried in cemeteries outside the settlements. Perhaps those buried below the floors were those associated with the building of the house or were especially loved and revered members of the group.

It is these graves and the extramural cemeteries which, paradoxically, provide us with our best evidence for the everyday life of the people buried in them. Throughout the fourth and third millennia, custom or piety seems to have dictated that the dead were buried with grave goods which were apparently intended to make life in the other world as comfortable as possible: food, clothes, ornaments, tools, weapons and even musical instruments and games are found. The afterlife is described in a few fragments of Sumerian texts, such as the myth of Inanna's descent to the underworld, in which the dead are described as 'Bereft of light, dust is their fare and clay their food. They reside in darkness and are clothed like birds' (Kramer in Pritchard 1955). It seems from this description as if any comforts had to be brought with you! The picture painted in other texts is no more cheerful. Enkidu describes the underworld to Gilgamesh in similar gloomy terms (Sandars 1960). Another text, the Death of Ur-Nammu (Kramer 1967), suggests that it might, however, be possible to improve your lot by sumptuous presents and feasts for the lords of the underworld, suggesting another use for some at least of the grave goods.

103

The study of funerary evidence has become immeasurably more sophisticated over the last five years or so as the papers presented in books such as Chapman's *The archaeology of death* show (Chapman *et al.* 1981). Archaeologists are becoming increasingly aware of some of the pitfalls involved in the simplistic assumptions which used to be commonly made. It is no longer enough to assume that a given group of graves necessarily mirrors everyday life; it has to be shown to do so. The graves must contain a representative sample of individuals who reflect the population profile, in terms of age and sex ratios, as well as in economic and social groupings. The interpretation of the funerary evidence can be further complicated by the realisation that in some societies religious belief or social custom, rather than economic or social status, may determine the type of goods buried with an individual. This means there may be no direct relationship between the furnishing of a grave and the position of its occupant in society during his lifetime. For example, taboos may prevent certain objects from being buried with certain classes of people, or may even dictate a total absence of grave goods from even the most important burials, as in the Christian and Islamic traditions. Conversely, certain groups may be buried with trappings which represent an ideal, rather than an actual position in society. The studies on the burial customs of gypsies published in Chapman (1981) illustrate this well.

There are few cemeteries in Mesopotamia which seem to provide a real cross-section of society; some seem to have been used by small, closely knit groups, such as the ED I cemetery at Kheit Qasim in the Jebel Hamrin, where the graves apparently contain the bodies of the people who lived in the adjacent, fortified, circular building. This seems to have been some sort of headman's house or border post (Forest 1983). The graves from the 'A' cemetery at Kish are also homogeneous, though in this case economically, not socially. They seem to belong exclusively to a group of prosperous citizens, with few graves being noticeably richer or poorer, than their neighbours (Breniquet 1984). There is one exception to these observations, and that is the Royal Cemetery at Ur. Here it seems arguable that the complete spectrum of society is represented, from the sixteen 'Royal' graves dominating the cemetery by virtue of their contents and their central position, to the simple inhumations, buried with nothing at all (Woolley 1934). It is from this cemetery that much of the evidence for daily life in the second half of the third millennium will be drawn, but first we must look at the evidence from earlier burials.

Tepe Gawra has produced some of the most extensive burial remains of the Uruk period. This period begins in level XIa and is marked by the building of the great round house (cf. chapter 5). Unfortunately, the dating of many of the burials is far from clear and the conclusions of the author of the report, who did not excavate there himself, differ widely from those of J.-D. Forest, who has recently reassessed the evidence (Forest 1983). According to Tobler, the author of the report, the round house is associated with only three graves, one below the floor of room 1, an adult with no grave goods, and two below the floor of room 125, one of the secondary rooms built up against the exterior wall of the round house. There is no description of goods from these graves either, so that they too were probably simple inhumations. Forty-five inhumations were attributed to the same level and lay outside the building, as did two built tombs also tentatively assigned to level XIa (Tobler 1950).

By contrast, Forest associates a cemetery of twenty-seven tombs built of mudbrick, or mudbrick and stone, with the round house. These tombs contain the remains of nine adults and eighteen children and are the first proper tombs to be identified at the site, although *pisé* coffins are found from level XIV. These tombs seem to mark the introduction of a new burial rite associated with a particular group within the society. (Tobler dated these tombs to the slightly later level XI, so he too would see a new burial rite at about this time.) The possibility that this group is socially defined is an obvious one; the skeletal material was not analysed for detailed information on age at death, but the report states that children and young adults heavily outweigh adults by a ratio of 2 to 1. Grave goods were found in sixteen of the tombs and were found with both children and adults. They consisted mainly of pottery bowls and ornaments, such as beads and pendants. Forest sees the fact that some tombs were much more richly furnished than others as reflecting differences of sex rather than wealth, and suggests that only males were buried with artefacts. The hypothesis is difficult to test: the sample is small, it is not possible to sex the bones physically in most cases, because of poor preservation, and few of the grave goods can be sexually linked. There are, for instance, no weapons, no mirrors or spindles. One adult was buried with two neonatal skeletons and it is reasonable to suppose that this is a female burial. She has no grave goods, but the hypothesis can hardly be validated by one example.

Whether this aspect of Forest's reconstruction is correct or not, it is fairly clear that this group of tombs is not representative of the population as a whole. The far higher number of inhumations in level XIa, forty-seven according to Forest, indicates that the tombs do belong to a well-defined minority group. The presence in the tombs of so many immature skeletons indicates that neither age nor profession was the distinguishing criterion, and Forest's suggestion that these bodies represent the remains of the people who lived in the round house is an attractive one. The parallel with Kheit Qasim is immediately apparent. The study of the burial customs at Gawra in the early Uruk period, even in the absence of a range of grave goods, clearly suggests that there were already important divisions within society, even if we cannot yet define the exact nature of these divisions.

These divisions seem to become more marked in the succeeding levels, as the tombs become richer and more sophisticated. There are still disagreements between Tobler and Forest about the dating of individual tombs, but both agree that the tombs are found between levels XI and VIII, that is to say to a period covering the second half of the fourth millennium and the beginning of the third. Tobler would place rather more

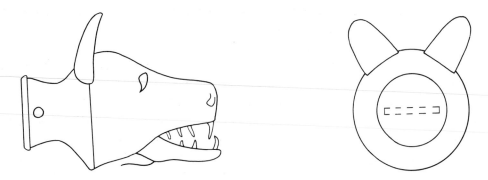

6.1 Electrum wolf's head from a tomb at Tepe Gawra

of the tombs at the end of this time-span than Forest does. The tombs continue to contain bodies of both sexes and all ages and are consistently richer than the contemporary inhumations. For the first time at Gawra we see significant quantities of gold appearing in the tombs, together with other exotic materials such as lapis and ivory. Some of the artefacts show a high standard of technical expertise, indicating the presence of craftsmen either at Gawra itself or in the area from which the artefacts were imported. The magnificent obsidian bowls suggest that some at least of these prestige items were manufactured on the site, as they would have been somewhat difficult to transport as finished articles. The outstanding single artefact is undoubtedly the tiny electrum model of a wolf's head from tomb 114 (Fig. 6.1). It has separately made ears, teeth and lower jaw and the whole stands only 23 mm high. It was probably attached to a wooden staff as there are two holes in the tubular neck and may have been a terminal to a ceremonial wand or staff of office.

Tomb 114 contained other remarkable objects too, including a number of gold beads and rosettes, two maceheads and a whetstone with a gold band round it. The tomb also contained a lapis stamp seal engraved with the figure of a couchant animal, and six red jasper pebbles. These pebbles may have been the counters in a game of some description, but it seems possible that they were part of a simple abacus. Tokens are known to have been used for accounting (see chapter 7) and the earliest numerical system we have from this area seems to be a sexagesimal one, that is to say that things were counted in groups of six as well as by the better known decimal system. The status of the person buried with these magnificent objects is clear and they also give us some clues about the spheres in which the person had been active in his lifetime. The wand and the jewels point to wealth and to ceremonial functions, the maceheads to a military role, and the seal and possibly the pebbles to economic functions. These are the fields in which a local chief might be expected to have been active, and it is tempting to interpret the remains in this way. Objects from other tombs are less easy to interpret;

some objects such as the so-called hut symbols are impossible to decode in the present state of our knowledge. Remains of grain and animal bones from at least four tombs suggest that the deceased were also provided with food and drink for the afterlife.

One other feature also marks these tombs out and that is their locations. They are all associated with major building in levels X, IX and VIII. The function of these buildings is disputed. Tobler sees them as temples, while Forest regards them as impressive private houses, belonging to the people buried in the tombs. This is an attractive thesis, but if it is accepted there are no buildings left which could qualify as religious, a conclusion which seems a little surprising in the light of the prevalance of religious architecture at contemporary sites such as Uruk in the south. If the absence of temples is accepted, then it hardly seems likely that the inhabitants of the tombs were priests and their families and supports the theory that they belonged to the chiefs. Whatever their exact status, this group had access to large amounts of prestige goods, like lapis and gold, coming from places as far away as Badakshan. Other foreign contacts, this time with Anatolia, are suggested by the plans of the houses which have been called megarons, and by impressed pottery which can be matched with pottery from eastern Anatolia. Anatolia has also been shown to have been the source of the obsidian found at Gawra. The élite group did not have a monopoly on these prestige goods; lapis, gold and carnelian are all found in the inhumations as well. Maceheads and a bone pipe or whistle were discovered in the graves, but no single grave was as richly furnished as the richer tombs. Prosperity was clearly not confined to the ruling élite, although it was most marked in that group.

The ED I cemetery at Kheit Qasim in the Hamrin valley has already been mentioned as another example of a cemetery which seems to contain a well-defined group of people (Forest 1983). As at Gawra, they seem to be associated with a particular building. They too were buried in brick-built tombs, but various features distinguish these from the Gawra examples. The Kheit Qasim cemetery has two distinct phases, each of which has somewhat different characteristics. In the earlier phase, the tombs seem to have been arranged in a pattern which itself suggests the hierarchical nature of the society. The smaller graves cluster round two parallel rows of impressive, rectangular, brick-built tombs (Forest 1983). The skeletal remains were in poor condition, but a preliminary study suggests that, unlike Gawra, there were few children buried here. On the basis of an analysis of the contents of the tombs, the larger ones, many of which contained metal objects such as daggers and other blades, are thought to have housed male bodies, while the smaller ones are thought to have been those of women. If this hypothesis is shown to be true, it is perhaps rather surprising that the only two cylinder seals found should come from graves thought to be those of women. It is possible that the observed dichotomy is not a straightforward sexual one, but one based on other criteria such as profession. The presence of weapons in the large tombs would then suggest a society where the soldiers enjoyed a higher status than the administrators identified by their seals. Further analysis may well point to other models.

Another unusual feature of this cemetery is the evidence for the placing of what seem to be funerary offerings on low brick platforms outside the tombs. These deposits frequently consist of copper blades of different types and were sometimes found pushed into the actual masonry of the platforms. Parallels for this sort of rite are known from cemeteries a little further to the east in the Zagros mountains of Iran (Van den Bergen 1973). The fact that the best parallels for this ritual come not from Sumer, but from Iran, underlines the position of the Hamrin as a border, open to influences not felt on the plain itself. The careful layout of the earlier cemetery at Kheit Qasim, and the fact that some of the tombs were reused a number of times, strongly suggest that the graves were marked in some way so that their positions were known, or that they were partly visible above the ground. No evidence for this was recovered from Gawra, but this may have been due to the methods of excavation and the rite was, as we have already shown, somewhat different.

We must now look at the evidence from the south of Mesopotamia; some of the best evidence for the early part of our period comes from the so-called Jemdat Nasr cemetery at Ur. A recent reassessment of the evidence indicates that this cemetery covers a much longer time than its name would suggest (Kolbus 1983). The graves are all inhumations and the contents of the earliest graves compare most closely with Protoliterate material from the Diyala, but others contain material of both ED I and ED II date. The graves can also be divided into two groups on the basis of their contents, one group being much more richly furnished than the other. Many of the richer group, distinguished by the presence of stone bowls, are located together in trench X and also seem to be of similar date. Their contents compare with the material from the Diyala. In his analysis of this cemetery Forest agrees with Kolbus's redating and suggests that there is a significant correlation between the side on which the body was buried and the type of grave goods; bodies on their right sides are correlated with metal goods, while those on their left sides correlate with jewellery. This leads Forest once again to suggest a sexual dichotomy with women being buried on their left sides and men on their right. Forest also notes the presence in a number of graves of specific pots, which he suggests may be the remains of funerary offerings of food and drink. This idea is strengthened by the evidence for food offerings which we have already mentioned from Gawra and by slightly later evidence from Abu Salabikh and Khafaje.

The evidence from these three widely separated sites at Gawra in the north, Kheit Qasim in the Hamrin and Ur in the southern plain point to the existence at around 3000 BC of societies where a class structure of some sort was beginning to appear, with differential distribution of wealth and status, which were at least in part hereditary. This is suggested by the presence of rich grace goods in the burials of young people, and by their location in close association with the prestige buildings. None of the cemeteries discussed has yet provided us with a representative sample of the population as a whole, so the deductions that can be made are obviously limited. The evidence also indicates fairly clearly that death and burial were already attended by a number of ceremonies and rituals, although the ideology which inspired them cannot, at the moment, be reconstructed. In the absence of any but the most simple of texts from this period, it may never be possible to do so with certainty.

From the succeeding ED II period we have graves from the site of Khafaje in the Diyala and from the 'Y' cemetery at Kish at the northern end of the Sumerian plain. The graves at Khafaje were found below the floors of houses and a total of 168 cover the whole of the Early Dynastic period (Delougaz *et al.* 1967). All ages and both sexes are represented, but no detailed evidence on age was recorded so we still cannot be sure that we have an entirely representative sample. It does seem possible that this is the case, especially as the houses cover the whole range of size from single room to mansion, so that the complete economic spectrum is probably represented. (Bone preservation is a major problem on the Sumerian plain and in the Hamrin valley as the salt in the ground water is absorbed into the bones and then forms crystals as the bones dry out. The salt crystals force off the surface of the bone and finally cause the whole bone to decay.) The most striking difference in the tombs at Khafaje at the end of ED I is that, for the first time, the tombs were built of plano-convex brick and have vaulted roofs. In the ED I period all the burials were simple inhumations. In the tombs single burials are the rule, but double and triple burials are found. There is even one tomb which contained five skulls, only two of which seemed to be in their original position, the others having been unceremoniously shovelled to one side to make room for the newcomers. This certainly suggests that these tombs were used as family vaults in some households and were reopened a number of times. Even allowing for this, not enough tombs and graves have been found to account for all the people who could have lived in the houses, so it seems that an extramural cemetery was probably in use at the same time, although this has not been located. Pottery containers are the commonest type of grave goods from Khafaje, and a few stone and copper ones were found too, together with a sprinkling of more exotic items like pins, blades, axes and cylinder seals. Some graves are better furnished than others, inhumations continue alongside the vaulted tombs, but none stands out as exceptionally wealthy or unusually poor. This is a little surprising in view of the range of floor areas noted in the houses below whose floors they were found, a range of size which is usually taken to indicate a range of prosperity. Perhaps it should be more realistically correlated with family size instead, nuclear families inhabiting the smaller houses and extended families the larger ones.

At Khafaje, as at Kheit Qasim, there is some evidence to suggest ceremonies connected with the burial rite. As many as thirty-six simple conical bowls were found in one grave, grave 92, which contained three bodies, while seventeen came from the

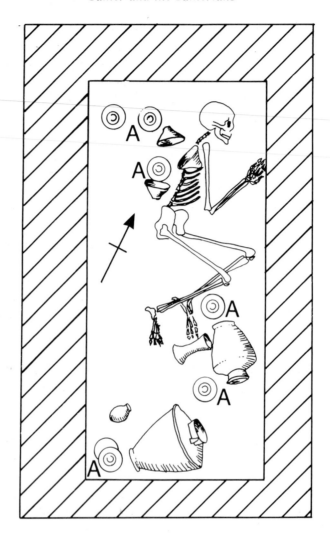

A Conical bowls

6.2 Grave 99 from Khafaje, showing conical bowls probably used for funerary offerings

double burial in grave 108 and ten solid-footed goblets from the single grave 51. When discussing a similar concentration of simple, mass-produced vessels from graves at Abu Salabikh, Postgate suggested that these cups might represent some sort of libation or liquid offering which was part of the funeral service. At Abu Salabikh one grave, grave 80, contained 135 conical bowls (Martin, Postgate and Moon 1985). Ten came from grave 99 at Khafaje (Fig. 6.2).

The 'Y' cemetery at Kish, which dates to the ED I/II periods, is also dug into an area of domestic housing, apparently of ED I date. Some of the graves seem to be contemporary with the houses, but the majority appear to be intrusive, having been dug down through the 'flood stratum' which covers the houses. It is to this intrusive group that the distinctive cart burials, formerly known as chariot burials, belong. There are at least four of these burials, and possibly as many as seven, each of which contained a large, wheeled vehicle (Moorey 1978). Their dating has been the subject of much debate, but Moorey has now shown that an ED II date is the most likely option, both on the basis of the rather meagre stratigraphic evidence and after comparison with better stratified material from the Diyala. One of these graves contained a minimum of five people, a two-wheeled cart drawn by an ox or cow, and a quantity of pottery. The only metal was a rein ring decorated with the figure of an onager, close in style to the slightly later example from the Royal Cemetery at Ur. In another of these graves a four-wheeled cart was identified, jacked up on a platform with the pole projecting in front of it. This cart too had been drawn by bovids and two more rein rings were recovered. The cart seems to have been backed down a ramp and then placed on the platform, while higher up the ramp were found the skeletons of four equids. The number of bodies in this grave was impossible to determine, but the grave was richer than the first and contained a number of copper tools and weapons as well as the rein rings. Beads of lapis and carnelian were found, together with two model boats, one of clay and the other of bitumen, and a quantity of pottery.

The excavator saw these cart burials as the graves of princes and described the carts as chariots (Watelin and Langdon 1934) but Moorey's less emotive term seems more appropriate. Some of the simple inhumations are as rich in metalwork as the cart burials, and indeed have produced some of the most sophisticated artefacts, such as the lattice-work copper stand made by the lost wax process. More significantly perhaps, the only two cylinder seals from this cemetery have come from the simple graves; if the cart burials were really those of princes or nobles, then it would be from these that we would expect to find seals, which were an essential tool of the trade for any senior figure in society. Watelin's claim to have discovered evidence for human sacrifice in the cart burials, which would suggest royal status for their occupants, is impossible to substantiate. As we have seen from evidence from the Diyala, the presence of more than one body in a burial is not of itself enough to support the idea of human sacrifice; multiple burials in family vaults are common. The cart burials may well represent the burials of a specific group within society, but there is little basis for regarding them as royal.

Scattered evidence from Early Dynastic burials at other sites like al Ubaid, where ninety-six graves were excavted by Woolley (Martin 1982), adds little to our knowledge, and it is to the Royal Cemetery at Ur that we have to turn for new information. 1,850 burials were found here by Woolley, dug into an area west of the later royal tombs of the Ur III period and south-east of the ziggurat. The exact boundaries of the cemetery were not established, although the south-east limit was traced, but Woolley considered that it lay just outside the ED town and was dug into the rubbish tips which marked the town's edge (Woolley 1934). These rubbish tips also served to raise the level of the surrounding marshland. The cemetery was apparently first used at the beginning of ED III and almost 400 graves belong to this phase. It continued in use into the Agade period and beyond (Pollock 1985), with almost the same number of graves attributed to the later periods. 750 graves were impossible to date as the stratigraphic context was unknown and the contents were not diagnostic. Numerically and chronologically, this cemetery provides us with the most substantial body of evidence that we have for burial customs in the third millennium. Its value is enhanced by the great variety in the types of burials and in their contents. The sixteen great 'Royal' graves are well known for the glamour and glitter of the objects they contained and for the evidence of what is usually described as human sacrifice on a massive scale (Fig. 6.3), though the accuracy of this description has been questioned. These sixteen tombs all belong to ED IIIa, the first phase of the cemetery's use, and seem to have formed its nucleus, as they lie in roughly parallel lines down the centre of the cemetery area with the other contemporary graves clustered round them. Woolley suggests that the position of these key graves may have been marked by some sort of superstructure, perhaps small funerary chapels. We have already seen that a similar suggestion was put forward by Forest about the burials at Kheit Qasim. If a superstructure did exist, it was probably fairly short-lived and probably fell into ruins during the lifetime of the cemetery, as some of the latest graves actually overlie the royal graves.

One other very distinctive group of graves was noted by Woolley and this was the so-called 'burnt' graves. These burials were not proper cremations, as the body seems to have been laid in the grave in the ordinary way, generally wrapped in matting, but sometimes in a coffin of reeds or clay, and then a fire was lit close to the head. Burning is normally confined to the head and upper part of the body. Fifteen graves certainly fall into this category, and a further ten may do so. The graves are not well furnished, with one exception (grave 156) and this lack of grave goods makes dating difficult. The majority seem to belong to the ED period with two examples, 1490 and 1646, probably belonging to the Agade period. Out of the twenty-five graves which show signs of partial cremation, four contain cylinder seals and a further nine contain metal artefacts. The importance of fire in the burial rite would suggest that the graves belong to a group of people with beliefs in common which distinguished them from the majority of the people buried in the cemetery. There is no evidence to suggest what these beliefs were, or it may, on the other hand, have been their profession, or their origins, which set them apart in this way.

Apart from these two, very distinctive, but very different classes of burial, the majority of the graves from all periods are simple inhumations; the body is often wrapped in a mat or, less frequently, deposited in a coffin. However, the contents of the graves vary so widely in quality and quantity that it would seem that the bodies

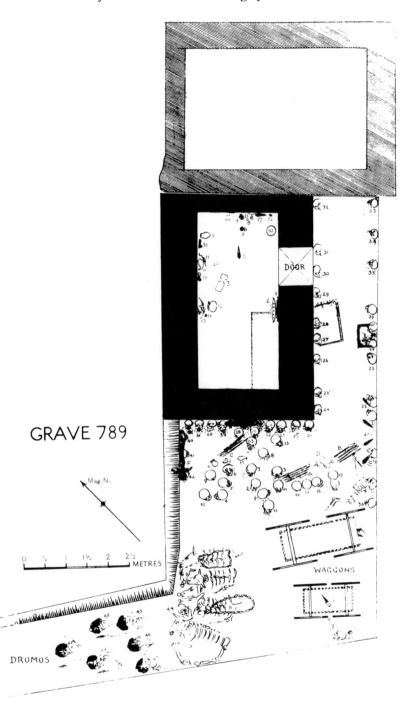

GRAVE 789

Mag N.

0 ½ 1 1½ 2 2½ METRES

DROMOS

6.3 Royal tomb from Ur

represent a wide spectrum of society. Children and infants are seldom present and were probably buried below the floors of the houses in which they lived, but most other sections of society seem to be represented. Single burials are the rule, but double, and in one case at least (grave 1266), triple burials occur. By a freak of preservation, some of the bones are well enough preserved to allow some deductions to be made about the physical appearance of the people buried. Most of the best-preserved material comes from the royal tombs and both the main female burial in RT 800, whose name was the lady Puabi, and the man in PG 779, Meskalamdug, were small. Puabi was under five feet tall and Meskalamdug about five feet five inches; the other male skeletons examined were also about the same height. It is interesting in view of the artistic representations of the time that Puabi is described as having had a prominent nose, certainly one of the characteristics of the statues which have survived. Professor Keith, who studied the bones, remarks on the good condition of the teeth, and attributes this to a 'civilized diet' (Keith in Woolley 1934). More accurately, it probably indicates that grain was being well processed, without too much stone debris in the flour and that the diet was low in sugar. The muscle attachments on Puabi's legs and ankle bones led Keith to suggest that she habitually squatted on her heels. He also suggests, on the basis of the moulding on the inside of the skull, that Meskalamdug was left-handed. Modern studies of skeletal material are few and far between because of the difficulty of retrieving a sample in good enough condition to be properly studied. It has already been mentioned that the salt in the soil is extremely destructive of bone.

It would, of course, be highly speculative to describe a whole group of people on the basis of a detailed examination of a few specimens but, together with the evidence of the art, it seems possible to suggest that the inhabitants of Ur in the Early Dynastic period were small and well-built, with a large cranial capacity, good teeth and large noses! The attribution of racial groupings on the basis of the measurements of the length/breadth ratios of skulls which Keith and his contemporaries used is no longer considered methodologically sound so there is no way of attempting to distinguish Sumerian from Semite on the basis of the skeletal evidence.

The evidence from the cemetery also allows us to make some deductions about the clothes these people wore. Three types of cloth were identified, a fine weave, a coarse weave and a cloth with long threads on one side, which may have formed tassels or a pile. Woolley even tentatively suggested that the finish may have imitated a fleece, a material often portrayed in art. Many of the bodies in the richer graves seem to have worn clothes decorated with beads and rings of shell or metal, which may also have served as fasteners. The court ladies seem to have worn long-sleeved jackets opening down the front, with bands of beads at the wrist, but no evidence was discovered for their skirts or trousers. They also seem to have worn a fine veil, or head covering, beneath their magnificent head-dresses decorated with gold ribbon and sometimes with great combs like a Spanish mantilla comb. Men wore a front-opening shirt or

III A votive couple from Nippur

jacket, with buttons and a belt supporting a dagger or knife. On their heads they wore something like the modern kaffir or headcloth, with a string of beads or metal ribbon to hold it in place. Cloaks, fastened on the shoulder with a long pin, were common to both sexes. Both men and women seem to have used cosmetic paints, and red, black, green and blue pigments were found in the graves, usually in bivalve shells.

It is interesting to note that the archaeological evidence for dress, such as it is, does not agree well with the evidence of the pictorial art, where men are frequently shown with bare torsos, fleecy skirts and shaven, uncovered heads (Fig. 6.4). Women are usually depicted wearing a sort of toga, again often of a fleecy material (Fig. 6.5). Their

6.4 Male dress, Early Dynastic period

6.5 Female dress, Early Dynastic period

head-dresses vary from elaborately pleated headcloths to high, bulbous hats which look as if they were made of felt. Perhaps the explanation is to be found in the functions which the men and women are generally performing when they are represented in the art. Here they seem to be specifically undertaking ritual tasks for which special clothes may well have been worn. Woolley also found a number of blades which he identified as razors and which could have been used to shave heads as well as chins. Many of the graves also contain other aids to beauty such as little reticules containing a number of small instruments suitable for cleaning nails and ears.

We have already described in chapter 5 the houses in which these people lived and noted that, even in the grandest of them, there was little trace of furniture. Important people shown on seals and plaques sit on elaborate chairs and thrones, often with a small table before them supporting a tray of food, but it has also been suggested that even important people like Puabi seem to have spent a good deal of time squatting on their heels. Perhaps furniture was reserved for ceremonial occasions and rugs and cushions were preferred for domestic use, though they have left no trace in the archaeological record. Evidence for other types of furniture does occasionally survive and the remains of a great chest 2.25 m long and 1.10 m wide were found in Puabi's tomb. It was decorated with bands of inlaid shell and semi-precious stones and was probably used as a wardrobe. Puabi's body lay on a bed or litter, but apart from this almost the only evidence we have comes from the art, as we have already noted. People probably ate and drank sitting on the ground, as they do today, eating from a communal dish and using the knives they carried in their belts. Their food could have been very varied, judging from the plant remains found in the tombs, but the staples seem to have been unleavened bread, dates, fish and a variety of vegetables. The remains of pig, sheep and goat were all found in the Royal Graves, together with tunny fish, chick peas and crab apples (Ellison *et al.* 1978). Judging from the texts, beer was the most common drink and on the banquet seals is almost certainly shown being drunk through long straws from a communal jar (Fig. 6.6). Date wine may also have been made and at least for the better-off the food was probably varied and plentiful. The rations issued to the temple workers, on the other hand, were extremely monotonous, consisting almost entirely of the staples of barley, beer and fish.

The tools and other artefacts buried in the graves can sometimes help us to deduce the profession of the buried person. The soldiers with their weapons, the court ladies with their jewellery and the musicians with their instruments are easy, but others are less clear-cut. Some bodies are found with tools like chisels and saws, so may have been carpenters, while one Sargonid grave contained what seemed to be the tool-kit and raw materials of a bead-maker. Many contain fish hooks and spears, which may represent the fishermen, who seemed to have formed an important element in the economy. We know from texts from Lagash that there were large numbers of fishermen specialising in different types of fishing on the temple staff there in the ED period (Schneider 1920).

6.6 Banquet scene on Early Dynastic cylinder seal

There are no graves which we can say with certainty belonged to agricultural labourers, who must, numerically, have formed the largest category of workmen in the population. This is probably because they were so poor that they were buried with only the most basic requirements. This also points to the dangers of relying on the evidence of graves alone to reconstruct the composition of past societies.

Entertainment could have been provided by a variety of musical instruments – lyres, harps, drums and cymbals – to which people danced and sang. Gaming boards and gaming pieces were found in a number of graves, like the famous example from the Royal Cemetery, where the rules of the game have just been discovered on a clay tablet. Dice, very similar to modern ones, are also known and may have been imported from the Indus valley. Scenes like those on the Ur standard show lavish feasts in progress to celebrate military victories, but these were probably confined to the leader's immediate entourage. Other important festivals were probably celebrated in the same way and entertainment might have been provided by wrestling matches (Fig. 6.7), which are depicted on some of the stone plaques discussed in chapter 8. Slightly later texts suggest that singing and feasting were an important part of any celebration, public or private, so that life certainly had its lighter moments.

Ur stood on the banks of the Euphrates and the finds of model boats in many of the graves underlines the importance of the river and of the adjacent marshes in the life of the city. The model boats were made in many different materials, of silver, pottery and of bitumen, but nearly all were the same long elegant shape, still to be seen in the

6.7 A wrestling match shown on a stone plaque

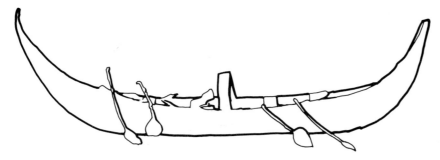

6.8 A silver model of a boat from the Royal Graves at Ur

southern marshes of Iraq today, where they are used for fishing and for transport of all sorts (Fig. 6.8). In the past they were used for raiding parties as well. The river was a vital resource, it supplied water for human consumption and brought fertility to the fields, while the teeming fish were a vital element in the diet. It was also a crucial artery of communication and a busy trade route. It was almost certainly easier to move goods, such as grain, in bulk, by water rather than by land. The country was broken and transport was by carts with solid wooden wheels. Such carts were found at Kish, in the 'Y' cemetery, as we have already mentioned, and were drawn by either oxen or donkeys. A curious sledge with runners in stead of wheels, if the reconstruction is to be believed, was found by Woolley in the grave of Puabi. This seems to have been another type of vehicle in use at the time. Donkeys provided the most common pack animal and, as the domesticated horse had not yet been introduced into southern Mesopotamia, were probably ridden as well.

Nothing in the private graves at Ur provides us with any clues which would enable us to refine our distinctly impressionistic picture of the Sumerian after-life as we have already described it, but the sixteen royal graves with their multiple burials do raise some apparent anomalies. Why, given the gloomy view of the underworld which seems to have prevailed, were so many people prepared to follow their masters and mistresses into the tomb? It has been suggested that the retinues were forced into the graves and then murdered, but Woolley was convinced that this was not the case. He suggested that the attendants had gone willingly into the tomb and had then drunk poison (Woolley 1934). As an explanation, he suggested that the status of the main person buried was such as to guarantee preferential treatment for their followers in the Nether World. Woolley saw the graves as those of king and queens, in spite of the difficulties raised by the fact that the names recovered from the graves do not occur on the King Lists and no unambiguously royal titles are found either. Titles like NIN which do occur can be used in other contexts. Another suggestion, that the occupants of the tombs had been participants in the sacred marriage, was effectively demolished by Woolley himself, but Moorey's theory that the tombs house priests and priestesses connected with the cult of Sin/Nannar at Ur cannot be ruled out (Moorey 1977). Whichever of these roles the deceased played in their lifetimes, Woolley's explanation of the rites associated with their burials would seem to remain valid, though his insistence on the willing submission of the other human victims may be a little romanticised.

The graves of the Sargonid period do not provide any evidence for radical change in the burial customs of ordinary people; the style of the artefacts changes gradually but the range of goods deposited and the associated rites do not. Most of the burials are still single inhumations, usually wrapped in mats, occasionally buried in a simple coffin. The bodies are still found in a flexed position with the hands in front of the face. They wear the jewellery they wore in life and take with them food for the afterlife, tools, weapons and their personal seals. The style of the seals and of the jewellery changes; the men now wear a simple metal frontlet, for example, instead of the more elaborate head-dresses of the ED. There are no Sargonid graves which can be compared to the earlier royal graves, but this cannot be taken as evidence that none existed, because excavation was far from complete and we know that Ur continued to be an important centre in the Agade period. Sargon's daughter, Enheduanna, was appointed high priestess and on account of both her birth and her position would have been buried with all pomp and ceremony. Her grave has not been located. The continuity in burial customs is another fragment of evidence to support the essential cultural continuity between the Early Dynastic and the succeeding Agade period.

In the succeeding Ur III period the situation changes again. The extramural cemetery, if it existed, has not been found, but the tombs of the ruling family were located above a corner of the older cemetery, just outside the sacred enclosure. Private graves all come from burials below the floors of private houses and, instead of being found in a fairly random way below courts and rooms, they now usually come from what seem to be private chapels, often placed behind the main living-room of the house. The chapels seem to have been partially open to the sky and usually had an altar and special hearths, apparently for burning incense. Infants, children and adults were all buried in these chapels, though the infants were usually found in pottery jars buried close to the altar (Woolley 1976). The creation of a special family mortuary chapel is a new development and for the first time we have good evidence for funerary offerings, which apparently continued to be made over a period of time. The evidence from earlier periods has been largely circumstantial and the presence of funerary chapels above the earlier royal tombs, for instance, was only guessed at. The new custom should probably be seen as a development from the old, rather than as a radical new departure. It seems probable that, as at Khafaje, an extramural cemetery was in use as well and may have been used by less prosperous members of the community.

The so-called royal graves of the Third Ur Dynasty do, on the other hand, show a number of new features. Even their attribution to the royal family has recently been questioned, but this still remains the most likely explanation for their distinctive features (Moorey 1984). In the Ur III period all except the first ruler, Ur-Nammu, were deified during their lifetimes. This divine status was reflected in their tombs which became shrines to the deceased god-king, whose worship continued after his death; for the first time the superstructure of these tombs, which housed the shrines, became more important than the burial vaults which lay below. The complex of tombs which lie under the south-east corner of Nebuchadnezzar's temenos and probably just outside the contemporary sacred enclosure, consists of three units (Woolley 1974). The central unit is the best preserved and the best constructed; it is also the earliest of the three and is massively built of burnt bricks stamped with the name of Shulgi, second ruler of the dynasty. It is not clear whether the tomb was built for Shulgi himself or for his father, Ur-Nammu. As the latter was never deified it seems more likely that Shulgi built it for himself. The southern unit is built of bricks stamped with the name of Amar-Sin, also known as Bur-Sin, Shulgi's successor, and the northern tomb is built of a mixture of bricks which seem to have been left over from the earlier constructions. As most of the bones recovered from this last tomb were female and as it is noticeably less well constructed than the others, it has been suggested that it was built for a queen consort rather than for a divine ruler (Michalowski 1977).

All three tombs are planned round a central courtyard like the private houses, but there the resemblance ends. The walls of the Shulgi tomb are 3 m thick and the external corners of the building are carefully rounded. The central court is paved to slope gently to a basin in the centre which caught any surplus ground water in the wet season. There are traces on the walls of the rooms of elaborate decoration in gold leaf and semi-precious stones. The minor rooms seem to have served as domestic offices, with a kitchen where ritual meals were probably prepared for the dead king and another which seems to have served as a store-room. At least two of the main rooms of the shrine house elaborate altars and offering tables for the worship of the ruler, while his body was probably originally interred in one of the two great vaulted tombs which lie below the shrine. The larger tomb is corbel-vaulted and was originally almost 6 m high, although the floor had to be raised before the bodies were finally laid to rest. The tomb was very thoroughly pillaged before the superstructure was completed and all that remains are a few scraps of bone and pottery. It is possible to deduce that at least seven people were buried in the vault, one of whom was a child. The second tomb was also robbed and the tombs in the other two mausolea suffered the same fate. The tombs were constructed first in a deep pit and a temporary shrine seems to have been erected while the final building was in progress.

The presence of several bodies in each of the vaults may indicate a continuation of the rite of human sacrifice seen in the Early Dynastic royal graves but, on the other hand, it may merely indicate that other members of the royal family also qualified for burial in the king's tomb and were buried during its construction. Once the tomb was sealed, after the disposition of the main burial, it was not reopened. A few fragments of text survive which seem to describe the rites which accompanied the burial of a king and one called 'The death of Gilgamesh' could be interpreted as meaning that the court was buried with the king, but the meaning is very obscure (Kramer 1944). Another fragment called 'The death of Ur-Nammu' (Kramer 1967) describes how, on his death, Ur-Nammu descended into the underworld and gave presents and a great feast to all the gods there, apparently to consolidate his own position. This suggests another reason for the rich offerings in the earlier royal tombs as well.

It was suggested at the beginning of this chapter that the best evidence for everyday life in Sumer could be obtained from the dead. The burials can provide evidence for the physical appearance of the people, for their clothes, food, jobs and amusements. The graves can also give us some insights into the structure of society, its external contacts, its level of technological achievement and even into its customs and beliefs. The essential continuity in burial customs is one of the most striking features of the period we have been looking at. It is not possible to detect any major changes in the burial customs of ordinary people. The relative importance of intra- and extramural burial may have varied but the position of the body, the goods which accompanied it, and the rites which were performed do not seem to alter in any significant way. The position of the kings is less clear and it is only in the Early Dynastic period that we have unequivocal evidence for human sacrifice, while it is not until Ur III that we can be certain that deified rulers continued to be worshipped after their deaths. The philosophy of the time is difficult to determine, the textual evidence is ambiguous and insufficient, but there is no indication that it was believed that a just man would enjoy a better afterlife than his less virtuous neighbour. On the contrary, what evidence there is suggests that your condition in the underworld reflected your social status on earth, not your virtue. Comfort seems to have depended on what goods you brought with you in your grave. These could be used as presents for the gods of the underworld or directly for your own bodily ease. It is these grave goods, meant to relieve the grey tedium of the afterlife, which provide us with the best evidence we have for reconstructing the everyday life of the people living in Sumer four thousand years ago.

Chapter 7

MANUFACTURING INDUSTRY AND TRADE

The artefacts in the graves and cemeteries help us to reconstruct the daily lives of the people with whom they were buried. They also pose a number of questions. How were they made and by whom, for instance? Some are so skilfully finished that they must be the work of professionals; some are mass-produced and suggest the existence of early 'factories', a hypothesis the texts support; many of the objects, as one might expect, seem to be the products of cottage industries. Much of the evidence relating to the manufacture of these and other goods comes from the texts; the archaeological evidence is not very helpful once the objects themselves have been studied. The texts suggest that the major centres of production were run by the great public institutions, by the temples and palaces, but we must remember that our information is biased by the accident of recovery. The vast majority of the tablets recovered come from public rather than private archives, reflecting the interest of the early excavators in temples and palaces. This means that small businesses, if they existed, are very under-represented. Although we have little direct, archaeological evidence, it seems possible that skilled craftsmen were working in the private sector too by the middle of the third millennium.

A money economy was not in use during the fourth and third millennia, but there was a well-regulated system of exchanges. The value of one article was expressed in terms of its worth in some standard commodity such as copper. At the beginning of the Early Dynastic period goods were 'priced' in terms of copper, but later in the third millennium silver became the medium of exchange. Law codes such as that of Eshnunna at the end of the third millennium contain a section at the beginning which lays down the fair prices for a range of goods, including corn and fish, in terms of silver (Pritchard 1969). These ratios were not immutable, but responded to market forces. In times of famine for instance, grain became very much more expensive in terms of silver. An extreme example of this can be seen in the prices Ibbi-Sin was forced to pay for grain just prior to the final collapse of his empire, a collapse which seems to have been induced by a series of natural disasters which were followed by the *coup de grâce* administered by a coalition of his enemies (Kramer 1963).

There seems to have been a flourishing internal trade in manufactured goods within the Sumerian plain and many towns had manufacturing specialities. By the end of the third millennium the town of Isin seems to have specialised in leather working and to have produced a whole range of goods which were traded widely within Sumer (van de

7.1 A woman spinning from Mari

Miesoop 1987). Lagash, on the other hand, seems to have been a centre for the slave trade. Much has been written about Mesopotamia's external trade, but the importance of this network of exchanges within the country has been identified relatively recently (Crawford 1973).

Sumer's biggest industry, in terms of men employed, was agriculture and this has been discussed in chapter 3. Grain was undoubtedly the largest single export from the Sumerian plain and so could be said to have underpinned the whole economic system.

TEXTILE MANUFACTURE

The second most important industry in terms of exports was the textile sector, for which evidence comes primarily from the texts. These show that by the Ur III period, large numbers of women and girls were working in temple and palace workshops as weavers, producing a great variety of different textiles (Waetzoldt 1972). Archaeological evidence is sparser, but a plaque from Mari shows a woman, possibly a priestess, holding a spindle, and what little architectural evidence we have will be discussed later in this chapter (Fig. 7.1).

Many of the descriptive terms for these textiles are impossible to translate, but different weights of cloth are listed and a variety of tufted cloth is also described. The representations of clothes on the statues of the period give us clues as well. Some of the figures seem to be wearing sheepskins with the fleece on the outside; some seem to be wearing lighter weight garments which mimic the pattern of fleecy curls in another material and some of the women depicted seem to be wearing very finely pleated

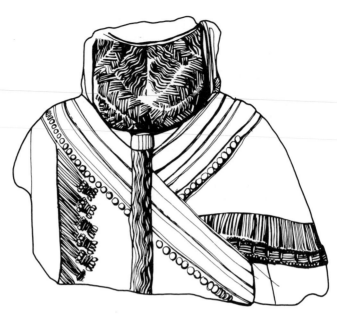

7.2 Decoration of tassels and beads on robe of the late third millennium

dresses which look as if they were made of lawn, or very light-weight cloth. It is perhaps rather surprising that the statues show hardly any evidence of embroidery, although there are some statues of Isin-Larsa or Ur III date which seem to be wearing robes with embroidered decoration, or perhaps drawn threadwork, on the front (Fig. 7.2). The robes are also apparently decorated with beads forming a fringe (e.g. Strommenger 1964, fig. 129). Several earlier statues, especially those of Manishtusu of the Agade dynasty, are also depicted wearing robes with quite elaborate fringes, knotted into decorative patterns, but these do not seem to appear before the Agade period (cf. Amiet 1976). The high, so-called *polos* headdresses worn by the priestesses of Mari (Strommenger 1964) may perhaps have been made of felt, illustrating another manufacturing skill which it would be reasonable to find in an economy where sheep were so important and where there were longstanding ties with nomadic herdsmen.

The archaeological evidence is, as we have said, minimal. The so-called Northern palace at Tell Asmar may possibly be an example of a small temple workshop and the presence of so many vats and other water installations (see fig. 5.6) suggested a textile working area to its excavator; leather working is also a possibility, and so is weaving. Certainly, a textile factory was located here in later levels, now destroyed (Delougaz *et al.* 1967). There is also a weavers' pit in the Giparu, or palace of the priestesses, at Ur in the Ur III period (Weadock 1975). Seals from the Jemdat Nasr period depict weaving in one or two instances. In one, a horizontal loom is being used and two people are passing the shuttle backwards and forwards between them (Fig. 7.3). This could represent

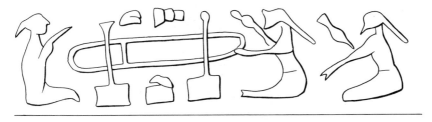

7.3 A horizontal loom on a seal of *c.* 3000 BC

carpet manufacture and the whole scene is suggestive of a cottage industry rather than large-scale, organised production (Amiet 1980, no. 275).

POTTERY MAKING

By contrast with the textile industry, the archaeological evidence for the manufacture of pottery, at least in the early part of our period, is relatively abundant. It even allows us to detect various changes in the industry, although the actual techniques of manufacture change little. The fast wheel, the last major innovation, was already in use in the early Uruk period and two-storey kilns are known to have been in use since the Hassuna period (Merpert and Munchaev 1971). It is noticeable that pottery becomes less ornate as our period progresses; burnished ware, which is a characteristic feature of the early and middle Uruk, does not appear in quantity after this in the south; painted decoration, very popular in ED I, especially in the Hamrin area, deteriorates sharply in ED II and polychrome wares are unknown after this. Reserved slip wares also die out in the course of the Early Dynastic. The repertoire of shapes diminishes too, and the rate of change slows down so that the same types of vessel appear over long periods of time. Some shapes occur from the Agade period throughout the Ur III and into the Isin-Larsa. All these changes, taken together, seem to indicate a declining interest in the potter's craft.

This is perhaps the result of the wider availability of metals and a growing prosperity which led to metal vessels being used for prestige purposes, in place of pottery ones. Lead vessels are found in increasing numbers from the Uruk period onwards and by the time of the Royal Cemetery a whole range of metal containers occurs, some of them aping pottery shapes, others, like the fluted gold tumblers from the tomb of Puabi (Fig. 7.4), in shapes which it would be difficult to produce in clay.

From the fifth millennium onwards, there seems to have been a dual system of pottery production in Mesopotamia; everyday vessels were probably produced in small quantities village by village, or even household by household. An example of this mode of production is probably to be seen at the Ubaid village of Abada in the Jebel Hamrin and at Qualinj Agha in northern Iraq in the Uruk period (Jasim 1985; Es-Soof

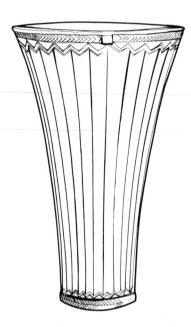

7.4 Gold goblet from the tomb of Puabi

1969). The second mode of production, in which high-quality wares were produced apparently by specialists for export to neighbouring settlements, is best known from Mallowan's famous excavations at Arpachiyah in north Syria (Mallowan and Rose 1935). Studies have shown that pottery from this workshop was traded over a radius of about fifty miles, pieces of an identical ware being found at Tepe Gawra (Davidson and McKerrell 1980). It is, of course, theoretically possible that potters from both sites were using clay from the same source, but as the source seems to lie much closer to Arpachiyah, where the ware is found in quantity, trade seems a more likely explanation. It is perhaps permissible to extrapolate from the Halaf into the Uruk, and to suggest that this same dual mode of production was still in operation 500 years later. If this was the case, then it is suggested that the high-quality Uruk burnished wares, which show a uniformity of design and execution, were probably mass-produced while other less sophisticated wares were produced locally.

Perhaps the best known of all the Uruk pottery shapes is the ubiquitous bevel-rimmed bowl or BRB. This coarse, ugly, but obviously functional vessel is found from Syria to the Iranian plateau; it was apparently made in a mould, though no mould has been found. This has led to the suggestion that the mould might have been of perishable material such as wood. It is crudely finished and instantly recognisable. From the archaeologists' viewpoint it is the ideal type-fossil as it occurs very widely and is almost indestructible. It would seem from a superficial visual examination of bowls from Hama, Syria, in the Copenhagen museum that these were made of local clay and the same seems to be true of other examples over a wide geographic area, suggesting that BRBs were made locally and do not emanate from some hypothetical centre of production. It was thought at one time that the bowls divided roughly into three standard sizes and that they were the ration bowls in which grain and other commodities were distributed to temple personnel. New measurements show that there is too much variation in size for this ration-bowl theory to be wholly convincing (Le Brun 1980). Various other explanations have been proposed, including the endearing suggestion that the bowls were the containers in which Sumerian workmen carried their midday meals to work, that they were the forerunners of the Thermos flask and the plastic box! Perhaps the most likely answer combines elements of several other suggestions. Could they have been bowls in which offerings were brought to the temple or rations were issued, which may later have been recycled for a whole variety of purposes including picnic ware? The most recent suggestion raises the possibility that they were bread moulds (Millard 1988). A multi-purpose function would go some way to explaining the variety of contexts in which the bowls are found. They occur frequently in temple precincts as well as in domestic areas. It would also explain their presence at sites outside Mesopotamia where Sumerian merchants may well have continued to worship as they were accustomed to do at home. The situation on the Iranian plateau may, however, have been rather different.

Let us now look at the evidence for the modes of production in the third millennium in a little more detail. The evidence is still scanty. Amiet has tentatively identified a number of scenes on cylinder seals, in the styles typical of the Uruk and Jemdat Nasr periods, which may show potters at work. Various types of pot are shown, of which the most common is a large jar. One seal from Susa (Amiet 1980, pl. 16, fig. 264) shows a pot on a tall stand which, it has been suggested, may represent a tournette or slow wheel. Two other seals on the same plate (figs. 267–8) show figures putting objects into domed structures which Amiet thought were granaries (Fig. 7.5). The discovery of domed pottery kilns at a number of third millennium sites including Abu Salabikh (Biggs 1974) raises the possibility that these are kilns rather than granaries (Fig. 7.5). Three are shown on this particular seal and, if they are kilns, offer good evidence for mass-production. The slightly later drilled seals quite frequently show squatting figures associated with numbers of pots and Amiet's fig. 324 may show a pot in the simpler type of single-storey kiln or clamp, a scene which is repeated on seal no. 1605 which comes from Uruk. Even if we can show that these seals do represent potters at work, we still do not know whether they were working in a temple precinct or in their own homes. There is some archaeological evidence for industrial production within the Eanna temple enclosure at Uruk in the Eanna IV/III phases, and there is excellent evidence for mass-production in Pit F at Ur. Here, below building level H, which was characterised by solid-footed goblets and the last occurrence of 'painted ware of Jemdat Nasr type', Woolley found a stratum, more than 5 m deep, consisting of kilns,

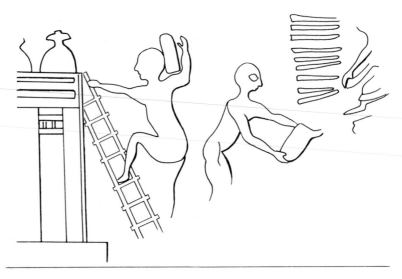

7.5 Kilns/granaries on Susa seal *c.* 3000 BC

pot wasters and clinker (Woolley 1955). Pottery was obviously produced here in quantity over a prolonged period of time prior to ED I, that is to say at a time contemporary with, and slightly later than, that typified by the heavily drilled seals we have already referred to. From the published plan (Woolley 1955, pl. 75) it is difficult to tell how many of the kilns were in operation simultaneously, as the plan conflates them all regardless of level. Most of them seem to cluster between 6 m and 8 m above sea level. The kilns themselves are of the usual two-storey type. The position of the kiln area within the town of Ur is also impossible to establish with certainty, but it seems reasonable to suggest that it was on the edge of the residential area, which then spread to cover the industrial area in the succeeding level H, as the town grew.

Returning to evidence for small-scale domestic production, we also have evidence for kilns, this time of the single-storey type in Uruk levels at Tell Rubeidheh in what is unquestionably a domestic context. One kiln was found with BRBs still inside it and had apparently also been used to heat-treat flint as well, preparatory to the making of the flint tools (Killick 1989). More small-scale pottery production, dating this time to the ED I period, was found at Abu Salabikh, where a kiln was found in a residential area associated with solid-footed goblets (Postgate and Moon 1982). Various kilns of later ED date have also been located at Abu Salabikh. Two groups were found associated with the 'A' cemetery at Kish (Moorey 1978), and in the Agade period a number of kilns was found on the outskirts of Tell Taya (Reade 1973). Edith Porada has suggested in a recent article (Porada 1984) that a seal of the same period and belonging to the Etana cycle may show pot-making in progress, with the rings of clay used in building large jars lying out to dry in a compound. If this really is pottery-making then we are

certainly looking at household production. It is perhaps significant that none of the
known public archives deal with pottery workshops, although, as we have seen, they
do deal extensively with other forms of manufacture taking place within the temple
and palace precincts. This might indicate that by the end of the third millennium small-
scale, local production was the norm, reflecting the decline in the importance of the
pottery industry.

METAL-WORKING

By contrast, large scale metal-working seems to have been concentrated in the public
sector. Texts from the Eanna precinct at Ur from level IV already contain references to
copper and a list of professions contains the word for smith. Artefacts from level IV and
from level III, which are thought to have originated in level IV, show a high level of
technical skill and are some of the earliest examples of *cire-perdue* casting from Sumer.
(All references in this section are drawn from Moorey 1985 and Muhly 1983 unless
otherwise stated.) The slightly later Archaic texts from Ur, which probably date to the
ED I period, already distinguish between copper and bronze, indicating some
knowledge of alloying and probably of the properties of different alloys. The
archaeological remains indicate a rapid increase in the use of metal from Protoliterate
times, with copper and lead being the most widely used metals. Gold is very rare in the
south although some outstanding examples of goldwork were found at Tepe Gawra
(Fig. 6.1 above). The most remarkable piece is the miniature head of a wolf made in
electrum. The workmanship is excellent, the head is beautifully modelled, its lower
jaw separately made and attached to the head by a pin. The teeth are of electrum wire. It
is not necessary to assume that the electrum is the result of deliberate alloying as
electrum does occur naturally, but other artefacts do show evidence of deliberate
alloying such as a true bronze pin from the same level VIII. It is usually assumed that
metals were imported into Sumer already smelted, probably in the form of ingots, to
avoid the expense and difficulty of transporting quantities of useless rock matrix to a
country almost devoid of the fuel necessary for smelting.

   In prehistoric times metal was used only for small objects like beads, pins and hooks.
The techniques used were simple too, cold hammering, annealing and open mould
casting. We do not know exactly when the closed mould was introduced, but the end
of the Uruk period saw a rapid increase in the amount of metal used and from the so-
called Sammelfund hoard from Eanna III come a small figure of a lion and pins
decorated with figures of calves, all made by the lost-wax process. Finds of this quality
seem to indicate the presence of skilled craftsmen, who in the south were probably
attached to the temple at this early period. There is, for instance, a report of a metal-
working area below the Stone-cone temple of Uruk IV, but Moorey and Muhly have
both challenged this interpretation of the finds here. (See most recently, however,

Nissen 1988). However, lumps of metal ore were said to have been found in approximately contemporary levels of the adjacent Anu ziggurat so that metal-working in the vicinity of one or other of the temples remains a possibility.

The suddenness of the increase in the use of metals at the end of the fourth millennium and the rapid increase in technical skills suggest the possiblity that contact with craftsmen from areas outside Mesopotamia, with a longer metallurgical tradition, may have been a factor in the development. Some of the ores used in Sumer seem to have come from the Iranian plateau where there was a long tradition of working the local deposits. Excavations at Tell-i-Iblis and Gabristan indicate a copper-working tradition going back to the early fifth millennium. This tradition included the use of copper arsenic alloys from the first half of the fourth millennium. True tin bronze is only widely used in the second half of the third millennium.

By the ED III period, however, the Mesopotamian craftsmen had mastered all the major techniques for working copper, lead silver, gold and tin. They also began to experiment with iron-working on a small scale, but iron was not to become economically significant for another thousand years or so. The Royal Cemetery at Ur has yielded the most impressive and extensive corpus of metalwork from prehistoric Mesopotamia and in it we find evidence for an astonishing range of techniques which were used to produce tools, weapons, vessels and jewellery. True tin bronze is found, together with the much commoner arsenical bronze; precious metals include gold, silver and electrum. All types of casting were employed, together with a range of decorative techniques which include granulation, *cloisonné* and the use of gold wire. It is difficult to pick out single items to exemplify the taste and skills of these expert craftsmen, but the objects cover many styles, from the classic simplicity of the fluted gold tumblers to the splendours of the well-known gold parade helmet and the delicacy and charm of Puabi's second-best diadem of lapis lazuli embellished with tiny gold figures of animals and fruits (Fig. 7.6).

Another interesting and remarkable group of objects comes from a number of different sites, some in the Diyala valley, some on the plain itself. These are copper figures of men and animals, found from ED II onwards. The figures are depicted singly and in groups: some seem to have been used as supports for small jars, some have no apparent purpose, like the figure of a man driving a team of four equids found at Tell Agrab. Similar figures in a variety of metals are also found decorating the rein rings which form part of the harness on carts and chariots. There are well-known examples from Ur and Kish as well as those shown on the Ur standard and on a number of cylinder seals. A second group of copper figures, usually showing a male figure with his hands clasped in the conventional gesture of prayer and his body tapering to a point, are used as foundation figures. A large number of them was found below the floor of the Construction Inférieure at Telloh, where one group was arranged in concentric circles, looking, according to the excavator, like a bunch of asparagus (Heuzey 1900). These

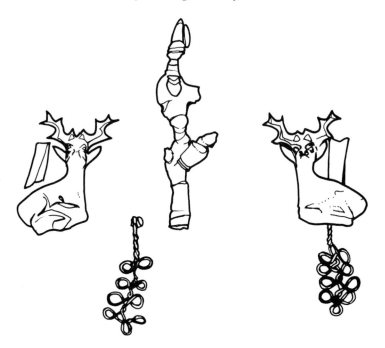

7.6 Decorations from Puabi's diadem

figures continue to be used until the end of the Ur III period, although the style changes and the later figures are shown carrying baskets on their heads. A final group of figures is found decorating large pins, possibly used for fastening cloaks and similar heavy garments.

As well as these decorative items, metal was widely used for more functional objects. The range of weapons found in third millennium levels is extensive and includes mass-produced blades in many sizes, apparently serving as arrows, spears and daggers. Axes too come in many shapes and sizes, some cast and some hammered with the tang beaten round a haft (Fig. 7.7). Helmets, and what is probably the remains of a shield, have been found at Ur, while the famous standard shows soldiers wearing leather cloaks with metal disks sewn onto them for added protection. Maceheads were another popular weapon, and seem also to have served as badges of office, but these were primarily made of stone, sometimes carved in high relief, like one from Telloh which was inscribed with the name of Mesilim of Kish. Tools are not often recovered, so that we are much less well informed about them. They seem to have been routinely melted down and recycled so that is is very difficult to tell how widely used they were. Stone and flint blades certainly continued to play an important part in the economy long after the introduction of metal. The texts do, however, mention large numbers of metal tools, including sickles and hoes, while Muhly quotes a passage from the late third

7.7 A Sumerian soldier with axe and spear

millennium Laws of Eshnunna which states that a workman issued with tools for the harvest must return the same weight of metal at the end of the season, even if some of it is scrap. From this we can suggest that temples and palaces had their own workshops where metal could be smelted down and recast as required.

The evidence for metallurgy in the Agade period, as in so many other areas, is limited, but enough remains to show that the skills of the craftsmen had certainly not diminished, especially as high-quality casting continued although true bronze became very rare again, possibly reflecting problems with the supply of tin. In spite of this, two superb examples of their workmanship have survived in the well-known head of Sargon from Nineveh and the more recently discovered seated figure of a man found near Dohuk (Fig. 7.8). Both pieces are beautifully and realistically modelled and their workmanship is made all the more remarkable by the fact that both are cast from pure copper. It is hard to believe that pieces of this quality were made by any but the most professional of craftsmen. It is also hard to believe that they could have been produced in conditions such as those found in one of the few workshops actually excavated. In level IVa at Tell Asmar, in among the houses, a small forge was found which contained a hearth with an underfloor draught, bins for fuel and a large flat stone apparently used

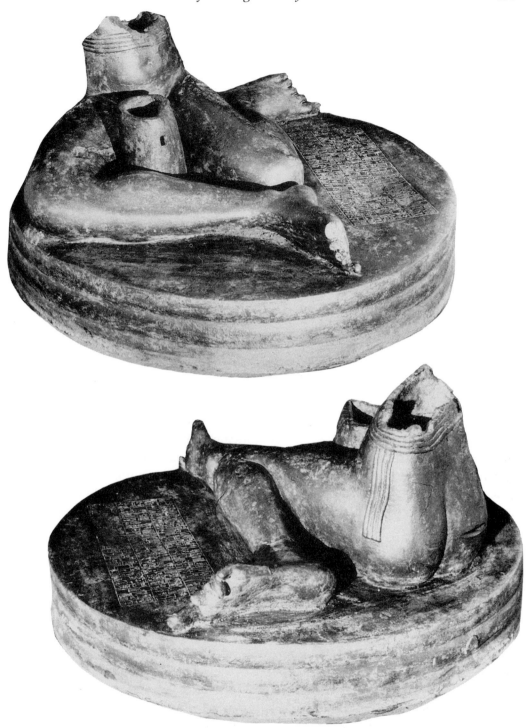

IV Copper figure of Agade date found near Dohuk

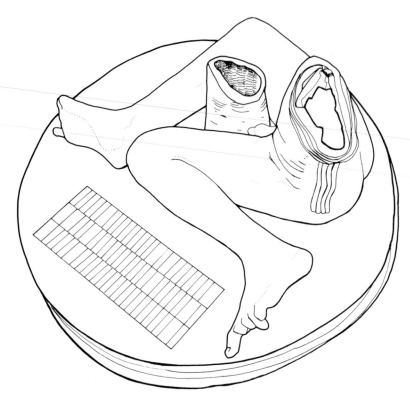

7.8 Copper figure of Agade date

as an anvil (Delougaz *et al.* 1967: 176). The workshop is squashed between two houses with direct access to a narrow lane and we can imagine that its owner fulfilled a function similar to that of a blacksmith in an English village, mending broken domestic and farm equipment and turning out a few simple tools. Here, then, we do seem to have evidence for metal-working unconnected with either of the big state institutions. The smiths may well have been freemen working on their own account. A slightly later text from Girsu lists two smiths who were free men, but other texts show that many were dependants of the institutions. The same word 'Simug' is used for both (Limet 1972).

In the Ur III period the evidence for metal-working again comes mainly from the texts, although a few fine pieces of jewellery have been found including a magnificent necklace of banded agate set in gold, which once belonged to a priestess at Uruk. The royal mausoleum of Shulgi at Ur also yielded scraps of gold leaf which seem to have been part of the architectural decoration. Gold leaf was used for this purpose as early as the Jemdat Nasr period, when the altar of the Eye temple at Tell Brak was decorated in this way (Mallowan 1947). The texts show quite large numbers of metal-workers employed by both the temple and palace to produce a whole range of goods from tools to jewellery. These workers were organised into groups under a foreman who, in his turn, seems to have been responsible to a general overseer. This was certainly the case at Ur. In addition, a parallel structure of officials seems to have existed who ran a sort of assay office; they issued the metals to the foreman and weighed the finished article to make sure all the metal was accounted for. They then counter-signed the receipts issued by the general overseer. In some provincial towns the governor himself seems to have been personally involved in the issue of metal from the treasury. The use of metal was obviously closely regulated, reflecting the relative difficulty of obtaining it from areas outside the Mesopotamian plain, but the metal trade was not solely in the hands of the state. Merchants, like the one whose house Woolley excavated in the Isin-Larsa town at Ur, also supplied quantities of copper. This involvement of private individuals seems to be a feature of the very end of our period, though the records are still very incomplete, making it difficult to be certain that such transactions had not been carried out over a much longer period. The full-time state employees were issued with regular rations, which varied considerably in quantity, perhaps reflecting varying levels of skill. Other craftsmen seem to have been taken on the payroll to complete specific commissions (Limet 1960).

We know little of the tools used by the smiths, except for the very basic equipment described from Tell Asmar. However, a workshop of slightly later, Old Babylonian date, was discovered in the outskirts of modern Baghdad at Tell edh Dhiba'i and here the finds included pot bellows, the nozzle from a tuyère and a variety of different crucibles, some with lips and some without (Fig. 7.9). A number of moulds was also found, one of which may be an ingot mould. This does not necessarily mean that smelting was being carried out. Ingots could be made from scrap as well (al Gailani 1965). With such relatively simple equipment, the Sumerian smiths seem to have been able to produce a wide range of goods of the highest quality, which even today can please and surprise us. Such evidence as we have suggests that much of the highest quality work in precious metals was carried out by craftsmen working for the major institutions, but finds from graves show that private individuals could acquire fine pieces too. Work with base metals, for which there was obviously a far greater demand, seems to have been carried out in both the private and public sectors. As with pottery and textiles, we seem to have indications of a dual mode of production.

STONE-WORKING

We have already mentioned statuary and maceheads as examples of stonework found in Mestopotamia. Stone bowls have also been frequently found, but there is little evidence for their manufacture. The lack of evidence may suggest that the bowls were imported ready-made or at least roughed out. All the stone used was, of course, imported. The usual method for manufacturing simple bowls involved the use of abrasive sand and a hard stone drill; once again these simple requirements would have left little trace in the archaeological record. More elaborate bowls, such as those of steatite/chlorite, were imported from various sources and will be discussed in the next

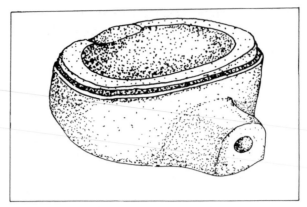

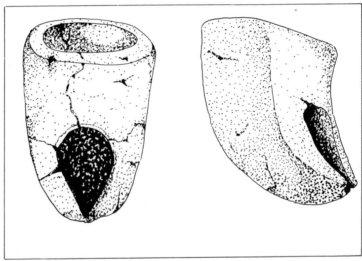

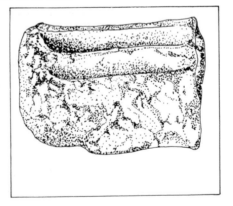

7.9 Metalworker's tools from Tell edh Dhiba'i (after Davey)

section of this chapter. The soft stone used for statues must have been reasonably easy to work and, once again, no elaborate equipment was needed. A workshop for the manufacture of votive statues was uncovered next to the Nintu temple at Tell Asmar and contained roughed-out blocks of stone and pieces of stone cushioned in bitumen to hold them firm while work was progressing. The small finds from these excavations have not been published so we do not know whether any tools were associated with the workshop. It is interesting to note that statues were also being mended here, an indication of the esteem in which such statues were held, or of the difficulty of acquiring suitable raw materials (Delougaz and Lloyd 1942). One or two examples of statues with metal insets are known from the Early Dynastic period, such as the charming figure of a woman with a diadem of copper found in a private grave at Ur (Woolley 1982). The harder stone popular for the manufacture of royal statues from the Agade period onwards may well have required a different set of tools, but once again the evidence is lacking.

OVERSEAS TRADE

As so many of the manufactured goods we have been discussing were made of imported materials, this seems an appropriate place to consider what is known of Mesopotamia's trading contacts. The evidence comes from a variety of sources, each adding another little piece of the jigsaw. We must look at foreign goods found in Mesopotamia, at Mesopotamian artefacts found in foreign contexts, at the raw materials themselves, some of which can be traced to their source by chemical finger-printing, and, of course, at the texts. The textual sources are particularly useful in the second half of the third millennium and complement the evidence from other sources, allowing us to reconstruct changes in the patterns of trade. These seem to reflect major historical events, apparently relating in some cases to political changes and in others to major movements of peoples, which disrupted the existing economic framework. It should be noted that the word 'trade' is being used very loosely in this discussion to cover the acquisition of foreign goods by any means, including foraging, pillaging and tribute. It is often almost impossible to distinguish archaeologically between these methods of moving goods from one place to another and even the texts are unreliable as rulers tended to use inscriptions to enhance their personal standing rather than to keep a factual record. With this end in view, genuine trade might be represented as tribute, and pillaging as trade.

Imported raw materials were in use in southern Mesopotamia from the Samarra period onwards, when carnelian beads were found with other imported materials in the graves at Tell es-Sawwan north of Baghdad (El-Wailly and Es-Soof 1965). The volume of imports increases steadily, especially during the Uruk period, when we have already noted the increase in the use of metals. These imports were increasingly used

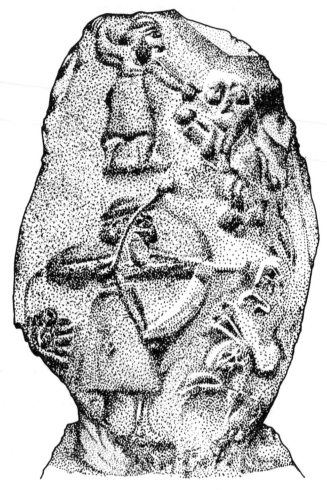

7.10 Lion Hunt stele

for utilitarian as well as decorative purposes, reflecting the relative ease of access. We begin to find metal bowls, especially of lead, as well as pins and other small pieces of jewellery. However, local resources continue to be used wherever possible, even for prestige objects. The Lion Hunt stele (Fig. 7.10), usually dated to the end of the Uruk or the beginning of the Jemdat Nasr period, seems to have been carved on a water-worn river boulder, presumably retrieved from one of the great rivers of the plain. The poor-quality deposits of stone near Eridu also seem to have been used for various purposes.

We know little of the mechanics of trade in the Uruk period, but recently discovered bones from Tell Rubeidheh show that the donkey was already domesticated and may have been used for overland transport (Killick 1989). Cattle too were used as draught animals, suggesting another way in which goods in bulk could have been moved. (The wheel had been in use from the end of the Ubaid period for the manufacture of pottery.)

In spite of the availability of wheeled land transport, the easiest way of moving bulky goods was still by water and the two rivers were vital arteries of communication. The Euphrates seems to have been especially important, judging from the remains of Uruk colonies found on its middle reaches at Habuba Kabira and Jebel Aruda. Further north, on the edge of the Anatolian plateau, new evidence for an Uruk presence has been found at Hassek and Arslan Tepe/Malatya. This latter has yielded Sumerian-style numerical tablets and cylinder seals in the Uruk style, convincing evidence for commercial activity (Weiss 1984).

Similar tablets found on the Iranian plateau, at Tepe Yahya and Godin Tepe, are thought to link these sites with Susa, as the language of the tablets seems to be proto-Elamite, rather than Sumerian. Other finds from these sites, including BRBs and cylinder seals, do, however, show some contacts with the Sumerian plain (Lamberg-Karlovsky 1973). Contacts between Mesopotamia and areas even further east in the Uruk period are proved by the finds of lapis lazuli at Tepe Gawra in late Uruk levels and at Jebel Aruda, as this semi-precious stone comes only from Badakshan, north of Afghanistan, and mines even further to the east (Herrmann 1983). The finds of lapis from Jebel Aruda, and from Gerzean Egypt, suggest that Mesopotamia was already acting as a middleman as well as importing for her own use, a role which became increasingly important in the second millennium.

We do not know how lapis was reaching Mesopotamia. There seem to be three possible routes. The first ran west from the mines to places like Tepe Hissar, south-east of the Caspian, which recent survey work has shown to be a lapis working site (Tosi 1984). From here, the route probably lay along what was later to become the great Silk Road from China, reaching Baghdad via the Diyala valley. A second route from the mines ran south-west to the vicinity of the modern city of Meshed; it then turned due south parallel with the present Afghan/Iranian border, through Shahr-i-Sokhta in Seistan, which was also an important centre for the manufacture of lapis and carnelian beads. From here, one branch of the road led westwards into the Bampur valley and thence to Susa, while another route, which does not concern us here, turned east towards Pakistan and the Indus valley. A third potential route lay up the Arabian Gulf, and small amounts of lapis were certainly brought into Sumer this way in the later part of the third millennium. The reports of lapis mines identified near Quetta in north-west Pakistan, if confirmed, may lead to a reassessment of the importance of this route. Recent finds of tin deposits in western Afghanistan suggest the possibility that tin, too, may have travelled along these routes.

Other goods were also coming up the Gulf by boat from late Uruk times onwards. The texts from Eanna IV at Uruk mention the import of copper from Dilmun, identified with the island of Bahrain. In the third millennium it was to become an extremely important entrepôt as well as a supplier of quality dates, and possibly pearls, from its own resources (Ratnagar 1981). In the Uruk period however, copper is the only commodity mentioned (Nissen 1986). It is curious, bearing in mind the textual

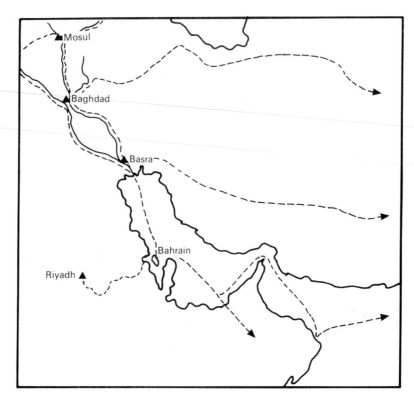

8 Major trade routes to Iran and the Gulf

evidence, that in contrast to the situation in the Ubaid period, little pottery of Uruk
date has been firmly identified from the Arabian coast. This may suggest that contact
was limited, and that the main thrust of Sumerian trade at this time was with Anatolia,
as the trading colonies on the Euphrates indicate. Copper was very probably being
imported from Anatolia down the Euphrates via sites such as Habuba, and there has
recently been a suggestion that Nineveh may be an example of a similar colony on the
Tigris (Algaze 1986). Other vital raw materials, too, were probably brought in from
Anatolia, including lead, silver, timber and perhaps stone.

At some moment, about a generation after they were founded, these settlements on
the Euphrates were abandoned. This event probably coincided with the end of Eanna
IV at Uruk, although it has been suggested that the desertion took place rather earlier,
at the end of Eanna VI (Surenhagen 1978). This view is not generally accepted. If this
abandonment was contemporary with the end of Eanna IV, it was accompanied in the
southern plain by discontinuities in the settlement pattern. A considerable number of
Uruk sites was abandoned and new, smaller, sites were established, some of which
have yielded typical Jemdat Nasr pottery (Adams 1981). There was no complete break
in cultural continuity. Writing, for example, continued to develop from a pictographic

to a syllabic and complex cuneiform system without apparent discontinuity. These two features, taken together, seem to suggest the possibility of a considerable displacement of peoples. This had its most visible effect on the edges of the plain, and on the smaller settlements, while leaving the major centres of population, which housed the scribes, relatively untouched. This displacement could have been caused by one of the many minor climatic fluctuations which affected subsistence on the north Syrian plain, forcing its inhabitants to migrate to other, more hospitable areas. Whatever caused the abandonment of Habuba and other similar sites, the effect was to cut the established trade routes with Anatolia and apparently to shift the focus of the quest for raw materials southwards to Dilmun and the Gulf.

In the Gulf, Mesopotamian artefacts are again found in the Jemdat Nasr period, both in Bahrain and further south in Oman along the line of oases running inland parallel with the coast, where typical Jemdat Nasr polychrome ware has been found in burial cairns (Rice 1985). Southern Arabia has rich deposits of stone, including steatite and diorite, as well as copper, and could have supplied the goods which were no longer coming in down the Euphrates, although there is as yet no firm evidence for the exploitation of the Arabian copper mines as early as this. The first steatite/chlorite bowls are, however, found in Sumer in graves of the Jemdat Nasr period and copper becomes more plentiful too. It is hard to see what, other than raw materials, could have been traded in exchange for the Jemdat Nasr pottery and its contents as the local Arabian economy was not as highly developed as that in Sumer and there is no evidence for manufactured goods which could have been traded. Nor is there evidence for Sumerian settlements in the Gulf region: no tablets have been found and even seals and seal impressions are rare. This makes it evident that the trade was organised on a different basis from that of the earlier trade with Anatolia, and suggests that it might have been dependent on caravans sent out from Sumer on an *ad hoc* basis.

A second route which assumed a renewed importance in the Jemdat Nasr and ED I phases was the north–south route through the Hamrin valley. This route has been much used in the later Ubaid period and then during the Uruk seems to have gone out of favour and the whole area suffered from a recession. The road originated in the area near Susa and then followed the foothills of the Zagros mountains northwards through the Hamrin before turning west to cross the Tigris near Nineveh, on its way into the north Syrian plain. The route through the Hamrin is marked by a string of fortified circular buildings, of which the earliest, Tell Gubba, dates to the Jemdat Nasr period. Slightly later ones are known from Razuk, Sleimah, Tell Abu Qasim and possibly from Tell Maddhur (Gibson 1981). It seems likely that these buildings may have served as strongholds at crucial crossing points on the trade route (see chapter 5). These sites are also linked by the discovery at most of them of a distinctive type of seal impression often found rolled onto the flat rims of pots, in the so-called Piedmont style (Fig. 7.11). This style is found along a wide arc of territory from Susa to north Syria and Collon has recently suggested that these seals mark a trade network from which Sumer was largely

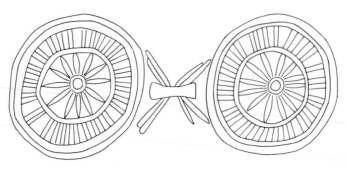

7.11 Design on a Piedmont seal

excluded, perhaps until the middle of the Early Dynastic period (Collon 1987). Not many of this type of seal are known from the plain of Sumer, perhaps because of the disruption we have already referred to which marked the post-Uruk period in this part of Mesopotamia. Susa may have been in a position to take advantage of Sumer's temporary weakness.

This weakness was of short duration and, by the end of ED I and the beginning of ED II, Sumer's contacts with Anatolia and Syria were being re-established. Scarlet-washed pots of this date were found in vaulted tombs at Mari and classic ED II votive statues come from Tell Chuera in north Syria, possibly indicating the re-founding of Sumerian merchant colonies on the route into Anatolia. Links with the east were also re-established. A large collection of stone bowls, some of banded calcite, and many apparently of eastern origin (Potts 1989), comes from the so-called Jemdat Nasr cemetery at Ur, now shown to have remained in use perhaps as late as ED II. The bowls are especially frequent in the later part of the cemetery (Kolbus 1983). From ED II onwards there is archaeological evidence for large quantities of raw materials pouring into Sumer from many different sources. It is probably to this period that the events reported in the myth of Enmerkar and the Lord of Aratta should be dated (Kramer 1952). This myth tells of Enmerkar's attempts to acquire lapis and carnelian from Aratta, usually thought to have been located in eastern Iran, in exchange for grain, which we have already said was Sumer's most important export. There is also textual and physical evidence for a great increase in trade with the Gulf which can be dated to a little later at the beginning of ED III. There are references not only to Dilmun/Bahrain but also to Magan and Meluhha. Magan is thought to be the name used to describe the Arabian mainland south of Bahrain, which became important for a whole variety of products including copper and diorite, a hard, black stone. It may also have been applied to part of the Iranian coast to the north. Meluhha was the furthest away from Sumer and there is no evidence for direct contacts between the two countries in the ED period. It supplied a whole range of goods, most of them luxuries, and is thought to be the designation for India (Ratnagar 1981).

There is one class of object which has been extensively studied for the light it can throw on the complicated trade networks of the second half of the third millennium. Bowls, formerly thought to be made of steatite, but now shown in many cases to be of chlorite/soapstone, have been subjected to detailed physical and stylistic analysis by Philip Kohl and some of his main conclusions will be briefly summarised here (Kohl 1974). Analyses of the material from which bowls in the so-called Intercultural style are made show that it comes from four main source areas. The first lay near Tepe Yahya on the Iranian plateau, the second east of Yahya, perhaps near Bampur; the third has not been precisely located, but seems to have lain in the Zagros mountains close to Susa, while the final group of mines lay on the Arabian peninsula, some south-east of Riyadh, and another group in Oman.

Almost all the pieces of chlorite found in Sumer, excluding those from Adad, come from the source near Tepe Yahya, where there was a thriving chlorite workshop in level IVb. The rest came from the Gulf sources, apparently via the workshops on Tarut, an island just north of Bahrain. Most of the finds from Susa and Mari come from the same Gulf source, while a seond group of bowls from these sites probably comes from the source near Susa. Finds from sites in the Gulf, from Adab and a few from Susa come from the sources on the Arabian peninsula. The distribution pattern is complex and raises a number of questions. Susa was obviously an important distribution centre and Adab seems to have had a special relationship with the centres in the Gulf, although at the moment there is nothing to help us explain what this was. Mari is also very rich in chlorite objects, some of which do not seem to have come up the Euphrates from the Gulf as one might have expected, but to have come across country from the Iranian plateau, via Susa.

Kohl's analysis of the decoration on these pots has produced another puzzle. The most distinctive decoration is in what has been christened the Intercultural style and shows elaborate scenes apparently mythological in content. The same scenes appear on pots originating in all the different areas. Workshops were found at Tarut near Bahrain as well as the one already mentioned at Tepe Yahya, and both were decorating pots in this style. Why were these factories, in different parts of the world, supplying different customers, producing pots whose iconography was indistinguishable? One answer might be that they met the specifications of the importing city, but this does not seem wholly convincing as the motifs often seem to be quite foreign to the Mesopotamian tradition. They include the Indian humped bull and dancing figures with feathered head-dresses. For the moment the problem remains unsolved.

Other chlorite vessels carry less complicated designs; some carry patterns apparently derived from textiles, fleecy curls being particularly popular. The so-called hut pots represent the façades of buildings, buildings which seem to be made of rushes like the *mudhifs* of the Iraqi marshes today (Fig. 7.12). On the other hand, they may represent circular tents or *yurts*. One or two examples show more elaborate buildings and a sherd from Tepe Yahya is decorated with a stepped façade which might represent a ziggurat, a type of building which occurs for the first time in the Early Dynastic

7.12 Decoration on a 'Hut pot'

period. All three types of decoration seem to go out of fashion in the Agade period when the pots become much scarcer and those there are are decorated with a monotonous dot and circle design. All types of chlorite vessels seem to have been regarded as highly desirable, judging from the prestige contexts in which many of them are found, but this makes precise dating more difficult as they seem to have been handed down as heirlooms and so are sometimes found in contexts later than that in which they were manufactured.

The earliest chlorite vessels so far recovered come from the Jemdat Nasr cemetery at Ur, which, as we have already seen, probably continued in use until ED II. These bowls are plain and undecorated and are similar to examples from Tarut. Next in time come the finds from the Sin IX temple at Khafaje and level VIII of the Inanna temple at Nippur, both dated to late ED II, but possibly continuing into ED IIIa. The majority of chlorite objects come from ED III contexts, from the Royal Cemetery at Ur and from the Ishtar and Ninni-Zaza temples at Mari. There are reports of isolated finds from Agade levels, but the contexts tend to be unsatisfactory and the heirloom factor cannot be discounted. Bowls with the dot and circle decoration are found in greater numbers in Ur III and Isin-Larsa contexts.

Apart from the chlorite bowls, there are few classes of artefact found in Sumer which we can be fairly certain were made outside the plain. Two types of carnelian beads form an exception to this. There is a type of fine, long, barrel-shaped carnelian beads which Chakrabati suggested in a recent article were almost certainly made in the Indus valley (Chakrabati 1984) and the much larger and better known class of etched carnelian beads which again were produced in the same area (Reade 1979). Both types of bead are first found in ED IIIa and the etched ones occur in diminishing quantities into the Ur III period. Being small and valuable, such beads must have been ideal trade goods, as too were the occasional finds of other Harappan goods such as dice and figurines of monkeys (Dales 1968).

The evidence for Mesopotamian artefacts in foreign countries, although very limited, suggests the same pattern of trade. We have already mentioned Jemdat Nasr pottery from the Gulf and it is not surprising that pottery of Early Dynastic type is also found at a number of sites, including Umm-an-Nar, an island site south of Bahrain with a good anchorage. The pottery found here seems to have originated in the south of the Sumerian plain (Mynors 1987). Inland, at the oasis site of Hili 8, plano-convex bricks were found in a level dated to ED II by the excavator (Potts forthcoming). There is little evidence from the Iranian plateau, but a fine statue from the cemetery at Shahdad has a number of Sumerian features. In the Indus valley the evidence is again minimal, but a few pieces of chlorite have been found in lower levels at Mohenjodaro decorated in the Intercultural style (Chakrabati 1984).

All this evidence, taken together, indicates that there was a flourishing southwards trade in the Early Dynastic period. Dilmun, as we have seen, was already an entrepôt in the early third millennium and its importance probably increased throughout the ED. It is mentioned on plaques of Ur-Nanshe of Lagash in early ED III. It is rather surprising that there are no traces of contact with ED Mesopotamia on the island of Bahrain itself, where the earliest city probably dates to ED III. It is possible that, at this time, Dilmun designated a wider area which included part of the mainland and perhaps Tarut to the north. The contact may have been via one of these areas and on the island of Tarut there was an important centre for the manufacture of chlorite bowls, apparently dating back to ED II. Tarut has also produced a votive statue of a nude male (Fig. 7.13) and a small figure of lapis, both of which show strong Sumerian influence (Rice 1985).

Further south lies the island of Umm-an-Nar, which has already been mentioned as having yielded ED pottery; it may perhaps have been the port through which materials like copper and chlorite were traded from the interior. Copper was extensively processed at the site of Maysar. This region is probably part of that known to the Sumerians as Magan. These Gulf ports also acted as middlemen in the trade with the Indus valley, forwarding etched carnelian beads and other exotica on the Sumer by a 'down-the-line' type of trade. Some lapis seems to have been coming up the Gulf too, but the major supply route for lapis remained the overland route through Iran.

Evidence for contact with the north is surprisingly sparse in the ED, although we have already mentioned the Sumerian statues found at Tell Chuera. It seems probable that in spite of the lack of evidence metals, stone and woods were still coming into Sumer from the north down both the Tigris and the Euphrates. The Ishtar temple at Assur is evidence of a Sumerian presence here in a city which traditionally controlled much of the traffic on the Tigris (Andrae 1938).

The Agade period saw a great expansion in foreign contacts, though it is difficult to tell how many of Sargon's so-called conquests were genuine and how many were

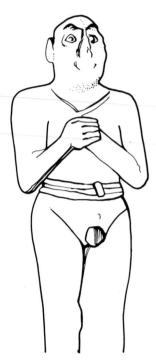

7.13 Figure from Tarut

raiding and foraging expeditions in search of raw materials. This problem of interpretation is illustrated by the accounts of Naram-Sin's 'conquest' of the king of Magan, which culminated in the capture of the king and the mining of diorite in the hills of Magan. Diorite was the favourite stone of the Agade kings and was used for their royal statues so it is tempting to ask whether this conquest was anything more than a mining expedition (Muhly 1973). Magan was too far from Sumer for the idea of political control to be convincing. The later kings of the dynasty also continued to be active in Magan and to make their statues of black diorite.

It is in the reign of Sargon, the first king of the Agade dynasty, that we have the first textual evidence for direct contact even further afield, with Meluhha, the Indus valley. There is a famous inscription in which Sargon boasts that the boats of Dilmun, Magan and Meluhha moored at the quays of Agade (Sollberger and Kupper 1971). It is probably to this period that the site of Ras al Junayz, on the south-east tip of the Arabian peninsula, should be dated. Tosi has suggested that this may have been a staging-post for the Meluhhan boats on their long journey from the Indus up to the head of the Gulf (Tosi 1984). Weights and seals (Fig. 7.14) identical to those in use in the Indus valley were found on the island of Bahrain, enabling us to track these Harappan merchants further along their route (Roaf 1982). It is even suggested that there may have been colonies of foreign merchants resident in some of the major Sumerian cities

7.14 An Indus valley seal

about this time or a little later (Parpola *et al.* 1977). Perhaps it is these colonies which commissioned cylinder seals like the examples recovered from Ur and from Tell Asmar which are decorated with typical Indus motifs. There is also an Agade seal which appears to show a Meluhhan interpreter translating for a party of foreigners to a local ruler (Lamberg-Karlovsky 1981).

Once again, the evidence for contacts with the north and east is far sketchier, but the legend of Sargon and the merchants of Purushkanda, a legend in which the merchants, inhabitants of a town in central Anatolia, appealed to Sargon for help, may represent a folk memory of actual events. Sargon claimed in his inscriptions to have reached the silver mountain, which could perhaps be identified with the silver-rich mountains of this region. Slightly later, Naram-Sin built his great storehouse and fortress at Brak on one of the important routes south of the Anatolian plateau, another indication of the importance of these northern areas as suppliers of vital raw materials. The virtual disappearance of true tin bronze in the later Agade period strongly suggests problems with the supplies of tin, probably imported from Afghanistan, and some of the Agade activity on the northern borders of their empire may be traced to a search for replacement sources. Recent survey work just north of the Cilician gates has identified a source of tin here, but it is not known whether it was being exploited in the late third millennium (Yener and Ozbal 1987).

After the fall of the Agade dynasty Gudea of Lagash continued the tradition of making royal statues from black diorite, suggesting continued contacts with Magan. The inscriptions of Ur-Nammu, first king of the succeeding Ur III dynasty, also stress the importance of links with Magan where the sites of Umm-an-Nar, Hili 8 and Maysar continued to flourish. It seems to have been a prosperous period for these sites, but it came abruptly to an end about 2000 BC when Umm-an-Nar was deserted, and there is a break in the occupation sequence at Hili 8 between levels II and III (Potts forthcoming). After this, contacts with Mesopotamia seem to focus on Bahrain, where a new city, City

II, was founded at about this time. The founding of this city is dated by the find of an Isin-Larsa tablet associated with the foundation levels of the city wall. A cylinder seal bearing the name of king Gungunum of Larsa and dated to 1925 was also found in City II. It is at about this time, or perhaps a little earlier, that the earliest of the great Barbar temples was founded on Bahrain, a temple which had certain generic similarities with Sumerian examples of the third millennium, being built on elaborately prepared foundations with an oval enclosure wall. These parallels should probably not be given too much weight and the internal arrangements of the building are very different from anything in Mesopotamia.

One explanation for this shift in the pattern of trade may be found in rivalry between the Gulf states for the carrying trade linking Sumer with the rich deposits of Omani copper, and for the role of middleman in the trade with Meluhha. The finds of Persian Gulf seals with Indus inscriptions on them in City II at Bahrain indicate that it had taken over again as the main entrepôt in this trade. Contact between Sumer and the Indus valley seems to become more spasmodic, probably due to the decline of the Harappan civilisation, but occasional finds of Harappan seals are made until Kassite times in the middle of the second millennium. It is also about 2000 BC that the first major settlement was founded on the island of Failaka at the northern end of the Gulf, probably by settlers from Bahrain. This new city shared the trade with Bahrain and seems to have had a substantial Mesopotamian element in its population, as much of the pottery found there is identical with that from the mainland of Mesopotamia.

The merchants who conducted this trade were men of substance, but once again, as with manufacturing industries, it is difficult to tell how much of the enterprise was state-controlled and how much private capital played a part. In the Ur III period, for which the records are fullest, it is clear that much of the trade was financed by the temples; earlier, in the ED period, the palace was a major partner, but by the Old Babylonian period private capital seems to have taken over. It is entirely possible that the obvious bias in our sources is at least partly responsible for distorting the picture, but at present the evidence shows a real switch from public to private finance. The dangers of the trade were considerable, the rewards great. Large profits were made and votive offerings of boats were deposited in the temple of Ningal at Ur to ensure future success. These third millennium seafarers were the predecessors of the famous Arab merchants of the Middle Ages who sailed as far as China in their search for luxuries, but for the Mesopotamian sailors the search was primarily for the raw materials without which Sumerian civilisation would have crumbled and the history of the ancient Near East would have been radically different.

Chapter 8

WRITING AND THE ARTS

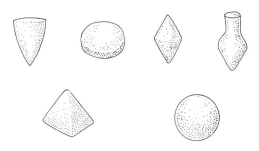

8.1 Tokens

The elaborate economic framework which we described in the last chapter was only possible because the Sumerians had developed what is probably the earliest writing system in the world. Even Egyptian hieroglyphics are thought to be slightly younger. The earliest attempts at keeping records seem to date back to the pre-pottery Neolithic period, when small clay tokens have been recovered in a limited number of shapes at several different sites from Çatal Hüyük in Anatolia to Jarmo in Iraqi Kurdistan. These tokens, it is thought, were used to represent various commodities. In time, certain tokens seem to have come to represent certain types of goods, sheep or cattle for example (Fig. 8.1). Different sizes and shapes also came to represent different quantities, so that it was possible to keep a simple record of transactions by this means. Schmandt-Besserat has elaborated this initial idea to suggest how a more sophisticated writing system may have developed from these simple beginnings (Schmandt-Besserat 1986). Her ideas are not universally accepted, but at the moment represent the most coherent attempt at explanation that we have.

The next stage in the process was for these tokens signifying the commodities involved in a single transaction to be placed together in a clay ball or *bulla*. For added efficiency the types of tokens enclosed in the ball were also impressed on the outside which could be stamped with a seal as well. It proved rather difficult to take good impressions of some of the tokens so attempts were made to incise their shapes onto the surface of the clay balls instead. This was perhaps the genesis of the idea of inscribing symbols onto clay. One serious problem with Schmandt-Besserat's idea is that X-rays are now showing us that the contents of these *bullae* do not always correspond with the marks on the outside (Lieberman 1980). The ball was not a particularly easy shape to

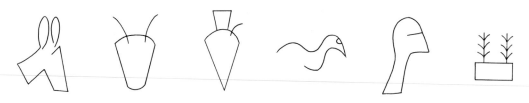

8.2 Pictograms

handle, so that when drawings of the tokens began to supersede the tokens themselves, a flattened tablet of clay began to be used instead. (Some of these early tablets are still impressed with the actual tokens rather than being incised, indicating the strength of the tradition.)

The earliest tablets we have come from level IV of the Eanna precinct at Uruk. Two tablets, which may even be earlier than this, were found at Tell Brak, but unfortunately they were not well stratified and so cannot be exactly dated (Finkel 1985). The vast majority of these early tablets still record single transactions with the commodity and the quantity incised or impressed on them. If left in the sun to dry, these tablets become hard enough to last for thousands of years. In later times especially important documents were baked to give them even greater strength. Eighty per cent of the documents from Uruk levels are economic, but other types of document were already being written, even at this early stage. There are lists of professions for example, and in order to record this sort of information important changes had to take place in the initial concept that each shape represented a particular object which it closely resembled (Fig. 8.2). These early signs are called pictograms and it is not possible to tell what language they were written in because a picture of a cow can be read as 'cow', as 'vache' or as 'bukra' depending on the language spoken by the reader. The next development was for the pictogram to take on not only the meaning of the object portrayed but also the sound value of that word, usually equivalent to a syllable. For instance the Sumerian word for head was 'sag' so that the picture of a head now had the sound value 'sag' as well. This enabled the scribes to begin to build up ways of writing complex words for which there was no pictogram available, thus greatly enlarging the amount of information they could store or transmit.

Once the idea of spelling out words syllabically was adopted it is possible to recognise the language in which the tablets are written and it is at this moment, at the end of Uruk IV, that we can say that the language of the tablets is certainly Sumerian. Other changes began to take place at the end of Uruk IV as a new type of stylus or writing instrument was introduced. The earliest styli, often made from a reed, had one pointed end used to incise lines and one circular one used to impress the clay. At the end of Uruk IV/III a new type of stylus is found with a triangular section instead of a circular one and this was used to impress wedge-shaped marks onto the tablet. The other end remained pointed but was used relatively little. The advent of the stylus with the triangular end affected the shape of the signs, which became more geometric and more abstract with the wedge becoming the basic building block of the different signs. It is also from these wedges, called *cuneus* in Latin, that the script got its name, cuneiform or wedge-shaped writing.

These changes in the script were accompanied by changes in the layout of the tablets. Instead of just containing one entry on each one, the tablets began to be divided up into boxes, each with its own entry, though the order of the signs was still rather haphazard. Gradually, the signs became more regimented and more and more information could be fitted on to tidily ruled out surfaces; the order was also standardised and tablets were read from left to right instead of from right to left. At about the same time, the last great change took place and the signs were swung through 90 degrees to lie on their backs. The reason for this is not entirely clear, but seems to relate to the way the tablet was held by the scribe to minimise the dangers of smudging the wet clay. This final development seems to have taken place about the middle of the third millennium (Fig. 8.3). An excellent account of these developments is to be found in a book by Christopher Walker called *Cuneiform* in the Reading the Past series (Walker 1987).

As the technical skills of the scribes increased, the amount of information they could transmit began to increase too. The majority of tablets probably continued to be economic in purpose but historical and literary compositions began to appear, together with letters and dedicatory inscriptions of all sorts. These dedications provide us with some of the earliest historical texts we have. They record the names and deeds of some of the early kings of the Early Dynastic period and provide a useful cross-reference for the so-called historical records which, in the case of the early King Lists for instance, seem to describe an ideal, rather than an actual, state of affairs. There are also dictionaries and scientific and mathematical treatises used by the scribes in their capacity as surveyors and astronomers.

Scribes were highly trained bureaucrats and specialists, who must have wielded a great deal of power as the majority of the population was illiterate, even at the highest level. State documents and private letters all begin with the phrase 'Say to X' or 'Say to my lord the king', indicating clearly that at least originally, when the formula first came into use, the recipients were unable to read for themselves. Descriptions of the training of scribes have survived and show that it was a long and thorough process. The profession often ran in families and, as one might expect, there are few records of female scribes, though Enheduanna, the daughter of Sargon of Agade, was a famous author of hymns and laments (Fig. 8.4).

Cuneiform was in use from the end of the fourth millennium BC till the first century AD. It was used for a range of languages besides Sumerian and the later Semitic dialects of Mesopotamia. It became the script in which international diplomacy was conducted

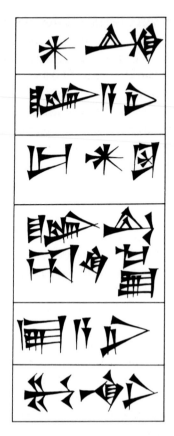

8.3 Developed cuneiform as it was written in the Ur III period

8.4 Enheduanna, daughter of Sargon of Agade

at the time of the famous Amarna archives. It showed itself to be amazingly versatile and amazingly tenacious, and yet in spite of this we still know very little about its origins. We have described one way in which it might have developed from the use of clay tokens and it has been suggested that this development probably took place on the Sumerian plain. There is another area which has a claim to be the home of cuneiform too and this is the area to the south-east of Sumer known as Elam. Tablets in the proto-Elamite language in a cuneiform script are found at Susa and over a wide area of modern Iran, at about the same time as the first tablets occur in south Mesopotamia. The exact relationship between these two very early forms of cuneiform remains to be worked out.

SEALS AND SEAL IMPRESSIONS

Another, much more limited form of recording information was in use long before the development of cuneiform and later was often used in conjunction with it. From the very early Neolithic, stones or pieces of clay decorated with simple patterns are found. Some are found pierced for suspension and seem to have been used as amulets, others may have been used to stamp patterns on cloth or other fabrics, but some may have been used as seals to make the owner's mark upon an object. The first stamps which we can confidently identify as seals come from sites in north Mesopotamia in Halaf and Ubaid levels. At Tepe Gawra three sealings were found in the Halaf sounding, one with a geometric design, the other two with representations of animals (Homes-Fredericq 1970). The backs of these sealings showed impressions of cloth, suggesting that they had been used to secure goods wrapped in sacking or perhaps jars whose necks were often covered with cloth which could be tied down with string. This in its turn could be secured with a wad of clay stamped with a seal. By the end of the Ubaid period stamp seals are found in some numbers in the north, but continue to be very rare in the south. They are now made of a wide variety of materials from clay to semi-precious stones, like carnelian, and are decorated with both geometric and naturalistic designs. The first representations of humans appear together with animals, snakes and plants. In the Uruk period the repertoire of designs expands again to include what appear to be ritual scenes (Fig. 8.5).

It is in the Uruk period, in the south of the country, that a new type of seal appears. This is the cylinder seal, shaped like a cylindrical bead, usually pierced lengthways and decorated with scenes which, when rolled on a piece of wet clay, produce a continuous frieze. The designs on the cylinder seals could be very much more varied and complex than those on the stamp seals, which gradually became less popular. The cylinder seals could also be made to cover a much larger surface area. This was important as one function of a cylinder seal was, as its name suggests, to seal items in transit from one place to another or to seal boxes or even rooms so that their contents

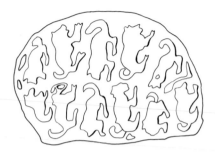

8.5 A stamp seal

could not be tampered with. Seals were also used as signatures in a society which, we have already seen, was largely illiterate. An extension of this function was to validate records of transactions and to record the agreement of the parties to a contract. Both the parties to an agreement, together with the witnesses, would roll their seals on the relevant tablet which recorded the terms of the deal and the whole transaction might be further strengthened by having the seal of the appropriate city or palace official affixed too. A seal impression also performed some of the functions of a modern credit card so, with all these varied legal and economic functions, it is easy to explain why the loss of a seal was treated as a most serious matter in the Ur III period and had to be publicly announced at various points in the city of its owner. Presumably if this was not done in due form, the unfortunate owner might find himself responsible for shady deals and bad debts accumulated by the thief (Steinkeller 1977).

Cylinder seals have been the object of special study by archaeologists, partly because they are intrinsically most attractive objects and partly because they can tell us a great deal about the periods in which they were made. Information can be gathered from the materials of which they are made. These can often give us some idea of the range of overseas contacts at the time, as seals are frequently made of stones like lapis, which can be traced to known sources. From the middle of the third millennium they are often inscribed, not only with the name of the owner, but sometimes with his office, 'Servant of the king X', for instance, which can supply useful historical data. The style in which they are decorated changes through time and it is now possible to identify the styles typical of any given period, so that seals provide an extremely useful auxiliary dating tool, though, being small and portable, it is easy for them to get displaced in the archaeological record. (For a recent comprehensive book on seals see Collon 1987.) Perhaps the potentially most interesting information can be gathered from the subject-matter of seals, which again changes considerably from period to period. It is possible to suggest that the subject-matter popular in any given period may reflect some of the preoccupations and interests of the people for whom the seals were made in the first place. It has also been suggested that the subject-matter may, in some cases, be linked to

8.6 An Uruk period seal with a pastoral scene

the profession of the owner. Apart from these two speculations, the pictures on the seals certainly supply us with information about the everyday life of the time which we cannot get from any other source.

Let us look first at the possibility that the subject-matter is related to the preoccupations of the period. The earliest seals we have from the Uruk period are large and fat with finely executed, well-thought-out designs. It is, incidentally, hard to see these as in any way experimental designs and this has led to the suggestion that earlier seals in perishable materials such as wood or ivory may have existed. The subject-matter of these seals falls into two major categories, which overlap. One group depicts agricultural scenes, such as feeding the flocks, while the second shows what seem to be ritual scenes. These often include a figure in a special skirt which looks as if it was made of net. This figure is sometimes also shown making offerings to the altars of the gods, while on seals from Susa he is shown in more warlike activities. He also wears a distinctive hat a little like a modern Pathan hat and it has been suggested that he is some sort of ruler. We have already noted in the chapter on burials that the Uruk period saw the emergence of élite ruling grups, so that this figure may have belonged to one such élite. If the institution of kingship was a new one, it is reasonable that it should form one of the two major themes on the seals, together with agriculture, which as we have said before, was the economic base of the country (Fig. 8.6).

It is more difficult to explain a third group of seals which overlap in time with the ones we have just described. This third group used to be thought to belong to the slightly later Jemdat Nasr period, but recently all three types have been found together at sites like Habuba Kabira on the Euphrates. Stylistically the third group is distinguished by the heavy use of the drill, which produces a rather crude pattern on a surface which is often taller and thinner than on the better quality seals. The designs are difficult to interpret, but many of them seem to depict everyday activities such as

8.7 An early ED combat scene

pottery-making and weaving. It has been suggested that these seals may have belonged to the temple workshops which produced these goods. If this is the case, they seem to fall into a slightly different category.

All three types die out in the Jemdat Nasr and ED I phases, to be replaced with elaborate running patterns in what is known as the Brocade style. This often incorporates figures of fish and animals shown in a very schematic way. By the end of ED I, however, the new themes which are to become typical of the later Early Dynastic period begin to appear. It was a time when inter-city rivalry appears to have been intense and we find the first archaeological evidence for armies and organised warfare, so it is not surprising that combat scenes become one of the most popular motifs. These combats are not the ordinary fights between opposing armies, but splendid mythological contests between heroes or between heroes and animals, suitable seals for soldiers perhaps (Fig. 8.7). The other popular theme which is found from ED II onwards is the banquet scene, in which elaborate feasts are shown with the participants drinking, while listening to music in many cases, attended by their retinues (see Fig. 6.6), another appropriate theme for an age when large and prosperous households were to be found in abundance and petty courts flourished in many of the major cities of the plain. Sometimes the seals are divided into two registers and both these popular themes could be combined on one seal.

In the succeeding Agade period the banquet scene goes out of favour though the combats continue to be a favourite motif, now portrayed with greater realism in more formalised style (Fig. 8.8). Once again the period was one when fighting remained a major preoccupation of the rulers, resulting in the creation of the first empire the Middle East had seen. It is also a period when there was a good deal of literary activity and we know of hymns and prayers, for example, written at this time. These literary achievements may perhaps be paralleled in the glyptic art by the many seals which show scenes from the lives of the gods. The sun god is frequently portrayed, as are many less easily identified figures who seem to include Ea the god of sweet water and Inanna/Ishtar the goddess of love and war. Inscriptions also become an ever more

8.8 An Agade combat scene

important part of the seal cutters' repertoire. They first appear in ED III and in the Agade period are often included as a design element. This would seem to suggest an increase in the number of officials who could read and some slight increase in general literacy, though for most people the picture remained the only way of identifying the seal and its owner.

In the Ur III period this trend continues and the designs become extremely stereotyped, showing named officials being presented to either their spiritual or temporal lords to be confirmed in their office. It was a period which seems to have seen an explosion of bureaucracy and a standardisation of many areas of life from the weights and measures to the official art, so once again the seals, not surprisingly, mirror the tastes and the ethos of the times.

The suggestion that the subject of a seal may in some way reflect the profession or status of its owner is not a new one, but recent work by Rathje on seals from the Royal Cemetery at Ur (Rathje 1977) suggests significant correlations between the richest graves and banquet scenes on the one hand, and contest scenes and graves containing tools, weapons and other functional objects on the other. This has led to the deduction that the graves containing banquet scenes may have belonged to senior court officials, while those containing contest scenes belonged to people of lower status with 'administrative duties in economic and military hierarchies'. Rathje also notes that in the Great Death Pit the seal found close to the body with the bull lyre shows just such a lyre being played. Further work in this direction should yield interesting results.

We have another source of evidence which tells us more about these officials and

V Female head from Uruk

others like them. The devout man or woman often commissioned a statue of themselves with hands clasped in prayer to stand perpetually before the altar of their patron god as a constant reminder to that god of their virtue and their requirements. Many of these statues have survived and form the bulk of our evidence for sculpture in the round from the third millennium. The first examples we have of sculpture in the round come from the Uruk period and do not fall into quite the same category. Like so much of the evidence from the Uruk period, they are of a remarkably high quality and it is difficult to understand how pieces like these could have been produced with no obvious antecedents. The majority of them come from the site of Uruk, so we should be cautious about regarding them as typical. They probably represent the very best that could be produced for one of the premier shrines in the land.

The most magnificent piece is the mask of a woman's head, about life size and modelled with a delicacy and realism which was not surpassed for thousands of years. It is suggested that it may have formed part of a divine statue, but its purpose is unknown. A number of male figures is also known, carved fully in the round, shown naked but for the type of hat worn by the king figure on the seals and a large spade beard. The hands are clasped in front of the chest in a gesture of prayer. Once again the figures are finely modelled, as are several animal figures from the same period. Some fine-relief carving is also known from Uruk, of which the finest piece must be the great Uruk vase, a vase about a metre high, of translucent alabaster on which is depicted a scene of harvest offerings being presented to the goddess Inanna. The offerings include all the produce of the fields and are presented by naked men to a female figure who may be the goddess herself or perhaps her earthly representative, the high priestess. Other fine stone vases are known from Uruk with animals in high relief guarding the spouts, but none are of the quality of the Uruk vase itself. (Excellent photographs of all the pieces discussed can be found in Strommenger 1964.)

As in other fields, the Jemdat Nasr and ED I phases seem to show a falling-off in quality and relatively few statues are known, although one small votive statue of a woman from Khafaje shows that the art of stone-working had not been abandoned entirely. ED II has provided more examples, but it must be admitted that they are crude in the extreme compared with the Uruk statues. A large cache of votive statues was found at Tell Asmar buried below the floor of the Square temple, apparently during extensive renovations. It seems that they were regarded as too sacred to be thrown away and so were deposited in sacred ground below the floor of the shrines. The style of the human figures is schematic: the torso is shown in almost geometric form, the faces with their stylised features are almost caricatures, with inlaid eyes and corrugated beards and hair. Two figures stand out from the group by reason of their size and their enormous eyes. It has been suggested that the male represents the god Abu, while the female, who may have originally had a child nestling into her skirts, is his consort. If this explanation is correct, then these are two of the very rare representations of gods known from ancient Mesopotamia. It has also been suggested that they actually represent the ruler and his wife and that they are dedicated to Abu (Winter 1984). There is little attempt at modelling in these figures; the heads are perched immediately on the shoulders, and the bodies are supported by legs which are often schematically indicated as part of a supporting column of stone. We should perhaps be cautious again about regarding these as typical examples of the statuary of the period as they do come from what seems to have been something of a provincial backwater. Finer pieces may well have existed in the major shrines.

There is one piece from the Square temple which supports this suggestion. It is made of translucent marble, rather than gypsum like the others, and portrays a naked, kneeling man wearing only a high hat and a curious belt, which seems to have some ritual significance as it occurs on other similar figures and on the seals. The quality of this piece is much higher and is reminiscent of Uruk work; it also resembles a small number of other pieces of similar material found on various sites. There is another

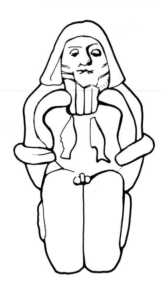

8.9 Kneeling figure from Telloh in naturalistic style

kneeling figure from Telloh (Fig. 8.9) and a fine standing figure of a man from Umma. Perhaps these pieces represent a particular workshop, or perhaps they are imports. They certainly stand out by virtue of both the workmanship and the material used. A statue of a woman from the Inanna temple at Nippur may also belong to this group. It is made of translucent green alabaster and the face is a gold mask. At the moment this piece is unique. We cannot even tell whether it represents a god or a worshipper.

ED III has produced a great many of these votive statues, in a rather more naturalistic style, although little attempt at portraiture can be detected. Perhaps this was not considered necessary as many of the statues now have their names and dedicatory inscriptions on the shoulder or back. The male figures are increasingly shown with bald heads instead of page-boy bobs, while the female figures wear more elaborate clothes, head-dresses and coiffures. Some of the finest statues come from the temples at Mari. Here, a number of the female figures are shown seated in chairs, wearing high *polos*-style hats and fleecy cloaks which envelop the head and body. One outstanding statue from Mari depicts the singer Ur-Nanshe sitting cross-legged in a pair of voluminous fleecy trousers, wearing a sort of pigtail down the back (Fig. 8.10). The expression of self-satisfaction is delightful, but the figure is something of a mystery as even the sex of the singer is unclear. The name is a masculine one, but the naked torso appears to show breasts. It has even been suggested that Ur-Nanshe may have been a Sumerian castrato!

The trend towards naturalism already noted in the seals at the end of the Early Dynastic period and into the Agade can be seen too in the statues. Relatively few have survived but French excavations at Susa recovered a number of Agade royal

8.10 The singer, Ur-Nanshe

monuments which had been carried off to Elam as booty. These are made of fine black diorite, the source of which is discussed in chapter 7, and return to the high standards of the Uruk sculptures. Most of the examples in the Louvre belong to statues of Manishtusu, the third king of the dynasty, and show him seated on an elaborately tasselled cushion or standing with clasped hands, wearing a long robe, a style of dress not seen before. The quality is high and it is frustrating that none of the heads of these statues have been recovered. Votive statues of ordinary people continue in the tradition laid down in the earlier period and fine heads have been found from sites as far apart as Assur and Adab. Naturally, not all the examples reach the same high standard, but the improvement in execution is obvious.

After the collapse of the Agade dynasty, the principality of Lagash seems to have escaped the ravages of the invaders and its governor, Gudea, continued to rule and to erect statues to himself and his immediate family which are very much in the same

8.11 Gudea of Lagash

tradition as the Agade ones. They are cut in black diorite and the heads are finely modelled, but their provincial origins are betrayed by the distortion of the bodies, usually squat and foreshortened, with the muscles heavily modelled (Fig. 8.11). It is a curious combination and leads one to wonder whether the heads were carved by a master craftsman and the bodies by his pupils. The establishment of the Ur III dynasty led to no major innovations in votive statuary; the quality continues to be high, the style naturalistic. Inlaid eyes seem to become less prevalent, perhaps as a result of the trend towards naturalism, and some changes in fashion can be traced in clothes and jewellery. All the statuary found so far comes from religious contexts and we have no evidence for its occurrence in private houses. So far as we can tell the Sumerians regarded statuary as a means to an end, the end being to obtain favours from the gods by reminding them constantly of the devotion and virtue of their servants on earth.

This same purpose seems to have been shared with some of the finest examples of stonework in relief which have come down to us. These are the royal commemorative stelae which were deposited in the temples to remind the god of the valour and success of his viceroy on earth. The earliest stelae have no inscriptions and so their purpose cannot be established with certainty. For example the Protoliterate Lion Hunt stele, roughly carved on a waterworn boulder, depicts a man with an elaborate bow, attended by a smaller man armed with a spear, killing lions. The larger man is wearing the same sort of Pathan hat seen on the king figures on the Uruk seals and this, together with the much later Assyrian traditions which link the king specifically with the lion hunt, suggests that this may be an early royal stelae.

Two more uninscribed stelae, of a slightly later date, are shaped like altars and show offerings being made by cloaked figures. They too are crudely executed, with the design covering the whole surface of the stone. On the first inscribed stele, the well-known Stele of the Vultures from late ED III, the design is divided into registers and the story is told in words as well as pictures. The stele commemorates the victory of Eannatum of Lagash over the neighbouring city of Umma and shows Eannatum leading his victorious army over the corpses of his enemies, while vultures pick at their severed heads. Many of the details of the soldiers' equipment can be matched by actual finds from the Royal Cemetery at Ur, including the splendid helmet worn by the king which matches exactly the one found in the tomb of Meskalamdug. On the reverse of the stele the god of battle, Ningirsu, is shown holding a net containing the enemies of Lagash.

The convention of dividing the surface of these stelae into registers continues into the Agade period, where the earliest example comes from the reign of Sargon and its many parallels with the Stele of the Vultures provide some of the many arguments for suggesting that there was a strong cultural continuity between ED IIIb and the Sargonic period. The Sargon stele, like the Vultures stele, shows the king leading his victorious army, but this time the king is bearded and bareheaded though his hair is done in the same style with a bun at the back. A more significant difference is that the net full of defeated soldiers is carried by the king himself not by a god. Sargon did not assume divine status like some of his successors, but here he seems to be carrying out a function formerly performed by a god. Two other fragmentary stelae are known from the first half of the Agade period. The first shows a file of finely carved prisoners (Fig. 8.12), obviously one register from a larger design, while the second, whose theme is similar, is now thought to record a land grant made by Rimush, the second king of the dynasty, after a military victory (Foster 1985).

The most striking artistic innovations seem to date to the later part of the period and the last of the Agade stelae, that recording the victory of Naram-Sin, is the outstanding piece. The sculptor returns to the earlier conventions and uses the whole surface of the stone to show the divine ruler striding up a great mountain, under the protection of his gods, to inflict a devastating blow on his enemies. Even the equipment and the clothes have changed, though that may be explained by the fact that this stele shows a lightly armed party of foot soldiers rather than the equivalent of the tank regiments shown on earlier stelae. As with the statuary in the round and the seals, the figures are skilfully

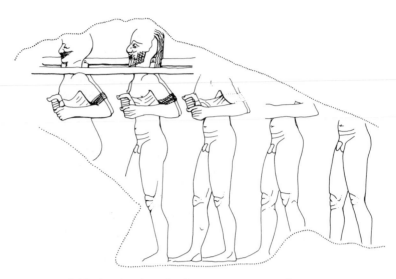

8.12 An Agade stele showing prisoners of war

portrayed in a naturalistic manner and the design is disposed to make the best use of the space available.

Unfortunately, this skill and liveliness does not seem to survive into the Ur III period. The great stele of Ur-Nammu, first ruler of the dynasty, which was found in the sacred enclosure at Ur, returns to the restrictions imposed by registers. The scene, however, is a peaceful one and shows Ur-Nammu before his god, apparently receiving instructions to build the great ziggurat at Ur itself. The stele is badly damaged and little can be said with certainty about the lower registers, which seem to show the actual building of the ziggurat and perhaps the celebrations which accompanied its completion. The figures are well executed and the space is well laid out, but the fire of the earlier stelae is missing. The tradition of royal stelae continues into the second millennium with one of the most famous examples of all, the stele of Hammurabi inscribed with his so-called Law Code, but the achievement of the Naram-Sin stele is not matched again.

Other, lesser examples of the stone carvers' skill are also known from the third millennium. A series of stone plaques has been found in Early Dynastic levels whose purpose is unclear and whose designs have more in common with the seal repertoire than with that of the monumental mason. These plaques are usually rectangular with a raised border, sometimes inlaid with shell, and a square hole in the centre. A number of uses has been suggested including door fasteners, wall decoration and commemoration. It is interesting that several texts mention the completion of transactions such as house purchases being marked by hammering a nail or peg into the wall (Hansen 1963). Several of these plaques are divided into registers like the stelae and some, such as those

8.13 Stone plaque showing a fisherman with his catch

of Ur-Nanshe of Lagash, record specific events such as the building of a temple. Others show banquet scenes, very similar to those on the seals, while contest scenes also occur, though the contestants are frequently human wrestlers rather than mythological creatures. Other scenes are found occasionally; one shows a naked figure pouring a libation before a seated goddess, while another shows a fisherman bringing in his catch (Fig. 8.13). On the whole the style is rather wooden, but some are of better quality and a few, which may date to the Agade period, use the whole surface of the plaque without registers. The earliest examples probably date to ED I and the latest to the Agade period, when they seem to go out of fashion.

Their subject-matter has also been compared to that of the shell plaques which are also found in ED contexts. These plaques too seem to have been used as wall decorations in some public buildings such as palace 'A' at Kish and the temple at al Ubaid (Fig. 8.14), while the most famous example, the so-called Ur standard, comes from one of the royal graves in the Ur cemetery. On one side it portrays a great victory

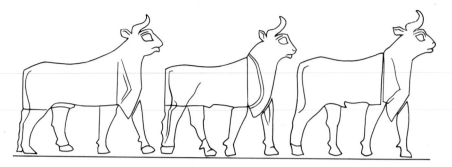

8.14 Shell inlays from the temple at al Ubaid

and on the other the feast which followed it. Fragments of other plaques from Mari also show warlike scenes, while another group of fragments shows priestesses going about their daily routine, which seems to have included weaving and perhaps midwifery. Shell inlay was also used to decorate boxes of wood, like the pieces found in the PCB building at Kish, and finds from the slightly later palace at Ebla in north Syria suggest inlay may also have been used to decorate stairs and furniture.

The art objects which have survived from the third millennium represent only a fraction of the pieces which must have existed. Whole categories of items have totally disappeared, including the embroideries and carpets which almost certainly existed. Yet even the fragmentary remains we have are enough to show us that objects of the highest quality, which have an immediate appeal across 5,000 years, were being produced in Mesopotamia from around 3000 BC. The majority of the pieces which survive come from the temples. Many of them were deposited by the kings and record their deeds, underlining once more the interdependence of what is loosely described as the palace and the temple.

𒀭 *Chapter 9* 𒀭

CONCLUSIONS:
THE DEVELOPMENT OF SUMERIAN SOCIETY

This book has described individually each of the 'building blocks' of what is rather loosely called Sumerian civilisation. The first two chapters looked at the basic parameters, the physical environment and the historical and chronological framework of the period. Then the way in which the inhabitants had used the environment was explored and the settlement patterns which characterised each phase of the 1,800 years covered by this study were summarised. An attempt to interpret what the observed changes in theses patterns may have meant in terms of political and historical developments followed. The internal characteristics of the more complex settlements, their layout and the major public buildings which dominated them, were then described and an attempt was made to relate these changes, too, to the wider issues of changes in the way of life and in political thought or ideology.

The life of private individuals was then explored, firstly by looking at housing in both rural and urban settings and then by looking at graves. Paradoxically, the grave goods tell us more about the living than their houses, for it was only in death that the accessories of everyday life escaped the endless recycling which was a crucial feature of the Sumerian economy. This recycling was the result of a chronic shortage of almost all raw materials on the plain. Although the graves help us to build up a picture of society in a material sense, they do not greatly help any attempt to understand the Sumerian view of the after-life and we are left with the puzzling contradiction between the evidence of the texts that life after death was a joyless affair, and the evidence of the royal graves at Ur which suggest that large numbers of attendants went willingly into the grave with their masters and mistresses.

The artefacts in the graves provide other types of information as well and give us insights into the overseas trading contacts of the society and into their sophisticated level of technological achievement. Without the grave goods we would be unaware of many of the skills of metal-workers in particular. It is suggested that the elaborate economic network they represent required the production of large quantities of manufactured goods and was a major factor in generating the need to make semi-permanent records of complex transactions. This seems to have stimulated the development of the system of cuneiform writing from the end of the Uruk period onwards. Cylinder and stamp seals acted as a secondary recording system of limited capacity, but one which was valuable in a largely illiterate society. The men who operated the bureaucracy which held the different sections of this stratified society together, and their masters, used the same recording system to perpetuate their virtues and their triumphs in an attempt to ensure their standing with the gods by inscribing them on various types of votive offerings. These often took the form of statues of themselves or of monumental stelae recording their deeds. These objects, where they survive, provide us with some of our earliest quasi-historical evidence and introduce us for almost the first time to individual people within society.

Each of these topics was looked at in isolation and we must now look at them all together to see whether any outstanding characteristics or regularities emerge which could be said to suggest a coherent pattern for the development of Sumerian society. Perhaps the most striking feature which emerges is that the Uruk period was of a different order from the periods which followed it. It was a period of crucial technological innovation over a vast range of fields. Arguably, it was the most innovative period in the history of Mesopotamia. It saw the introduction of writing, of the fast wheel, of extensive irrigation systems and of techniques of alloying and casting not previously found on the plain. Not all these skills were necessarily developed on the plain itself. Some may have been brought in by immigrants from the Iranian plateau, for instance, but they all appeared within the span of a few hundred years and transform life. No comparable innovations can be attributed to the succeeding Early Dynastic, Agade or Ur III periods; they seem to have built on the new techniques and refined them, but fundamentally the technological tool-kit remains unaltered. So too did the range of raw materials available to the craftsmen.

It was not only in the technological field that the Uruk period saw innovation. It also seems to have been the time when a formal system of government began to emerge. This system appears to have been based initially on the temple and was presumably vested in the priests as the earthly representatives of the god. It is the development of this formal system of government and its shift from one area to another in society which can be seen as the unifying thread which runs throughout the period. The evidence for the gradual emergence of a secular leader, possibly from temporary war-leaders, has been given in an earlier chapter. Such a man may have been appointed by the temple, or by the community as a whole. He may have been the head of an important family group. The first evidence for the emergence of a second focus of power comes in the art of the late Uruk period with portrayal of the figure in a net skirt and a Pathan-style hat who may represent such a war leader. He is shown performing various tasks including shooting prisoners (on a seal from Susa) and making offerings. By the time of the first archives in ED IIIa, it seems fairly clear that the secular ruler was still closely linked to the temple and had many religious duties in addition to his military and administrative responsibilities. The relative power of what can loosely be called church and state seems to have been in balance.

By the end of the ED period the balance of power seems to have been shifting in favour of the palace. The end of the period saw the first successful attempt at uniting the whole of the Sumerian plain under one king and the first short-lived attempt to expand the hegemony outside Sumer. The power of the king can be seen even more clearly in the Agade period when Sargon not only extended his area of military operations from the Upper to the Lower sea, but is also known to have appointed his daughter as high priestess of the moon god at Ur. This is usually quoted as an example of his eagerness to mollify the traditionalists in Sumerian society. Seen from a more political viewpoint, it should perhaps be interpreted as the palace extending its influence into the realm of the temple. Was Enheduanna being used to make a dynastic marriage with the priests of Ur in the same way that other royal children were married off to princes on the fringes of Mesopotamia? It has recently been suggested that the custom of appointing the king's daughter as high priestess was established in ED III and this might perhaps mark the beginning of the palace's bid for complete control (Winter 1987). This bid was certainly successful under Naram-Sin of Agade, Sargon's grandson, who, as we have already seen, was the first king to assume divine status. By so doing he was uniting in his own person all the powers of church and state. The king became not only a god, but head of the administration, head of the army, lord chief justice and high priest. His position must have seemed unassailable.

His successors certainly seemed to like the device and in his own dynasty and in the next one, with the exception of Ur-Nammu, the first ruler of the Ur III dynasty, they all followed in his footsteps. In the Ur III period vassal states such as Eshnunna on the Diyala were expected to worship at the shrine dedicated to the divine king of Ur and the political independence of Eshnunna at the end of the dynasty is marked by the secularisation of the shrine to the erstwhile divine overlord with a pottery kiln being built into the niche where the royal statue had stood.

It is not possible to tell what effect these political changes had on ordinary people, but the trend towards a more stratified society seems to have continued. In each town there was an increasing number of professional people with a tendency towards more and more job specialisation. Scribes, priests, diviners, merchants and all sorts of skilled craftsmen are recorded from the end of the Ur III period. This seems to reflect increasing technological specialisation and the developing of an ever more complex administration to support the divine king. It also provides evidence for the presence of an influential middle class, which was to become even more important in the succeeding Old Babylonian period. Society also seems to have become more cosmopolitan, with merchants travelling regularly to the north as well as to Dilmun in the south. There may even have been colonies of foreign merchants from as far away as India resident in certain cities (Parpola *et al.* 1977).

This gradual change in the balance of political power brought important changes in other areas too. Originally, all land was seen as belonging to the god of the city, or in concrete terms to his representative the temple. By ED III there is evidence for private landholdings of some significance, and the palace was also a major landowner. This gave the king control of a large proportion of the state's major resource, agriculture, so that the temple no longer had what seems to have been a monopoly of the means of production. The ruler's control of large areas of land also allowed him to accumulate personal wealth and to consolidate his own political position by making grants of land to the followers on whose support he could rely. These grants also had the effect of increasing the amount of land and wealth in private hands and led to the establishment of a third economic force in the land, though one which was not to become of enormous importance until after the fall of Ur III. The control of land gave individuals, too, access to a potential agricultural surplus, which could be used for the amassing of private fortunes, sometimes through extremely profitable trading ventures. Certainly by the end of the third millennium private merchants were heavily involved in long-distance trade, which seems previously to have been the prerogative of the major state institutions.

The emergence of the power of the ruler to balance that of the temple can be traced in the architecture as well. The earliest monumental architecture which we described was concentrated in the sacred enclosures like the Eanna precinct at Uruk, which contained temples and large non-temple buildings which seem likely to have had administrative functions. By ED II however, we see the first multi-purpose buidings which have no physical relationship to the temples and which seem to have housed a secular administration. By ED III we have buildings like the 'A' palace at Kish which have monumental doorways to match those of the temples and elaborate public rooms. It seems probable that these buildings housed the secular ruler and his administration. From the texts we know that both the ruler and his wife had this sort of household. The ultimate architectural expression of the domination of the king is the building of temples for the worship of the divine ruler. The increase in private wealth and the emergence of a fully stratified society, which are closely linked to the rise of the secular authority, can also be seen reflected in the house plans recovered from the late third millennium city of Ur. Here the houses range from spacious, well-laid out mansions with private chapels which are perhaps another manifestation of the decline in the power of the temple, to small hovels poked into any gap in the existing buildings.

Perhaps the graves illustrate the range of wealth even more vividly, especially at the Royal Cemetery of Ur. It seems that in Sumer, as in any other expanding economy, the increase in private wealth led to growth in demand for luxury goods of all sorts and so stimulated both trade and the manufacturing industries. By the middle of the third millennium ordinary professional people, minor officials for instance, seem to have possessed jewellery and cylinder seals which they took with them to the grave. They patronised the arts too and commissioned statues of themselves to stand in the temples praying for the welfare of the donor. They also made gifts to the gods which were meticulously recorded by the temple scribes. The votive offerings themselves reflect the changing pattern of government. The earliest *objets d'art* come almost without exception from the temple precincts, but from the mid-third millennium there is a change and although the objects continue to be found in the temples they, in practice, glorify the ruler. The Stele of the Vultures, for example, may be couched in terms of an offering to Ningursu but it is also a celebration of the military might of Eannatum of Lagash. Offerings also begin to be made 'For the life of the king' by his loyal servants. Finally, offerings are made to the divine king himself both during his life and after it.

The fall of the city of Ur about the year 2000 BC to the Gutian hordes was seen in contemporary thought as the end of civilisation itself. The defeat of Ibbi-Sin, last king of the Ur III dynasty, was the defeat of one of the gods; his dynasty had been in supreme control of the Sumerian plain for more than a century and had presided over what was in many ways the peak of Sumerian achievement. In fields like architecture and engineering, as well as in literature and the arts, new levels of technical excellence had been reached. The collapse of one of the oldest and most sophisticated kingdoms the ancient world had seen must have seemed like an unimaginable disaster which may well have had reverberations around the Near East, as well as in Mesopotamia itself. Its impact was perhaps made all the greater by the fact that it happened at a time of increasing political unease across the region. To the west new poeples like the Hurrians were moving into north Syria and then pushing south and east. The familiar pattern of small city-states was disintegrating, new languages, new fashions and even new animals like the horse were appearing, bringing with them new military techniques and a new threat. And yet, in spite of this, Sumerian culture continued to survive, and newcomers like the Amorite dynasty of Babylon adopted many of the customs and skills of its predecessors. The influence of the Sumerians and the civilisation they were instrumental in developing continued to be felt down the next two millennia. The last cuneiform documents, for instance, were found as late as the second century AD and Herodotus describes the great ziggurat of Babylon as it existed in his time. The ideas the Sumerians introduced were even more potent and traces of them can still be found in our world today. Some examples have already been given from both literature and mathematics. Many practical skills, such as the use of the wheel for both transport and pottery production, also seem to have originated with these extremely inventive and original people.

The emphasis in this book has been on description rather than explanation. The evidence is not yet available to allow anything but the most speculative explanations to be made, though it is perhaps possible to make certain tentative steps in that direction. There are few scholars today who would see these events as the result of an inevitable evolutionary progression, the outcome of some form of natural selection. There are probably very few scholars who would postulate any single causal factor. The advent of computers has had a much more profound influence on archaeology than just the ability to process huge bodies of information with relative ease; it has introduced some of the ideas of systems theory and enabled archaeologists to build complex multicausal models which seem to approximate much more closely to historical reality than the old monocausal ones. The factors which brought about the changes described in this book seem to have included minor climatic changes, resulting economic pressures exacerbated by the lack of raw materials on the Sumerian plain, the complex *Realpolitik* of the third millennium, of which we can only get glimpses, and even, perhaps, the presence of outstanding individuals of whom Sargon of Agade is the most obvious example. The possibility of external influences, of the diffusion of ideas from other civilisations, cannot be ruled out. It is possible that the idea of divine kingship may have originated in Egypt, where it appears to have been long established. It seems probable that most, or all, of these factors had some role in bringing about the development of the absolute monarchy which marked the end of the third millennium, but if we are to progress beyond such generalities it is of paramount importance that the archaeologists work closely not only with the scientists whose collaboration is already an integral part of work in the ancient Near East, but also with the linguists and the historians. It is only through their skills that we gain direct access to the people who brought about these momentous changes.

A study of Sumerian life might be thought to be a rather obscure and esoteric interest, a self-indulgence even, in a climate when practical applications are expected to be derived from every sector of the academic world; but such a study, as well as providing a training-ground for developing critical and communications skills with much wider potential uses, can provide us with insights into a number of problems which continue to plague the region today. It can give a valuable perspective on political problems, which are by no means unique to the modern world, and in the practical field it gives us case studies on problems like salinisation of the soil and desertification, which are of vital importance today. The search for an appropriate technology in this part of the world is also helped by a study of the methods employed by others who have successfully mastered the same environment in the past without the benefits of modern high technology. Even in a world where practical returns are required from scholars as well as industrialists, the archaeology of the Sumerians has much to offer. It also provides a field where much remains to be done and which will continue to stimulate and puzzle its devotees for many years to come.

REFERENCES

Adams, R.McC. 1965. *The land behind Baghdad*. Chicago.

　1972. Settlement and early irrigation patterns in ancient Akkad. In *City and area of Kish*, ed. McG. Gibson, pp. 182–208. Miami.

　1981. *Heartland of cities*. Chicago.

Adams, R.McC. and H.J. Nissen 1972. *The Uruk countryside*. Chicago.

al Gailani, Lamia 1965. Tell eth-Dhiba'i. *Sumer* 21: 33–40.

al Gailani-Werr, Lamia 1982. Catalogue of cylinder seals from Tell Suleimah, Himrin. *Sumer* 38: 68–88.

Algaze, Guillermo 1986. Habuba on the Tigris: archaic Nineveh reconsidered. *Journal of Near Eastern Studies* 45: 125–35.

Amiet, Pierre 1976. *L'Art d'Agadé au musée du Louvre*. Paris.

　1980. *La Glyptique Mesopotamienne archaique*. 2nd edn. Paris.

Andrae, Walter 1938. *Das wiedererstandene Assur*. Leipzig.

Banks, E.J. 1912. *Bismaya, or the lost city of Adab*. New York.

Beale, T.W. and S.M. Carter 1983. On the track of the Yahya large Kush. *Paléorient* 9: 81–8.

Biggs, R.D. 1974. *Inscriptions from Tell Abu Salabikh*. Oriental Institute of Chicago, vol. 99. Chicago.

Breniquet, Catherine 1984. Le cimetière 'A' de Kish. Essai d'interpretation. *Iraq* 46: 19–28.

Buckingham, J.S. 1827. *Travels in Mesopotamia*. 2 vols. London.

Bulgarelli, Grazia M. 1974. Tepe Hissar: preliminary report on a surface survey. *East and West* 24: 15–28.

Busink, Th.A. 1970. L'origine et l'évolution de la ziggurat Babylonienne. *Jaarbericht Ex Oriente Lux* 21: 91–142.

Cambridge Ancient History vol. I, part 2, 1971. 3rd edn, ed. I.E.S. Edwards, C.J. Gadd and N.G.L. Hammond. Cambridge.

Chakrabati, Dilip K. 1984. Long barrel-cylinder beads. In *Harappan civilization*, ed. G. Possehl, pp. 265–70. Warminster.

Chapman, Robert, Ian Kinnes and Klavs Randsborg (eds.) 1981. *The archaeology of death*. Cambridge.

Chicago Assyrian Dictionary, ongoing.

Collon, Dominique 1987. *First impressions*. London.

Cooper, Jerrold 1973. Sumerian and Akkadian in Sumer and Akkad. *Orientalia* NS 42: 239–46.

　1983. *Reconstructing history from ancient inscriptions: the Umma/Lagash war*. Malibu.

Crawford, H.E.W. 1973. Mesopotamia's invisible exports. *World Archaeology* 5: 231–41.

　1983. More fire installations from Abu Salabikh. *Iraq* 45: 32–4.

Dales, G. 1968. Of dice and men. *Journal of the American Oriental Society* 88: 14–23.

Davidson, T.E. and Hugh McKerrell (1980). Neutron activation analysis of Halaf and Ubaid pottery. *Iraq* 42: 155–67.

Delougaz, P. 1933. *Plano-convex bricks*. Studies in Ancient Oriental Civilization 7. Chicago.

　1940. *The Temple Oval at Khafaje*. Oriental Institute of Chicago, vol. 53. Chicago.

Delougaz, P. and S. Lloyd 1942. *Presargonic temples in the Diyala region*. Oriental Institute of Chicago, vol. 58. Chicago.

Delougaz, P. *et al*. 1967. *Private houses and graves in the Diyala region*. Oriental Institute of Chicago, vol. 88. Chicago.

Diakonoff, I.M. 1982. The structure of Near Eastern society. *Oikumene* 3: 7–100.

Edwards, I.E.S., C.J. Gadd and N.G.L. Hammond (eds.) 1971. *Cambridge Ancient History* vol. 1, part 2. 3rd edn. Cambridge.

El-Wailly, F. and B. es-Soof 1965. Excavations at Tell es-Sawwan. *Sumer* 21: 17–32.

Eliot, Henry W. 1950. *Graphic analysis*. Cambridge, Mass.

Ellison, Rosemary, J. Renfrew, D. Brothwell and N. Seeley 1978. Some food offerings from Ur. *Journal of Archaeological Science* 5: 167–77.

es-Soof, Behnam 1969. Excavations at Tell Qualinj Agha (Erbil). *Sumer* 25: 3–42.

Fathy, Hassan 1973. *Architecture for the poor*. Chicago.

Finkbeiner, Uwe (ed.) 1986. *Gamdat Nasr: period or regional style?* Wiesbaden.

Finkel, Irving 1985. Inscriptions from Tell Brak 1983/84. *Iraq* 47: 187–202.

Forest, C. 1982. Un bâtiment du Vème millenaire. *Archeologia* 162: 59–62.

Forest, J.-D. 1983. *Les Pratiques funéraires en Mésopotamie du Vème millenaire au début du IIIème*. Paris.

Foster, B.R. 1981. A new look at the Sumerian Temple state. *Journal of Economic and Social History of the Orient* 24: 225–34.
   1982. *Administration and use of institutional land in Sargonic Sumer*. Copenhagen.
   1985. The Sargonic victory stele from Telloh. *Iraq* 47: 15–30.

Frankfort, H. 1934. *Iraq excavations of the Oriental Institute 1932/3. 3rd preliminary report*. Oriental Institute of Chicago, vol. 17. Chicago.
   1939. *Cylinder seals*. London.

Frankfort, H., S. Lloyd and T. Jacobsen 1940. *The Gimil-sin temple and the palace of the rulers*. Oriental Institute of Chicago, vol. 43. Chicago.

Fujii, Hideo 1981. Preliminary report of excavations at Tell Gubba. *Al Rafidain* 2: 3–130.

Gibson, McG. 1972a. Umm-el-Jir, a town in Akkad. *Journal of Near Eastern Studies* 31: 237–94.
   1972b. *City and area of Kish*. Miami.
   1981. *Uch Tepe*. Chicago.

Gibson, McG. and R.D. Biggs 1977. *Seals and sealings in the ancient Near East*. California.
   1987. *The organisation of power. Aspects of bureaucracy in the Ancient Near East*. Studies in Ancient Oriental Civilization 46. Chicago.

Glassner, J.-J. 1987. *La Chute d'Akkade*. Berlin.

Haas, Jonathan 1982. *The evolution of the prehistoric state*. New York.

Hall, Edward T. 1969. *The hidden dimension*. New York.

Hall, H.R. and C.L. Woolley 1927. *Al Ubaid. Ur excavations*, vol. 1. Oxford.

Hallo, W.W. 1957. *Early Mesopotamian royal titles*. New Haven.
   1971. Gutium. *Reallexikon der Assyriologie* 3: 708–14.
   1973. The date of the Fara period. *Orientalia* 42: 228–38.

Hallo, W.W. and W.K. Simpson 1971. *The ancient Near East: a history*. New York.

Hansen, D.P. 1963. New votive plaques from Nippur. *Journal of Near Eastern Studies*. 22: 145–66.
   1978. Al Hiba 1968/76. *Sumer* 34: 72–85.

Hawkins, David 1979. The origin and dissemination of writing in western Asia. In *Origins of civilization*, ed. P.R.S. Moorey, pp. 128–66. Oxford.

Heinrich, E. 1982. *Tempel in Heiligtümer im alten Mesopotamien*. Berlin.

Heinrich, E. and A. Falkenstein 1938. Forschungen in der Umgebung von Warka. Vorläufige Berichte über die Ausgrabungen in Uruk-Warka 9. Berlin.

Herrmann, G. 1983. Lapislazuli. B: Archäologie. *Reallexikon der Assyriologie* 3: 489–92.

Heuzey, Leon 1900. *Une ville chaldéenne*. Paris.

Homes-Fredericq, D. 1970. *Les Cachets mésopotamiens protohistoriques*. Leiden.

Huber, P.J. 1982. *Astronomical dating of Babylon I and Ur III*. Occasional papers on the Near East no. 1, part 4. Malibu.

Jacobsen, Thorkild 1939. *The Sumerian King List*. Chicago.

    1969. A survey of the Girsu (Telloh) region. *Sumer* 25: 103–10.

    1982. *Salinity and irrigation agriculture in antiquity*. Malibu.

Jasim, Sabah Aboud 1985. *The Ubaid period in Iraq: recent excavations in the Hamrin region*. BAR International Series 267. Oxford.

Katz, Dina 1987. Gilgamesh and Akka. Was Uruk ruled by two assemblies? *Revue d'Assyriologie* 81: 105–14.

Keith, Sir Arthur 1934. Report on the human remains from Ur. In *The Royal Cemetery* by C.L. Woolley. *Ur excavations*, vol. 2. Oxford.

Killick, R.G. (ed.) 1989. *Tell Rubeidheh: an Uruk village in the J. Hamrin*. Iraq Archaeological Reports 2. Warminster.

Kohl, Philip 1974. Seeds of upheaval: production of chlorite at Tepe Yahya. Ph.D thesis, Harvard University.

Kolbus, Suzanne 1983. Zur Chronologie des sog. Gamdat-Nasr Friedhofs in Ur. *Iraq* 45: 7–17.

Kramer, Carol 1979. *Ethnoarchaeology*. New York.

Kramer, S.N. 1944. The death of Gilgamesh. *Bulletin of the American School of Oriental Research*. 94: 2–12.

    1952. *Enmerkar and the lord of Aratta*. Philadelphia.

    1963. *The Sumerians*. Chicago.

    1967. The death of Gilgamesh. *Journal of Cuneiform Studies* 21: 104–22.

Kupper, J.-C. 1957. *Les Nomades en Mésopotamie*. Paris.

Lamberg-Karlovsky, C.C. 1973. Urban interaction on the Iranian plateau. *Proceedings of the British Academy* 59: 1–43.

    1981. Afterword. In *Bronze Age civilization of Central Asia*, ed. Philip Kohl, pp. 386–97. New York.

Le Brun, Alain 1980. Les 'écuelles grossières' état de la question. In *L'Archéologie de l'Iraq*, ed. M. Barrelet, pp. 59–70. Paris.

Lees, G.M. and N.L. Falcon 1952. The geographical history of the Mesopotamian plain. *Geographical Journal* 118: 24–39.

Lenzen, H.J. 1941. *Die Entwicklung der Zikurrat*. Leipzig.

    1964. New discoveries in Warka S. Iraq. *Archaeology* 17: 122–31.

    1974. Die Architektur in Inanna in der Uruk IV Periode. *Iraq* 36: 111–28.

Lieberman, S.J. 1980. Of clay pebbles, hollow clay balls and writing: a Sumerian view. *American Journal of Archaeology* 84: 339–58.

Limet, H. 1960. *Le Travail du métal au pays de Sumer*. Paris.

    1972. Les méteaux à l'époque d'Agade. *Journal of Economic and Social History of the Orient* 15: 3–34.

Lloyd, Seton 1940. Iraqi government soundings at Sinjar. *Iraq* 7: 13–21.

    1947. *Foundations in the dust*. London.

Lloyd, Seton and Fuad Safar 1943. Tell Uqair. *Journal of Near Eastern Studies* 2: 131–58.

Ludwig, W. 1977. Mass, Sitte u. Technik des Bauens in Habuba Kabira-Süd. In *Le moyen Euphrate*, ed. J. Margueron, pp. 63–74. Strasbourg.

Mackay, E. 1929. *A Sumerian palace and the 'A' cemetery at Kish*. Chicago.

Maisels, Charles K. 1987. Models of social evolution: trajectories from the Neolithic to the State. *Man* NS 22: 331–59.

    1990. *The emergence of civilization*. London.

Mallowan, M.E.L. 1947. Excavations at Brak and Chagar Bazar. *Iraq* 9: 1–258.

1966. Tell Chuera in Nordost Syrien. *Iraq* 28: 89–95.

Mallowan, M.E.L. and J.C. Rose 1935. Excavation of Arpachiyah. *Iraq* 2: 1–178.

Margueron, J. 1982. *Recherches sur les palais mésopotamiens de l'âge de bronze*. Paris.

Martin, Harriet 1982. The Ubaid cemetery at Al Ubaid: a re-evaluation. *Iraq* 44: 145–86.

1983. Settlement patterns at Shurrapak. *Iraq* 45: 24–31.

Martin, H., J.N. Postgate and J. Moon 1985. Graves 1–99. *Abu Salabikh excavations* vol. 2. London.

Matthiae, Paolo 1980. *Ebla, an empire rediscovered*. London.

McAdam, Ellen 1981. Town planning and domestic architecture in ancient Mesopotamia. Unpublished D.Phil. thesis. Oxford University.

McCown, Donald H. and R.C. Haines 1967. *Nippur I. Temple of Enlil, scribal quarter and soundings*. Oriental Institute of Chicago, vol. 78. Chicago.

Mellaart, James 1979. Egyptian and Near Eastern chronology: a dilemma? *Antiquity* 53: 6–18.

Mellink, M.J. 1983. Archaeology in Asia Minor. *American Journal of Archaeology* 87: 427–42.

Merpert, N.Y. and R.M. Munchaev 1971. Yarim Tepe: 3rd preliminary report. *Sumer* 27: 23–32.

Michalowski, P. 1977. The death of Shulgi. *Orientalia* NS 46: 220–35.

1983. History as charter. *Journal of the American Oriental Society* 103: 237–48.

Millard, Alan 1988. The Bevelled-rim bowls: their purpose and significance. *Iraq* 50: 49–58.

Moorey, P.R.S. 1976. The late prehistoric administrative building at Jemdat Nasr. *Iraq* 38: 95–106.

1977. What do we know about the people buried in the Royal Cemetery? *Expedition* 20: 24–40.

1978. *Kish excavations 1923–33*. Oxford.

1984. Where did they bury the kings of the IIIrd Dynasty of Ur? *Iraq* 46: 1–18.

1985. *Materials and manufacture*. BAR International Series 237. Oxford.

1987. On tracking cultural transfers in prehistory. In *Centre and periphery*, ed. M. Rowlands *et al.*, pp. 36–46. Cambridge.

Mosely, C.W.R.D. (ed.) 1983. *The travels of Sir John Mandeville*. London.

Muhly, J.D. 1973. Copper and tin. *Transactions of the Connecticut Academy* 43: 155–535.

1983. Kupfer. B: Archäologische. *Reallexikon der Assyriologie* 6: 348–64.

Mynors, H.S. 1987. Mesopotamian ceramics of the third millennium BC with analysis of pottery from Abu Salabikh, Kish and Ur. Ph.D dissertation, University of Southampton.

Nissen, H.J. 1986. The archaic texts from Uruk. *World Archaeology* 17: 317–34.

1987. The chronology of the Proto- and Early Historic periods in Mesopotamia. In *Chronologies du Proche Orient*, ed. O. Aurenche *et al.*, pp. 607–14. BAR International Series 379 (ii). Oxford.

1988. *The early history of the ancient Near East*. San Francisco.

Oates, David 1982. Tell Rimah. In *Fifty years of Mesopotamian discovery*, ed. J. Curtis, pp. 62–71. London.

Oates, D. and J. Oates 1976. Early irrigation agriculture in Mesopotamia. In *Problems in economic and social archaeology*, ed. G. de G. Sieveking *et al.*, pp. 109–36. London.

Oppenheim, A. Leo 1954. Sea-faring merchants of Ur. *Journal of the American Oriental Society* 74: 6–17.

Parpola, S., A. Parpola and R.H. Brunswig Jr 1977. The Meluhhan village. *Journal of Economic and Social History of the Orient* 20: 129–65.

Parrot, André 1936. Les fouilles de Mari, deuxième campagne. *Syria* 17: 1–31.

Pollock, Susan 1985. Chronology of the Royal Cemetery at Ur. *Iraq* 47: 129–58.

Porada, Edith 1984. Pottery in scenes of the Agade period? In *Pots and potters*, ed. P.M. Rice, pp. 21–6. California.

Postgate, J.N. 1977. *The first empires*. London.

1979. Historical geography of the Hamrin basin. *Sumer* 35: 594–7.

1983. The West mound surface clearance. *Abu Salabikh excavations* vol. 1. London.

1984. Excavations at Abu Salabikh. *Iraq* 46: 95–114.

(ed.) 1985. *Bulletin of Sumerian Agriculture*.

1986. The transition from Uruk to ED: continuities and discontinuities. In *Gamdat Nasr: period or regional style?* ed. U. Finkbeiner, pp. 90–106. Wiesbaden.

Postgate, J.N. and J.A. Moon 1982. Excavations at Abu Salabikh 1981. *Iraq* 44: 103–36.

Postgate, J.N. and P.J. Watson 1979. Excavations in Iraq 1977/8. *Iraq* 41: 141–81.

Potts, D. (forthcoming) The chronology of the archaeological assemblages from the Arabian Gulf. In *Chronologies in Old World archaeology*, ed. E. Porada. 3rd edn. Chicago.

Potts, T.F. 1989. Stone vessels of the late third millennium B.C. from South Mesopotamia: their origins and mechanisms of exchange. *Iraq* 51: 123–64.

Powell, Marvin 1985. Salt, seed and yields in Sumerian agriculture. *Zeitschrift für Assyriologie* 75: 7–38.

Pritchard, J.B. 1955. *Ancient Near Eastern texts*. Princeton.

1969. *The Ancient Near East: supplementary texts and pictures*. Princeton.

1975. *The Ancient Near East vol. 2*. Princeton.

Rashid, Anwar 1963. Tell el Wilayah. *Sumer* 19: 82–106.

Rathje, William L. 1977. New tricks for old seals. In *Seals and sealings*, ed. McG.Gibson and R.D. Biggs, pp. 25–32. Malibu.

Ratnagar, Shereen 1981. *Encounters*. Oxford.

Reade, J.E. 1971. Tell Taya (1968/9); a summary report. *Iraq* 33: 87–100.

1973. Tell Taya (1972/3); a summary report. *Iraq* 35: 155–88.

1979. *Early etched beads and the Indus/Mesopotamia trade*. British Museum Occasional Papers 2. London.

1982. Tell Taya. In *Fifty years of Mesopotamian discovery*, ed. J. Curtis, pp. 72–8. London.

Redman, C.L. 1978. *Rise of civilization*. San Francisco.

Redman, C.L. and P.J. Watson 1970. Systematic intensive surface collection. *American Antiquity* 35: 279–91.

Rice, Michael 1985. *Search for the Paradise land*. London.

Roaf, M.R. 1982. Weights on the Dilmun standard. *Iraq* 44: 137–42.

1984. Ubaid houses and temples. *Sumer* 43: 80–90.

Roaf, M.R. and J.N. Postgate 1981. Excavations in Iraq 1979/80. *Iraq* 43: 167–98.

Safar, Fuad *et al.* 1981. *Eridu*. Baghdad.

Sanders, N.K. 1960. *The epic of Gilgamesh*. London.

Schmandt-Besserat, D. 1977. An archaic recording system and the origin of writing. *Syro-Mesopotamian Studies* 1: 1–32.

1986. An ancient token system: the precursor to numerals and writing. *Archaeology* 39: 32–9.

Schneider, A. 1920. *Die Sumerische Tempelstadt*. Eisen.

Sjöberg, A. 1976. The Babylonian E-dubba. In *Sumerological studies in honour of T. Jacobsen*. Chicago Assyriological Studies 20.

Sollberger, E. and J.-R. Kupper 1971. *Les Inscriptions royales sumériennes et akkadiennes*. Paris.

Speiser, E.A. 1935. *Excavations at Tepe Gawra: I*. Philadelphia.

Spycket, A. 1981. *La Statuaire du Proche Orient ancien*. Leiden.

Starr, R.F.S. 1939. *Nuzi*. 2 vols. Cambridge, Mass.

Steinkeller, P. 1977. Seal practice in the Ur III period. In *Seals and sealings*, ed. McG. Gibson and R.D. Biggs, pp. 41–54. Malibu.

Strommenger, Eva 1964. *The art of Mesopotamia*. London.

1980. *Habuba Kabira: eine Stadt vor 5000 Jahren*. Mainz.

Stronach, David 1961. Excavations at Ras al Amiya. *Iraq* 23: 95–137.

Surenhagen, D. 1978. *Keramik Produktion in Habuba Kabira-Süd*. Berlin.

Thesiger, Wilfred 1964. *The Marsh Arabs*. London.

Thompson, R.C. and M.E.L. Mallowan 1933. The British Museum excavations at Nineveh 1931/2. *Annals of Archaeology and Anthropology, Liverpool* 22: 71–186.

Thureau-Dangin, F. 1905. *Les Inscriptions de Sumer et Akkad*. Paris.

Tobler, A.J. 1950. *Tepe Gawra II*. Philadelphia.

Tosi, M. 1984. Early maritime cultures of the Arabian Gulf and the Indian Ocean. In *Bahrain through the ages*, ed. Shaikha Haya al Khalifa and Michael Rice, pp. 94–107. London.

Tunça, O. 1984. Recherches sur l'architecture religieuse protodynastique en Mesopotamie. *Akkadica*. Supplement 2.

Van den Berghe, L. 1973. Luristan à l'âge de bronze. *Archeologia* 63: 24–36.

Van Driel, G. 1979. Jebel Aruda 1977/8. *Akkadica* 12: 2–28.

1983. Jebel Aruda 1982. *Akkadica* 33: 1–26.

Van de Mieroop, Marc 1987. *Crafts in the early Isin period*. Leuven.

Vorläufige Berichte über die Ausgrabungen in Uruk-Warka. Berlin.

Waetzoldt, H. 1972. *Untersuchungen zur neusumerischen Textilindustrie*. Rome.

Walker, Christopher 1987. *Cuneiform*. London.

Watelin, L.C. and S. Langdon 1934. *Excavations at Kish*. London.

Weadock, Penelope 1975. The Giparu at Ur. *Iraq* 37: 101–28.

Weiss, H. (ed.) 1984. *The origins of cities*. Guildford, Conn.

Weiss, H. and T.C. Young 1975. The merchants of Susa. *Iran* 13: 1–18.

Winter, Irene J. 1984. Review of A. Spycket, *La Statuaire du Proche-Orient ancien. Journal of Cuneiform studies* 36: 102–14.

1987. Women in public: the disk of Enheduanna. In *La Femme dans le Proche-Orient antique*, ed. J.M. Durand, pp. 189–201. Paris.

Woolley, C.L. 1934. *Ur excavations*, vol 2: *The Royal Cemetery*. 2 vols. London.

1939. *Ur excavations*, vol. 5: *The ziggurat and its surroundings*. London.

1955. *Ur excavations*, vol. 4: *Ur. The early periods*. London.

1974. *Ur excavations*, vol. 6: *The buildings of the Third Dynasty*. London.

1976. *Ur excavations*, vol. 7: *The Old Babylonian period*. London.

1982. *Ur of the Chaldees: the final account*, ed. P.R.S. Moorey. London.

Wright, Henry T. 1969. *The administration of production in an early Mesopotamian town*. Ann Arbor.

1980. Problems of absolute dating in protohistoric Mesopotamia. *Paléorient* 6: 93–7.

1981. The southern margins of Sumer. In *Heartland of cities*, ed. R. McC.Adams, pp. 295–345. Chicago.

Yener, K.A. and H. Ozbal 1987. Tin in the Taurus mountains: the Bolkasdag mining district. *Antiquity* 61: 220–6.

Zarins, J. 1978. The domesticated equidae of 3rd millennium Mesopotamia. *Journal of Cuneiform Studies* 30: 1–17.

INDEX

Note: Place names are listed without the prefix Tell.